LEGENDARY LOCALS OF MYRTLE BEACH SOUTH CAROLINA

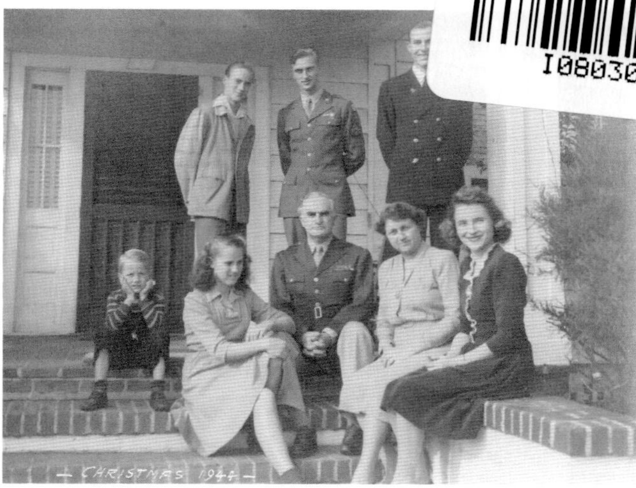

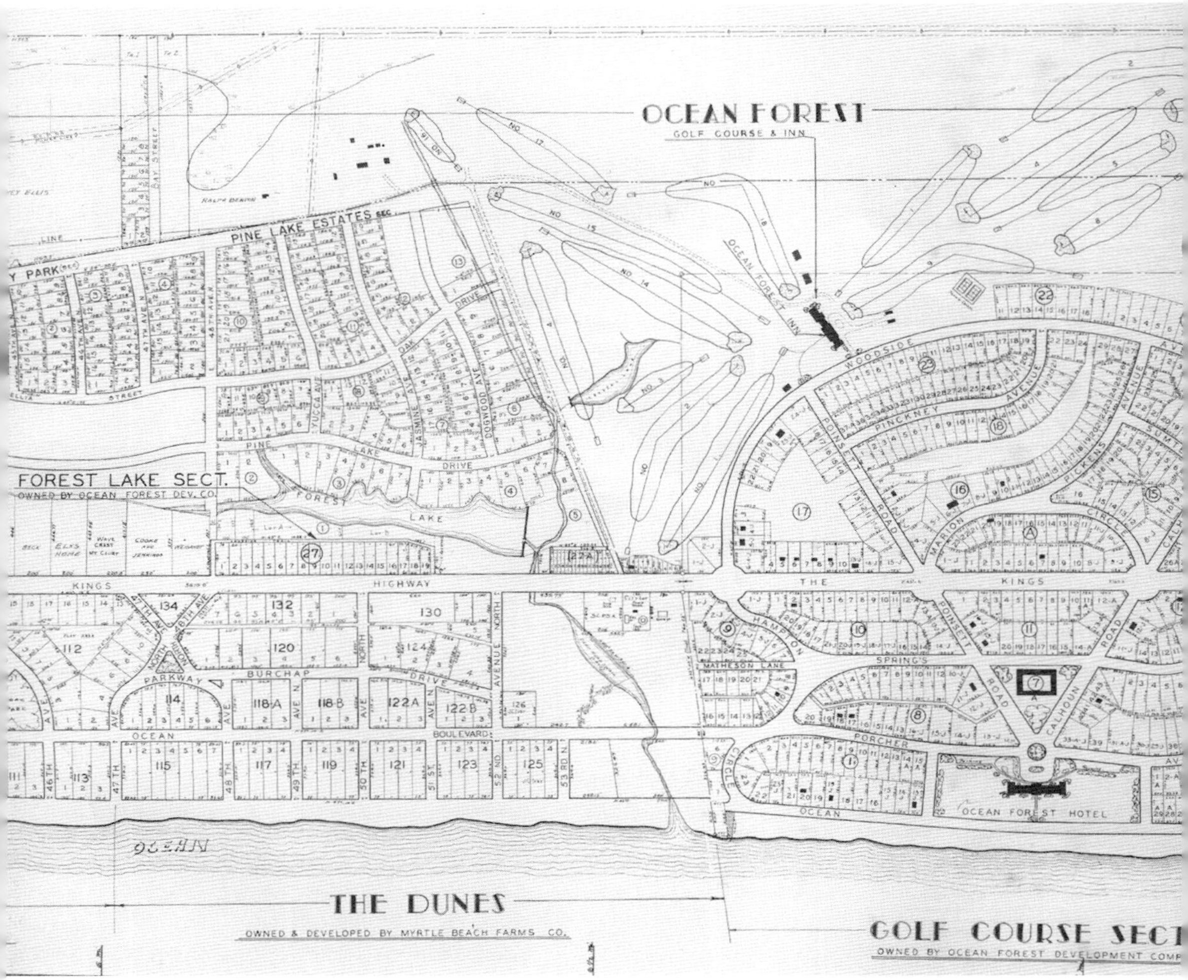

Map of Mrytle Beach

This is a portion of the map drawn by T.M. Jordan, a civil engineer, in July 1938. The city was broken up into sections running from south to north: Midway, Hurl Rocks, Withers Heights, Yaupon Circle, South Myrtle, Hotel, East Chester, Booker T. Washington, Washington Park, Kings Highway, Myrtle Heights, Oak Ridge, Knox Acres, Oak Park, The Dunes, Forest Lake, Fairway Park, Pine Lake Estates, Ocean Forest, Golf Course, Highlands, Colonial Heights, and Forest Dunes. These names are still used, and the new street signs reflect that. At one time, local phone numbers reflected these section names as well. Someone living in Myrtle Heights would refer to their phone number as "Myrtle Heights 1234." Over the years, new areas have been incorporated into the city limits. Some merged with preexisting areas, while other sections were added with additional section names. (Courtesy Chapin Memorial Library.)

Page 1: The Springs

The Springs Family is outside their family home on Highway 17 North towards the end of World War II, Christmas 1944. From left to right are (sitting) Albert, Alice, Brigadier General Holmes, Louise (mother), and Louise Springs (see page 11); (standing) Wilson, David, and Dr. Holmes. (Courtesy Springs family.)

LEGENDARY LOCALS

OF

MYRTLE BEACH

SOUTH CAROLINA

LESTA SUE HARDEE

LEGENDARY LOCALS

ISBN 978-1-4671-0143-1

Legendary Locals is an imprint of Arcadia Publishing
Charleston, South Carolina

Printed in the United States of America

Library of Congress Control Number: 2013952748

For all general information, please contact Arcadia Publishing:
Telephone 843-853-2070
Fax 843-853-0044
E-mail sales@arcadiapublishing.com
For customer service and orders:
Toll-Free 1-888-313-2665

Visit us on the Internet at www.arcadiapublishing.com

Dedication
In memory of my father and in honor of my mother and sisters for their unconditional love and unending support, I love you all.

On the Front Cover: Clockwise from top left:
James "Bonecrusher" Smith, world heavyweight champion (courtesy James Smith; see page 102); Lawrence Boulier, artist (courtesy Stacy McFarland; see page 16); Curtis Williamson of Santee Cooper presenting a check to Ashby Ward, director of the Myrtle Beach Area Chamber of Commerce (courtesy MBCC; see page 98); Janice McDonald, Miss South Carolina USA (courtesy Janice McDonald; see page 115); Zeb Thomas, Myrtle Beach Area Chamber of Commerce president and Thomas McInville, superintendent of building and planning for Horry County Schools accepting the Community Service Award 1977 (courtesy MBCC; see page 63); Sigmund Abeles, artist (courtesy Sigmund Abeles; see page 23); Mark Garner (right), owner of *The Sun News* preparing for the 20th annual Sun Fun Festival (courtesy MBCC; see page 45); Joan Borglund, Miss WCIV Charleston and Alma Lynn Thompson Hayden, Miss Sun Fun in the Sun Fun "Jail" (courtesy MBCC; see page 121); Anthony James, actor and artist (courtesy Anthony James; see page 22).

On the Back Cover: From left to right:
Justin Plyler, owner of the Gay Dolphin and Natia Resheed (courtesy MBCC; see page 67); Ashby Ward, director of the Myrtle Beach Area Chamber of Commerce (courtesy MBCC; see page 62).

CONTENTS

ACKNOWLEDGMENTS

Thank you to everyone who spent so much time searching their scrapbooks and boxes looking for old pictures. Thank you to the Myrtle Beach Area Chamber of Commerce (MBCC) and Brad Dickerson, for allowing me to dig through their archives. Thank you to the Archives at the Chapin Memorial Library (CML). To Jack Thompson, our own wonderful photographer who has documented Myrtle Beach through pictures over the years, I am filled with gratitude that you shared your photographs with me and I will always be in your debt (and I am serious about helping you digitize your collection). To the people I had not met before our interview who allowed me to take their cherished and irreplaceable photographs and letters with me to scan and copy—to you I especially thank for honoring me with your trust. To all of the people I did not put in this book—you are not forgotten—Myrtle Beach is and has been filled with so many memorable people that I hope to fill my next book with you.

INTRODUCTION

Myrtle Beach has long been a major tourist destination for millions of visitors over the years. Known for its white sandy beaches, amusement parks, gardens, and over a hundred golf courses, the tourists love to come back year after year and the true locals love to live here for many of the same reasons.

First inhabited by the Waccamaw Indians, later, with the help of land grants, several families including the Withers family settled here in the late 1700s only to have 18 members washed away by a hurricane in 1822. Devastated, the family soon left the area, and it was not until the Burroughs family opened up a logging camp in the late 1800s in what was then called New Town that things began to change. Mr. Burroughs had a vision, and he, along with a few other visionaries, changed the future of this little logging town. Myrtle Beach was incorporated in 1938 and celebrated its 75th birthday in 2013. The families that decided to take a chance and move here in the early 1900s and the families that arrived over the next few years helped build Myrtle Beach into what it is today. As with any new endeavor, one has to take a chance, and if someone keeps in mind that it only takes one—one idea, one person, one step—to succeed, great things are possible.

This book is filled with some of these stories of people who took a chance; someone had to open the first drug store, a guesthouse, a golf course, a bakery, a dance hall, and a movie theater. Who helped build the library, the first hospital, and the first church? Who was the first mayor? Who was the first real estate agent? Where is Knox Acres? Where is 10th Avenue North?

As with any vacation spot, there is more to Myrtle Beach than the average visitor sees, and there is more to the history than even some of the locals realize. This book aspires to create a journey to meet some of the people who made this history.

CHAPTER ONE

Early Settlers and Founders

History shows, through archeological digs and primary sources, that there have been people traveling through this area long before Franklin Gorham Burroughs acquired the land and began the establishment of what is known today as Myrtle Beach. During English rule, there were many land grants given to people willing to settle in the areas of Alston, Belin, Huger, and Withers. They brought their families and tried to tame the wilderness. They produced indigo, mined salt, and distilled turpentine. They built homes, planted their crops, worked the land, and raised their families. There were no roads, no support from a neighbor since the nearest neighbor was miles away, and the closest town was a couple of days' ride by mule and wagon through swampy, thick-forested, uncivilized land. One by one, they abandoned this area, moving closer to the cities and back to their plantations in other areas.

When Burroughs first acquired the land, he knew he would have to establish something for the workers, something more than just a place to sleep, work, and eat. He built the camp and extended it to include the commissary, which became the center of the camp. Seeing a need for an easier way to transport his turpentine and timber, Burroughs set in motion the building of an extension of the railroad—which up to that point only traveled north to south—inland to the towns and cities there. He also knew that this area had the potential to become something more than a turpentine camp, and said that the beach would eventually become a resort. He died in 1897 of pneumonia, leaving his business to his eight children.

The railroad was built, and along came the Seaside Inn—the first hotel. The first pavilion came next, where people would gather to dance and socialize. It was the beginning of the world-class resort, the paradise along the Atlantic Ocean that has become what is now known as Myrtle Beach.

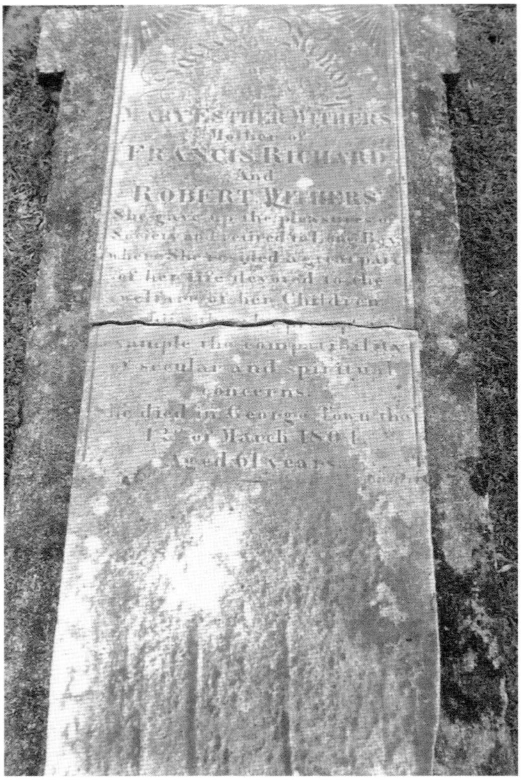

Withers Family

In the 1700s, this area was called Long Bay, a beautiful land inhabited by the Withers family. They received the property from a land grant, and their main crops were tobacco and indigo. In 1822, a powerful hurricane stalled over the area, inundating the residents with torrential rains, high winds, and a massive storm surge. The Withers home was picked up and carried out to sea, with 18 people sheltering from the storm inside. They, along with the house, perished in the waves. There are some who say that on a dark and stormy night they have seen a house lit by flickering candlelight, riding the waves, before disappearing into the mist. After the storm, the remaining family members abandoned the area. Mary Esther Stewart Withers's gravestone at Prince George Winyah Episcopal Church says it all in regards to the Withers family: "She gave up the pleasures of Society and retired to Long Bay, where she resided a great part of her life devoted to the welfare of her children." (Author's collection.)

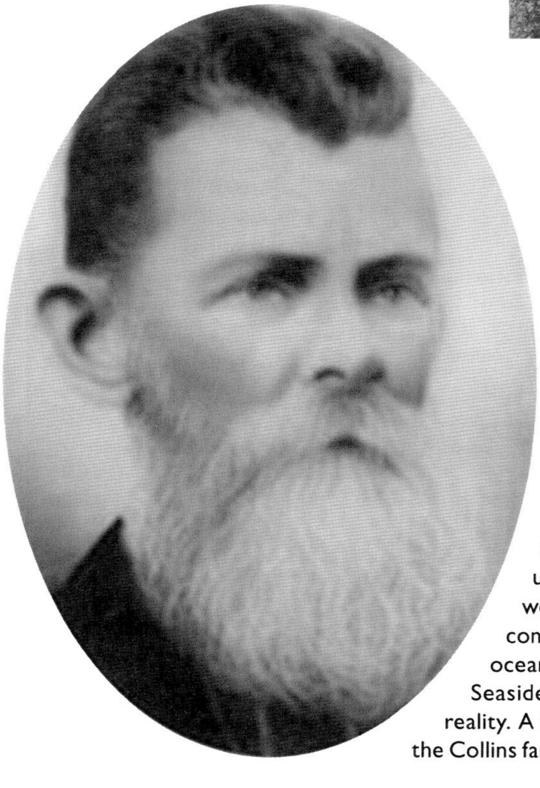

Franklin Gorham Burroughs

He arrived in Conway in the mid-1800s, where he eventually acquired most of the land that had been owned at one time by the Withers family. A true visionary, Franklin saw the potential along the coast as a world famous resort, but he unfortunately died in 1897 before those dreams were realized. The Burroughs and Collins Company completed the railroad to the beach, built the first oceanfront hotel in Myrtle Beach in 1901 called the Seaside Inn, and began to make Burroughs's dream a reality. A few years later, the Burroughs family bought out the Collins family. (Courtesy Burroughs and Chapin Company.)

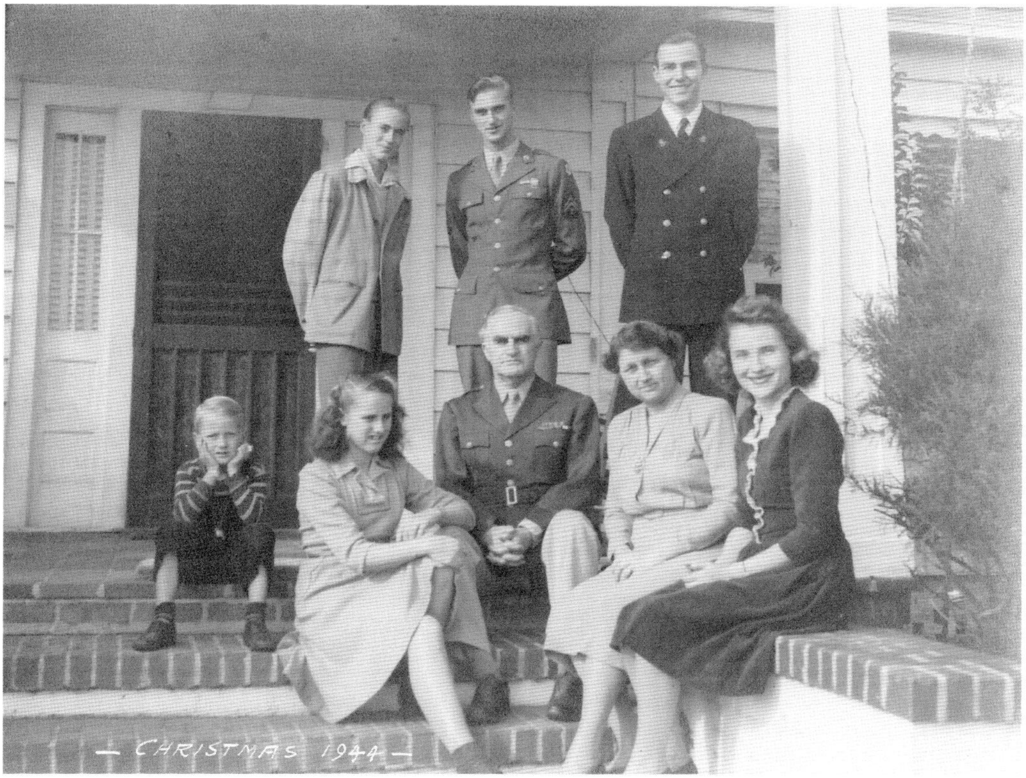

Retired Brig. Gen. Holmes Buck Springs
Born at Bucksville in 1879, Holmes Springs moved to Myrtle Beach from Greenville when the Woodside brothers came to build the luxurious Ocean Forest Hotel. He was vice-president and executive manager of the development firm Myrtle Beach Investment Company from 1926 to 1932. Deciding to move out on his own, he organized the H.B. Springs Real Estate and Insurance Company, which is currently run by his descendants. Over the years, he worked hard to improve this area, and was instrumental in acquiring the land for Myrtle Beach State Park (the first in South Carolina), and getting the first hospital built (the Ocean View Hospital). He married Louise Wilson, and they had six children, Louise, Alice, Dr. Holmes B. "Bobby" Jr., David, Wilson, and Albert. He was the first president of the Myrtle Beach Real Estate Board, and a member of the chamber of commerce and the Rotary Club of Myrtle Beach. Always an optimist, he regularly spoke about the "need of less selfishness, more brotherly love, and a spiritual awakening to save the world." When he died, Mayor Ramsey closed city offices during the funeral, and other businesses also closed in tribute to him. He was remembered in his obituary in *The Sun News* as a "distinguished soldier, churchman, business man and civic leader [who] long served his country, state and community with honor." (Courtesy Springs family.)

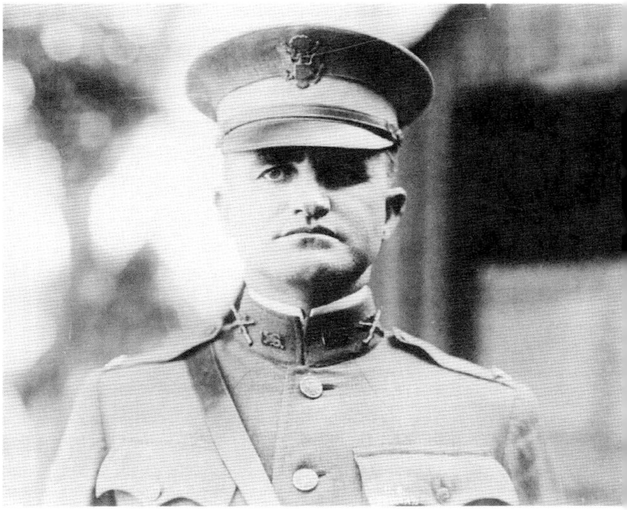

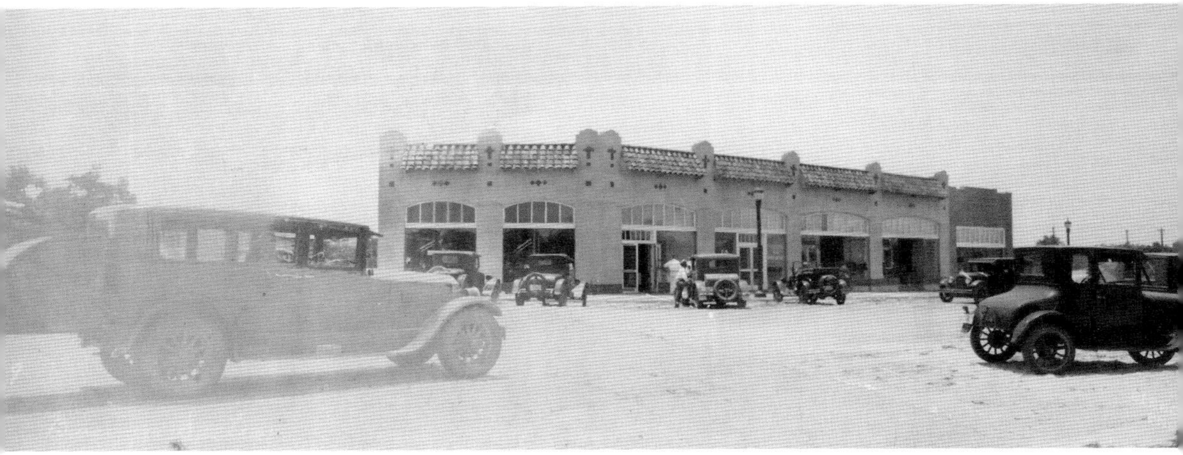

Chapin Company

In the mid-1930s, the roads were firm dirt and the mercantile store did not have the additions to the building that came later. The window in the fourth section reads "United States Post Office." The building was extended to the right several years later, and the post office was relocated to that section. The post office was there for many years until a new building was built on Oak Street. (Courtesy Chapin Foundation.)

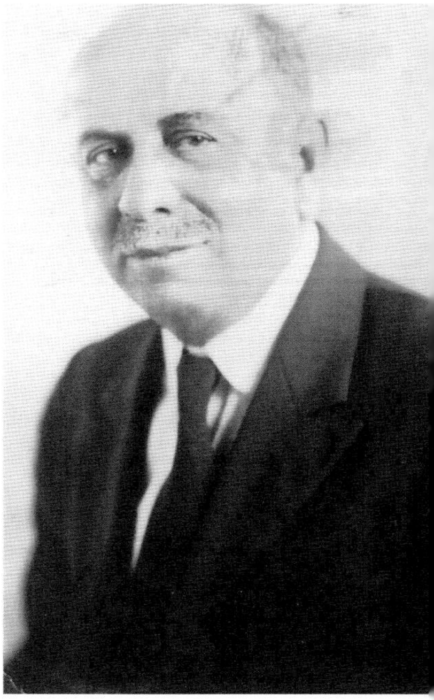

James Edward Bryan Sr.

Larger than life, Jim Bryan was born in 1876 in Horry County. First a teacher, he went to work with Burroughs and Collins (later Burroughs and Chapin) in Conway. He operated a store in rural Horry County for them before moving to Myrtle Beach in 1902. It was a stellar year for him, because he also married his sweetheart Susie Stone. They had seven children: George Waller "Buster," James Edward Jr., Leon Stone, Elnita, Geraldine, Emma Jay "Jakie," and Susan Dean Bryan. In 1926, when Chapin Company was built and Myrtle Beach Farms was formed, Jim was selected as president, a position he held until his death. After the formation of Burroughs and Chapin in 1912, he was a founding partner and president of Myrtle Beach Farms. He held both positions until his death. During his tenure, he also managed the Sea Side Inn and the Myrtle Beach Pavilion. He served on many boards, including the yacht club board of directors. Bryan had great hope for Myrtle Beach and its people, helping everyone who crossed his path. A man of strong character and compassion, he touched lives and his legacy lives on today. Bryan died in 1937 in Myrtle Beach at the age of 61. (Courtesy Sarah Bryan.)

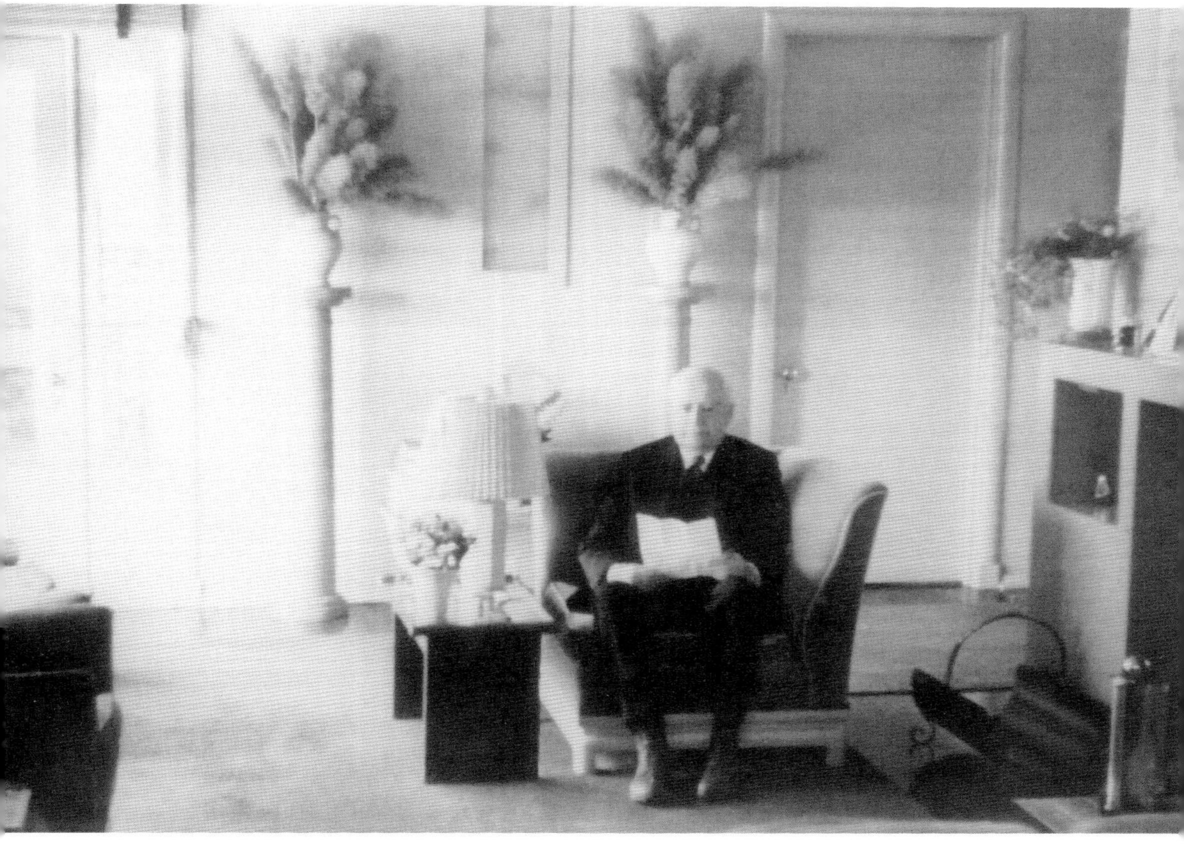

Simeon Brooks Chapin
By 1912, when Simeon Brooks Chapin arrived in Myrtle Beach, he too saw its potential and joined the Burroughs family in their endeavors, forming Myrtle Beach Farms Company. Chapin was a perceptive businessman and philanthropist, known for joining a community, seeing its needs, and generously contributing to them. He opened the Chapin Company—only the fourth store ever to be built in the area—which was the heart of the city for many years. Residents could do all of their shopping there, including clothing, furniture, hardware, and groceries. It also housed the library, a bank, and the post office at one time. Simeon donated land for parks and churches of all denominations and money for the library, and established the Chapin Foundation to carry on after his death. (Courtesy Chapin Foundation.)

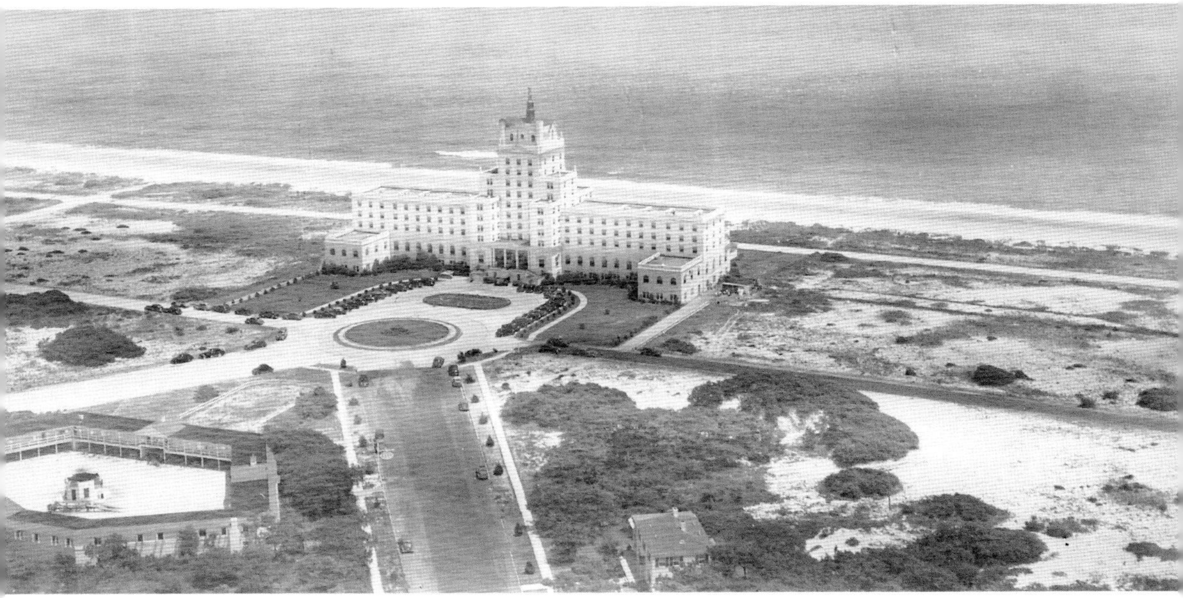

Woodside Brothers

The brothers (John T. born in 1864, J. David born in 1871, Robert I. born in 1873, and Edward F. born in 1874) were from Greenville, South Carolina. Col. Holmes B. Springs was working for the Woodside Bank in Greenville when he heard that John T. Woodside wanted to expand his business. Colonel Springs suggested that he speak with the Burroughs family in Horry County, as they were the largest landowners there. A meeting was established, and business was conducted. In 1926, they bought over 66,000 acres in Myrtle Beach with 12 miles of magnificent beachfront property. Woodside had a dream to build the first large luxury hotel on the land that stretched from the Atlantic Ocean to the current Highway 17 bypass. The vision for the property included the majestic hotel with golf courses, stables, and homes for the wealthy. The residents watched as the stately hotel was built to strict standards of luxury. However, due to the stock market crash of October 29, 1929, the Woodside brothers lost the property before it was completed. Woodside could not afford to stay in the hotel or make his mortgage payments. Myrtle Beach Farms repossessed most of the land, while the bank foreclosed on the building, the country club, and golf course. The latter was sold and became the Pine Lakes Country Club Golf Course, still in use today as one of the finest on the Grand Strand. The hotel was sold to other investors, and when completed in 1930, cost $1 million to build and was five stories tall. The "Million Dollar Hotel" was everything they envisioned. It catered to, and was frequented by, the wealthy. For many years, the hotel was filled to capacity. The ballroom would glitter with fancy dresses under the chandeliers. There were plays in the summer filled with Broadway stars and up-and-coming movie stars. Many locals worked the beach, the bar, the pools, and cleaned the rooms. Over the years, many proms were held in the grand ballroom. Slowly, the "Grand Old Lady" began to deteriorate and its upkeep was monumental, so it closed in June 1974. The hotel was imploded a few months later after Labor Day on September 13, 1974, much to the sorrow of many locals. The Woodside brothers may have lost everything during the Depression, but their legacy lives on with the businesses they built in Greenville and Pine Lakes Country Club in Myrtle Beach. There is a street in the Pine Lakes Section called Woodside Drive to commemorate the brothers and their contribution to Myrtle Beach. (Courtesy CML.)

CHAPTER TWO

Artists and Entertainers

A diverse and well-rounded community is filled with artists and entertainers. This area has always been overflowing with creative energy and artistic souls. The fresh salt air and the endless days of sunshine seem to energize and inspire the imagination. Myrtle Beach has painters, sculptors, and musicians. It also features writers, actors, dancers, photographers, comedians, jewelers, silversmiths, and sandcastle artists. Residents are fortunate to live in an area with such innovative minds willing to share their talents.

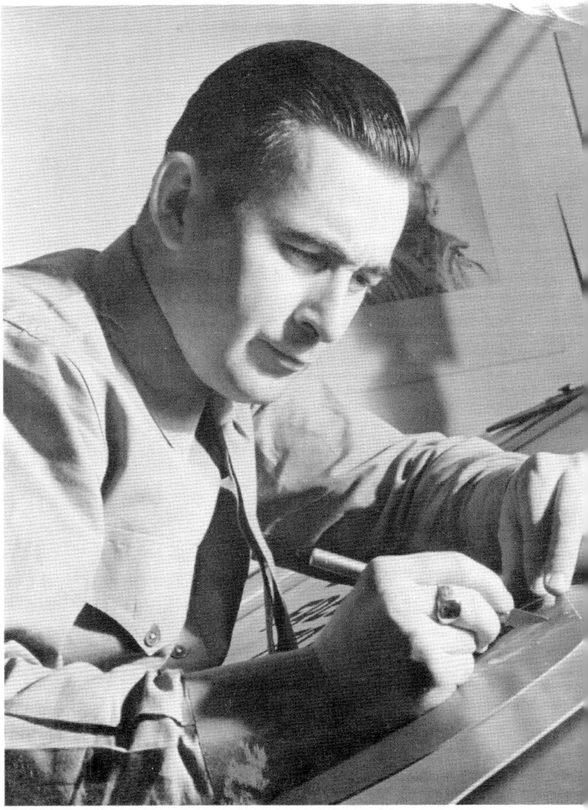

F. Lawrence "Larry" Boulier

Before moving to Myrtle Beach, he was an official artist for the Marines. Some of his work can be seen in the book *Marines at War* (1943) and the Marine archives. Over the years he became a very well known impressionist artist and exhibited his work all over the country. Boulier and his wife, Isla, moved to Myrtle Beach and soon built their A-frame house and matching art studio on Myrtle Street and moved into it in November 1958. He was the editor of several newspapers while here, including the *Conway Field* and *The Sun News*. One editorial stated what he thought Kennedy should have said in a debate with Nixon (which was passed on to Kennedy) and at the next debate, Kennedy said what Boulier suggested and sent a note to Boulier with a simple "Thanks, JFK." He was instrumental in forming the Conway Chamber of Commerce and the Waccamaw Arts and Crafts Guild. Larry opened the second art gallery here in Myrtle Beach, where he also held art classes for adults. It was located first at his home and then later at a formal studio on the northern end of the town. (Courtesy Stacy McFarland.)

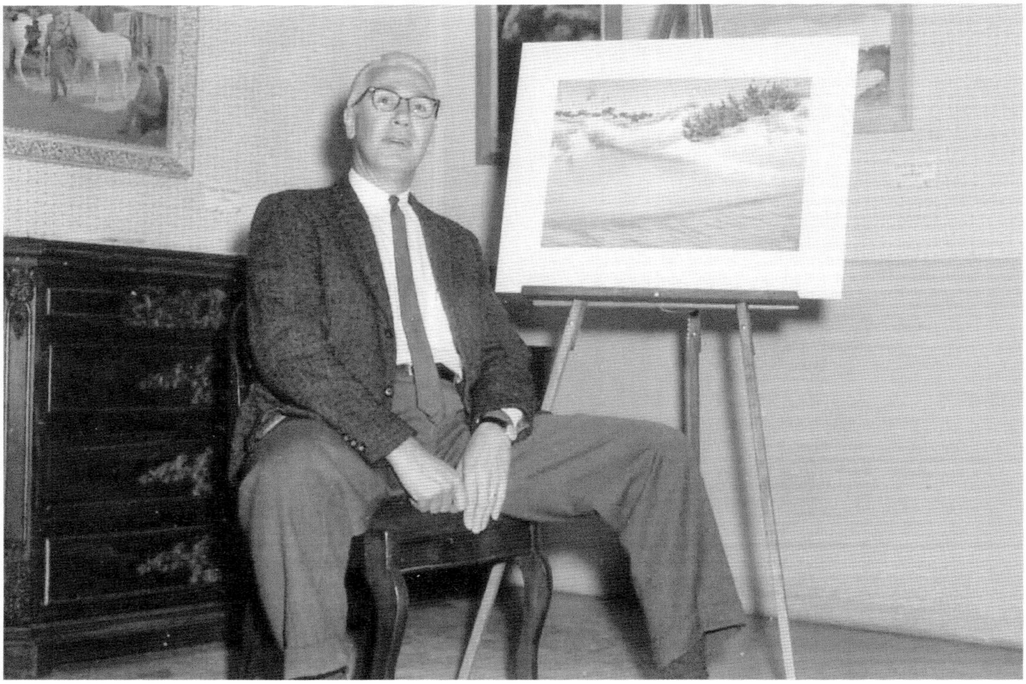

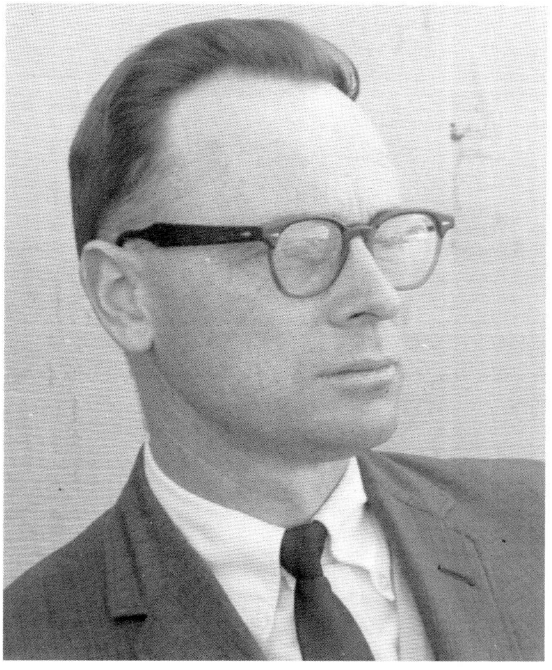

Charles Gay Joyner
He wrote and published *The Sandpiper*, a weekly magazine designed for tourists in the 1970s, and the *Camp Town Crier* while in Myrtle Beach. Active in the community, he was past president of the Myrtle Beach Civitans in 1970. After retirement in 1982, he and his wife Karyn moved to Hendersonville, Tennessee. Still writing, his column called "Joyner's Corner" can be found in *Carolina Country Magazine*. (Courtesy MBCC.)

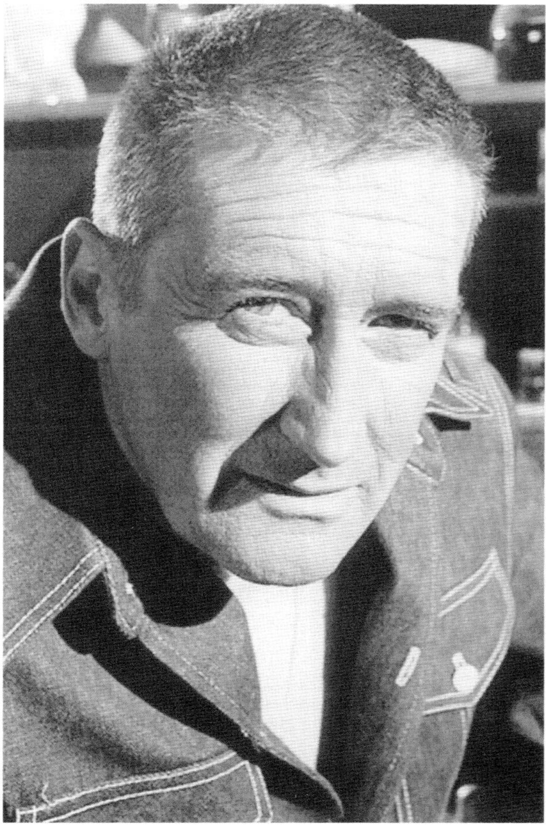

Mickey Spillane
Mickey came to Myrtle Beach in 1952 to judge a beauty pageant and decided to stay, eventually making his home in Murrells Inlet. A favorite among locals, he was very active in promoting Myrtle Beach and frequently participated in the Sun Fun Festival and other local events including books signings and lectures. As the award-winning author and creator of the Mike Hammer novels, he received the Mystery Writers of America Award in 1995 and was also inducted into the South Carolina Academy of Authors in 2012. Other local awards included a star on the Ocean Boulevard Walk of Fame and induction into the South Carolina Hall of Fame. (Courtesy MBCC.)

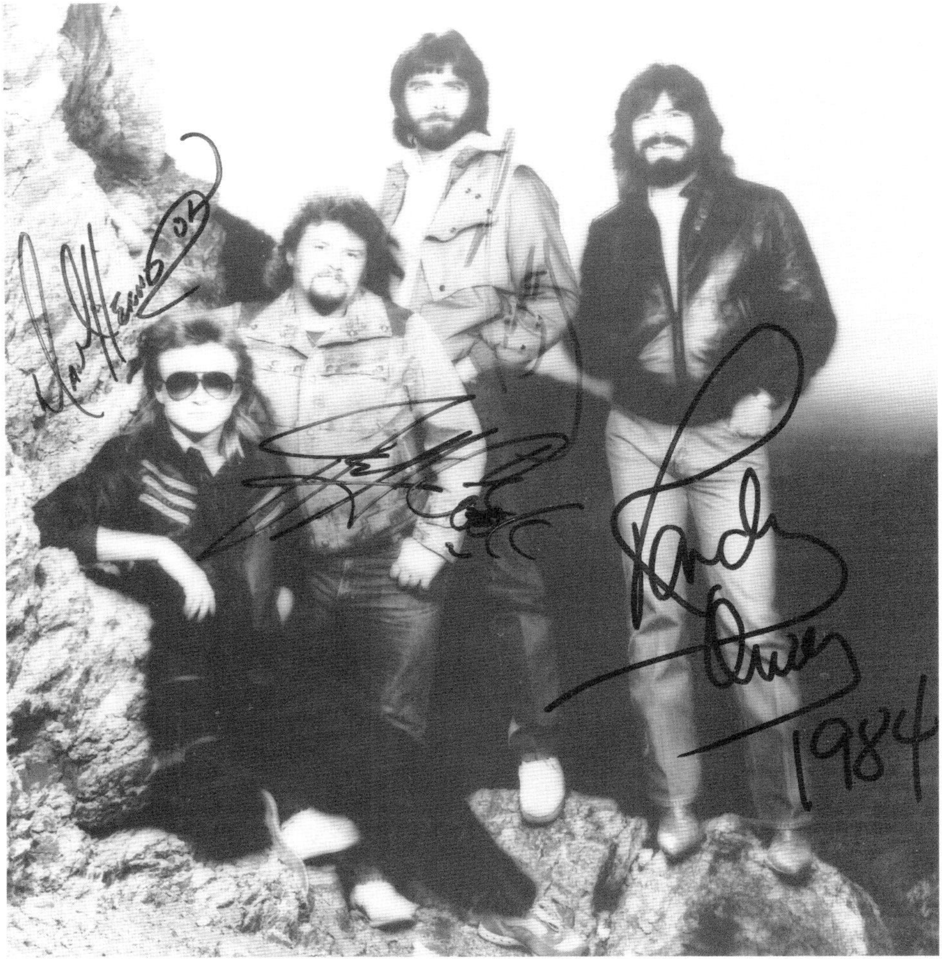

Alabama
When Alabama first came to Myrtle Beach in 1973, they had landed a summer job at The Bowery as the house band, called Wildcountry. Randy Owens, Teddy Gentry, and Jeff Cook were cousins who grew up together in Fort Payne, Alabama. After playing together as kids, then going their separate ways, getting jobs, and attending college for a while, they got back together and decided to form Wildcountry. In 1973, when they moved to Myrtle Beach, they would sing and play for hours on end for free and take home only what they earned in tips. They would return each year beginning with Easter weekend and play through Labor Day. In 1979, Mark Herndon (from Florence, South Carolina) joined them as the drummer. Each year, they would write more music and test it in front of their crowded audience at The Bowery, and each year they would be asked to come back. The audience loved their music. They changed their name to Alabama in 1977 after they signed a contract with GRT. In 1980, they signed with RCA and sold over four million copies of their album that first year. Even though they are originally from Alabama, the people of Myrtle Beach hold the band Wildcountry and Alabama dear to their hearts because of the hours of sweaty nights they played at the legendary Bowery. They went on to win the ACMA top vocal group of the year for 1981, and in 1982, they were named CMA entertainers of the year. They have not stopped winning awards for their music and songwriting to this day. On April 4, 2013, Owen, Gentry, and Cook returned to The Bowery for a command performance in a room filled to capacity with their loyal Myrtle Beach fans. (Courtesy Deacon Dawson.)

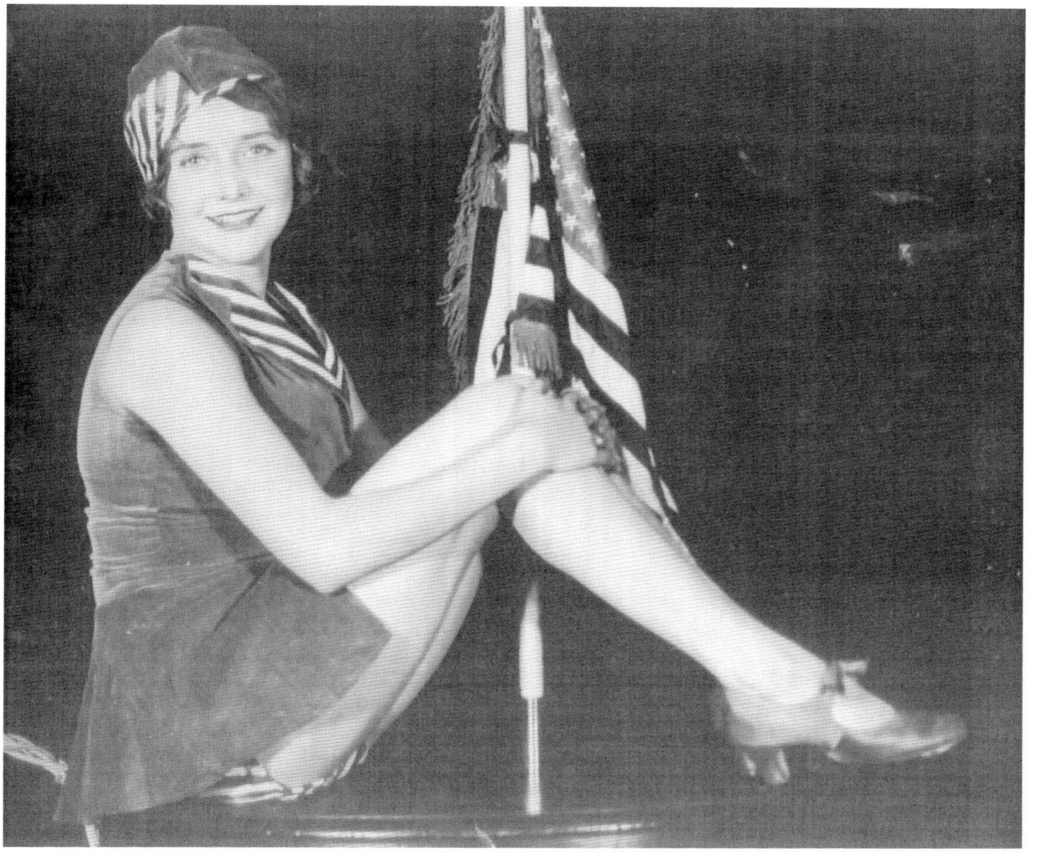

Julia Mayer

When she and her husband Bernard retired to Myrtle Beach, he repaired clocks and she opened the dance studio Myrtle Beach School of Performing Arts in their home in 1967. Because of the studio's popularity and traffic jams on her residential street, she eventually moved to a storefront on Broadway. Prior to moving to Myrtle Beach, they lived in the Washington, DC, area, where she danced professionally with the likes of Bill "Bojangles" Robinson, Gene Kelly, and James Cagney. She was named Ms. Senior Dance of America in 1983 and received the Charlie Award in 1985. At the age of 75, she made her off-Broadway debut in *Sole Sisters* at the La MaMa Theater. If someone asked her how she stayed so limber she would say, "I use WD-40 on my knees." And she did. (Courtesy Myrtle Beach School of Performing Arts.)

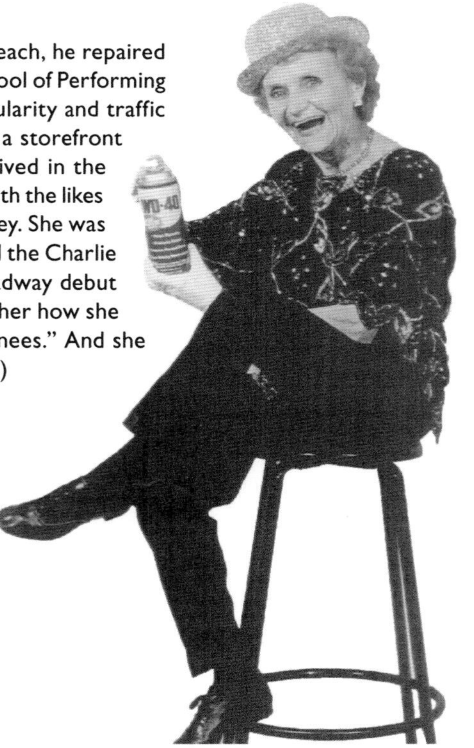

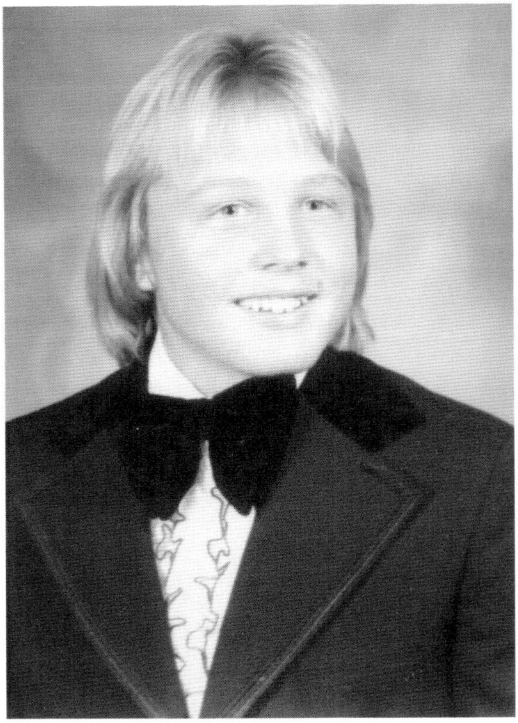

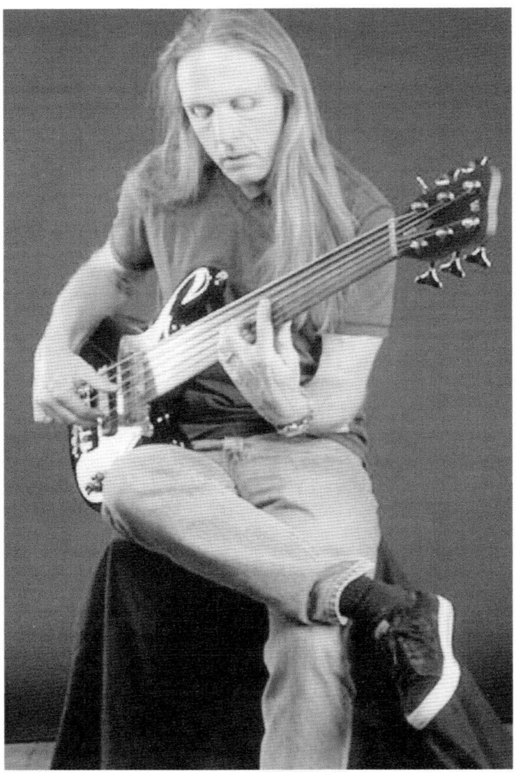

Steve Bailey
In school, Steve was known as a surfer until he started playing bass at the age of 12. Soon, he began practicing most of the day, and while his surfing suffered, his music blossomed. After college, he traveled the world playing with all of the greats, and one day he himself became one of the greatest bass players. Now people are honored to play with him. He was Bass Player of the Year runner-up in 1994 and 1996, has several solo albums, and can play a 13th chord in tune on a six-string fretless bass. Bailey teaches bass and has authored several books on the subject. He is married with two lovely daughters, still loves to surf, and still calls Myrtle Beach home. (Courtesy Steve Bailey.)

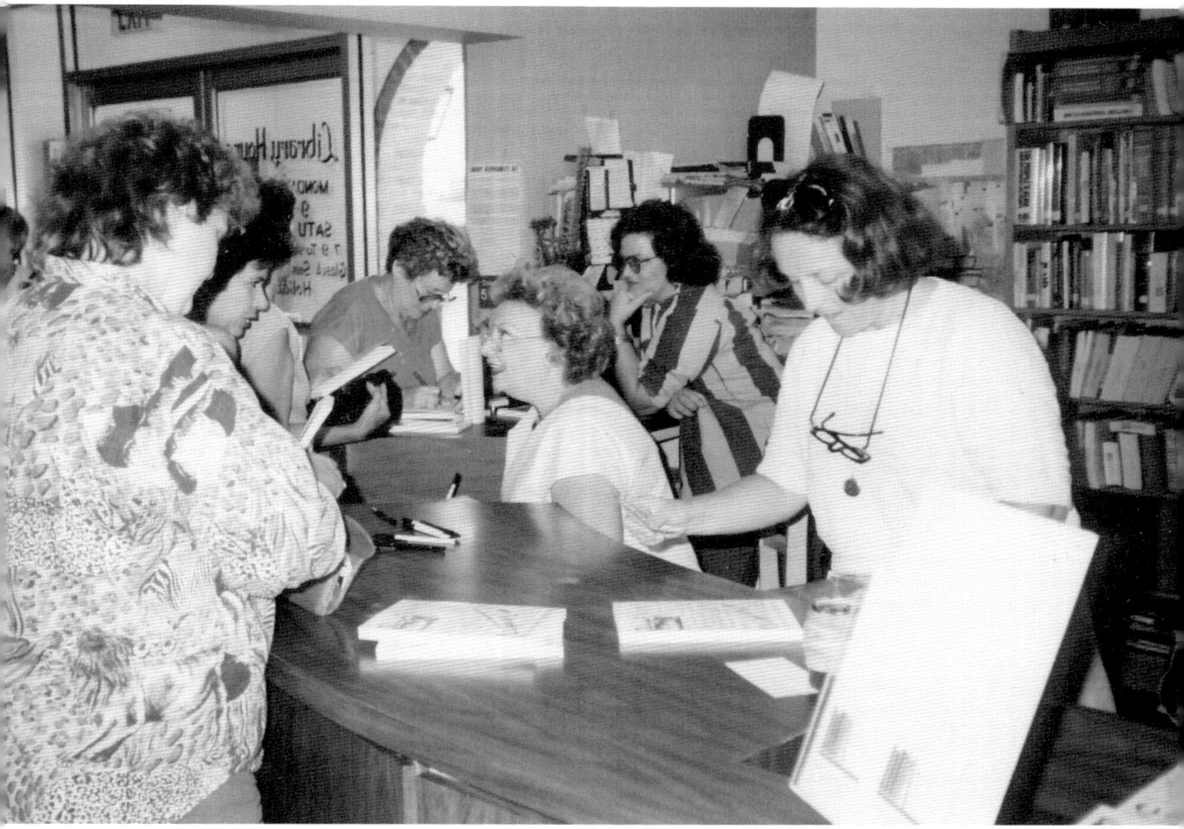

Nancy Rhyne

Even though she was born in North Carolina, most of her books were set in South Carolina, and because of this focus the South Carolina Federation of Media Women recognized her for her outstanding contributions. She is the author of over 20 books including *The Grand Strand: an Uncommon Guide to Myrtle Beach and its Surroundings*, *Carolina Seashells*, *Tales of the South Carolina Low Country*, and *More Murder in the Carolinas*. Always a fabulous storyteller, Rhyne has mesmerized people with her stories and lectures, and her author signings are filled with her fans. She is seen here at a book signing at Chapin Memorial Library for her book *Murder in the Carolinas*. (Courtesy CML.)

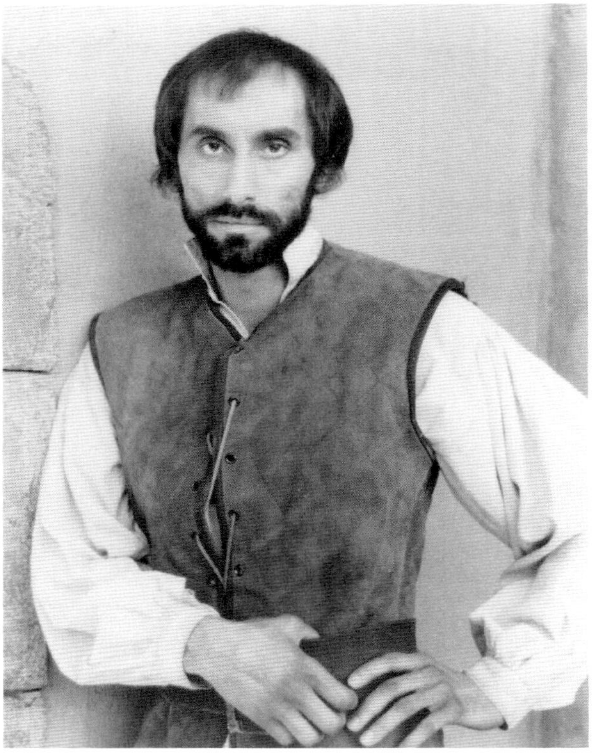

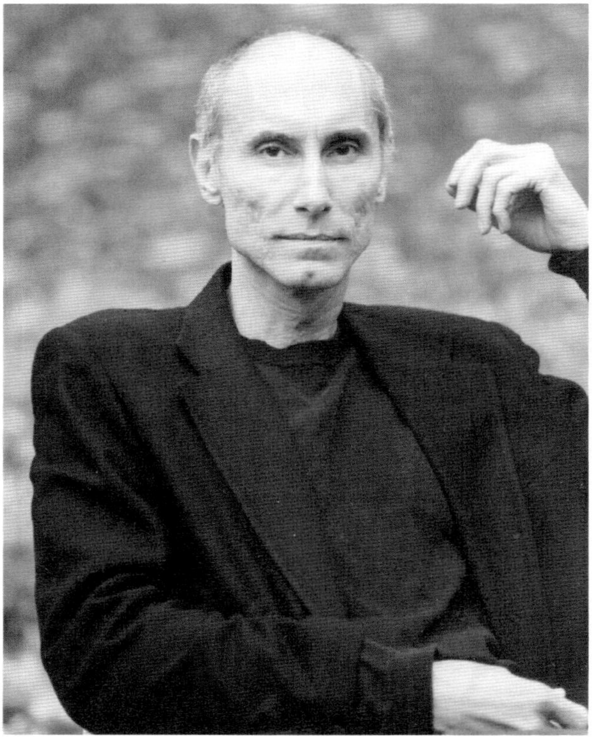

Anthony James

Anthony James was born in Myrtle Beach on July 22, 1942, to George and Marika Anthony. His father, George, was Greek and immigrated to the United Sates in 1919, then moved to Myrtle Beach in 1933 and entered the restaurant business. His mother, Marika, was also from Greece and came to Myrtle Beach in 1940 when she married George. They were well known for having the Seven Seas Restaurant and later the Mayflower Restaurant on Ninth Avenue North. His father passed away in 1951.

After finishing school, James—or Jimmie as some people still refer to him—decided to pursue a dream and moved to Los Angeles, where he changed his name to Anthony James and became an actor. His mother decided to start fresh and relocated with him.

Anthony James has starred in many films over the years, including *In the Heat of the Night*, *Return from Witch Mountain*, *The Naked Gun 2 1/2: The Smell of Fear*, and his last film, *Unforgiven*. His résumé also includes a long list of television guest spots including *Charlie's Angels*, *Buck Rogers in the 25th Century*, *Hawaii Five-0*, and *Married with Children*. James decided to retire from acting in 1992 and devote his full time to his other love, his art. He has established himself as an artist who paints modern, colorful, dramatic, emotional, large-scale abstract paintings, with exhibits in New York, Boston, and Miami. His work can be seen today at Renjeau Galleries. (Top, courtesy Anthony James; bottom, courtesy Karen Watson.)

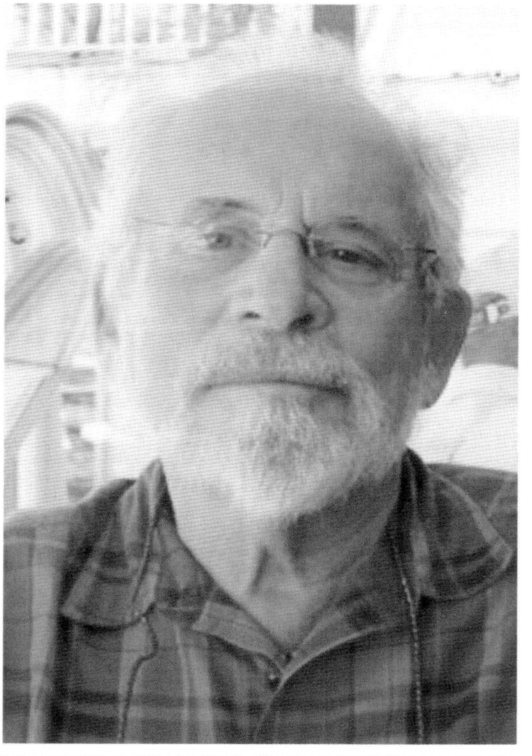

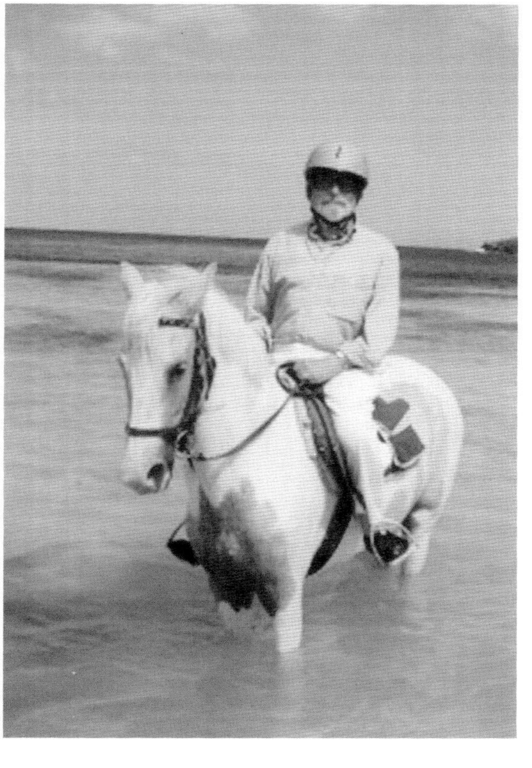

Sigmund Abeles

Sigmund Abeles was born in New York City, where he now resides, but grew up in Myrtle Beach. His mother, Henrietta, decided to move to Myrtle Beach for a fresh start in 1936. She designed and built Paul's Guest House at 506 North Kings Highway, which she named after her father. Growing up in Myrtle Beach during the 1940s and 1950s was an adventure for little Sig; this was a new town and things changed daily. Sitting on the front steps of his home, young Sigmund watched the world go by. He saw massive sculptures on their way to Brookgreen Gardens, and quite often during the war he'd see the trucks loaded with Nazi war prisoners from a POW camp in town. One day when he was outside having a snack, he looked up to see Pres. Franklin D. Roosevelt, Winston Churchill, and Bernard Baruch drive by in a large open limousine.

Sigmund's first experience of art was the sculpture at Brookgreen Gardens. His mother would let him take the car down and he would sit and look at the statues, then draw and paint them. He met the painter Gerald Tempesta in 1950 when he was still in high school after Tempesta decided to relocate here and Abeles became his apprentice. He learned a great deal from him and another friend and mentor, Truman Moore, a great artist in his own right. After receiving an AB in fine arts from the University of South Carolina in 1957, Sig moved back to New York to attend Columbia University, where he received an MFA in painting.

In 2007, Myrtle Beach welcomed Sigmund Abeles home with a show at the Franklin G. Burroughs–Simeon B. Chapin Art Museum called "Sigmund Abeles: From Whence I've Come," which opened with rave reviews. The show included over 40 paintings, prints, drawings, pastels, and sculptures created from 1951 to 2007.

Over the years, Sigmund was married a few times and has three children: David, Shanna, and Max. After his mother passed away in 1983 he donated Paul's Guest House to CASA, an organization that helps battered women and children, which Chapin Company helped move to an undisclosed location. (Courtesy Sigmund Abeles.)

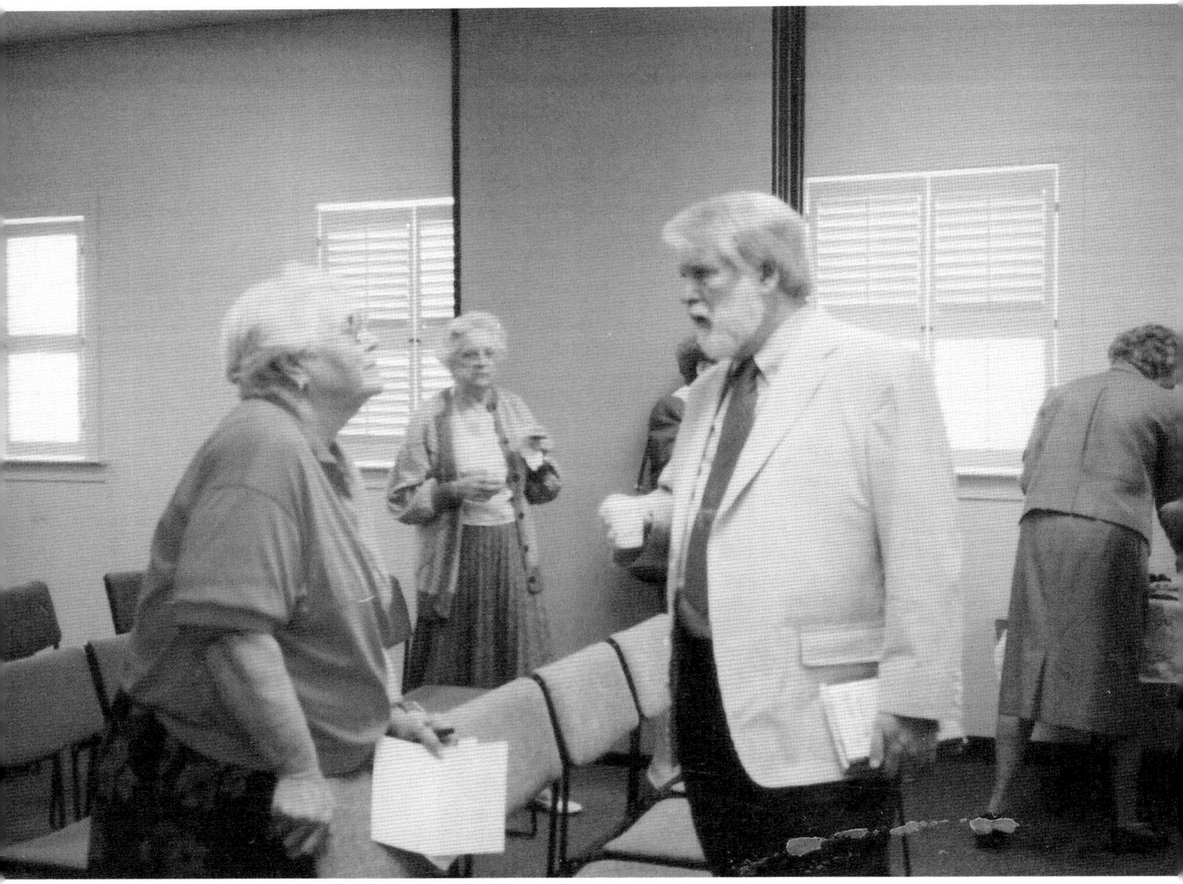

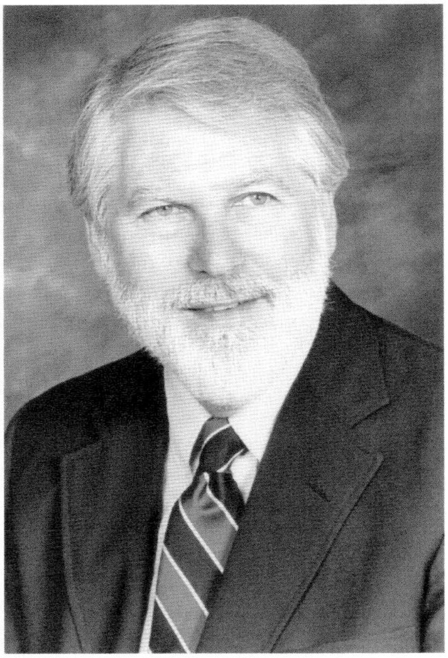

Dr. Charles W. Joyner

Joyner was the first in his family to go to college, majoring in history and English and eventually earning two doctorates, one in history from the University of South Carolina and one in folklore from the University of Pennsylvania. He is a Burroughs Distinguished Professor of Southern History and Culture at Coastal Carolina University. Always one to keep busy, he has written several books including *Down by the Riverside: a South Carolina Slave Community*. He, along with Dr. Orville Burton, is the editor of *Slavery and Anti-Slavery: A Transitional Archive Database*, which is filled with over five million primary documents. The foremost authority on the American South and slavery, Dr. Joyner has lectured all over the world and makes Myrtle Beach his home. (Courtesy CML.)

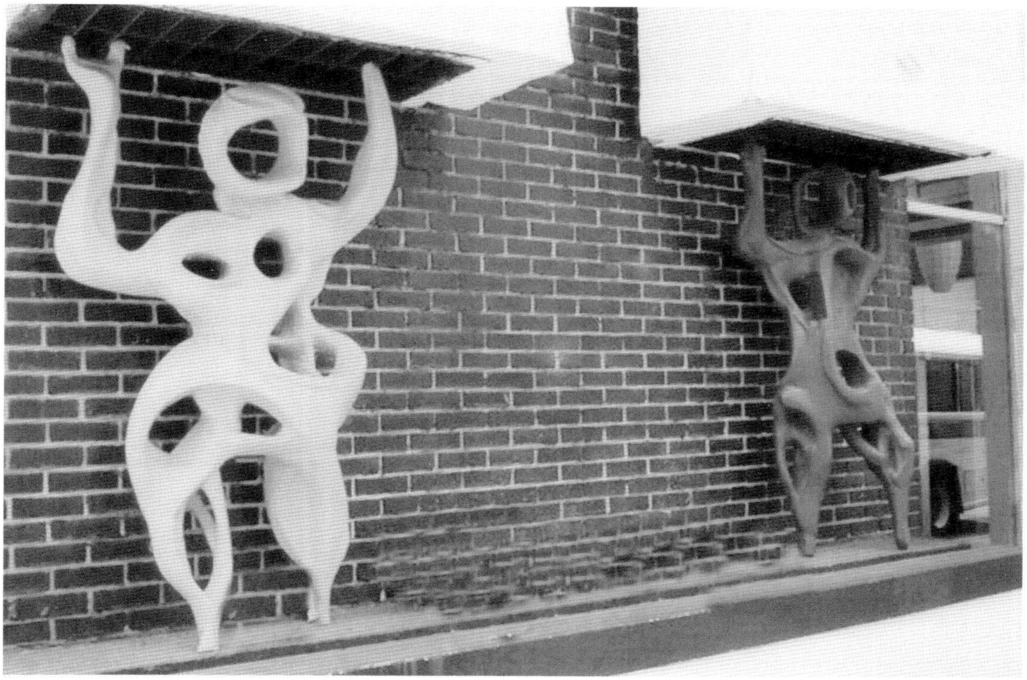

Gerard Tempesta

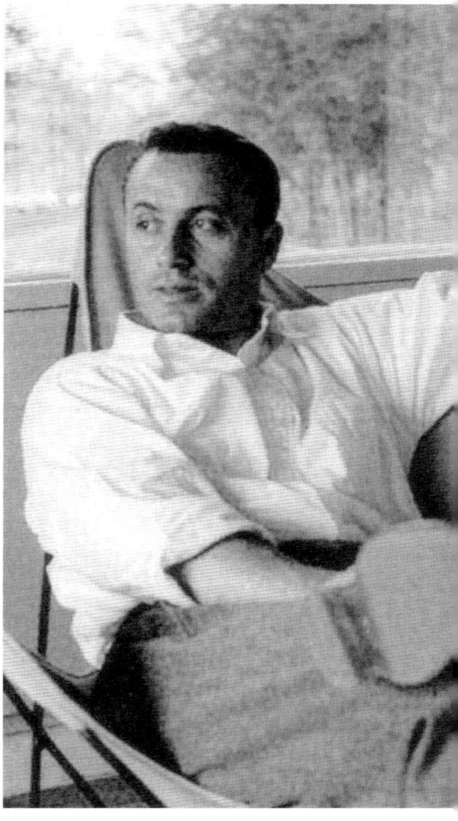

Gerard and his wife, Sarah, made their home here in 1951–1953 when he opened the area's first art gallery, Tempest by the Sea. The father of Abstract Spiritualism, he was born in Italy and immigrated to the United States with his family when he was 11. They settled in Massachusetts. Drafted into World War II, he was in the 82nd Airborne Division, fighting campaigns at Normandy on D-Day and the Battle of the Bulge. He also designed the 101st Airborne Division's insignia, the Screaming Eagle. He studied art at the Boston Museum School and was the protégé of Giorgio de Chirico in Rome. He continued to paint all of his life, notably horses, where he uses his signature ribbon effect. When he lived here in the 1950s, he would sit for hours at the first Patricia Hotel, where people would come in and he would paint their portraits. When the Rivoli Theater opened, his sculptures adorned the front entrance. His abstract of a man and a woman proudly greeted theatergoers for years. Sigmund Abeles was his protégé, becoming his apprentice and now an acclaimed artist living in New York. Harry Love, another local artist, nominated Tempest for the South Carolina Hall of Fame, into which he was inducted in 2009. In 2007, he was recognized by the South Carolina legislature in a joint resolution citing his artistic accomplishments and service during the war. Ever the artist, his work touched many people all over the world and can be found in many collections including the Vatican Museum. Tempest, an artist, sculptor, and architect, died in Myrtle Beach on July 26, 2009. (Above, courtesy Diane Moskow-McKenzie; right, courtesy CML.)

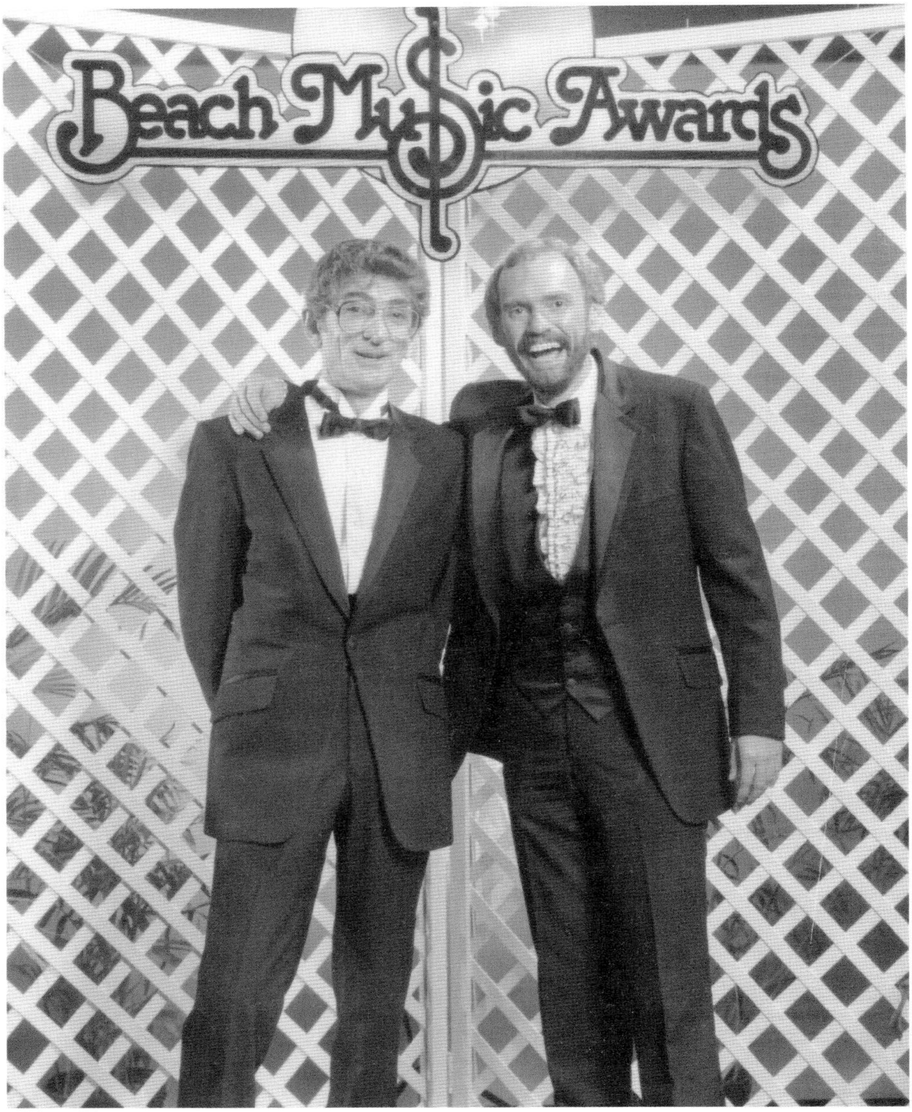

Richard O. "Dick" Biondi and Deacon Dawson

Pictured here are Dick and the Freakin' Deacon at the first Beach Music Awards. Dick was on the local airwaves during the 1970s. One of the original DJ "screamers," he called himself "The Wild I-tralian." He was a favorite among the locals. Known for being the first DJ in the United States to play the Beatles on the air in February 1963, he has been on the air for over 60 years. Inducted into the Radio Hall of Fame in 1999, he can now be heard on late night Chicago's WLS-FM.

The Freakin Deacon Dawson, a radio personality on the airwaves in Myrtle Beach for over 25 years, arrived in Myrtle Beach in 1976. One of the DJs with WKZQ, he moved to WYAK and later to WSYN. He even had a stint at the old Myrtle Beach Pavilion, where he broadcasted his show at the Magic Attic. One of his notable awards was *Billboard Magazine's* 1983 Radio Personality of the Year. Along the way he started acting, which he is still involved in. He has worked with Andy Griffith, Danny Glover, and Gene Hackman. Deacon is also a commercial artist, photographer, and natural comedian. (Courtesy Deacon Dawson.)

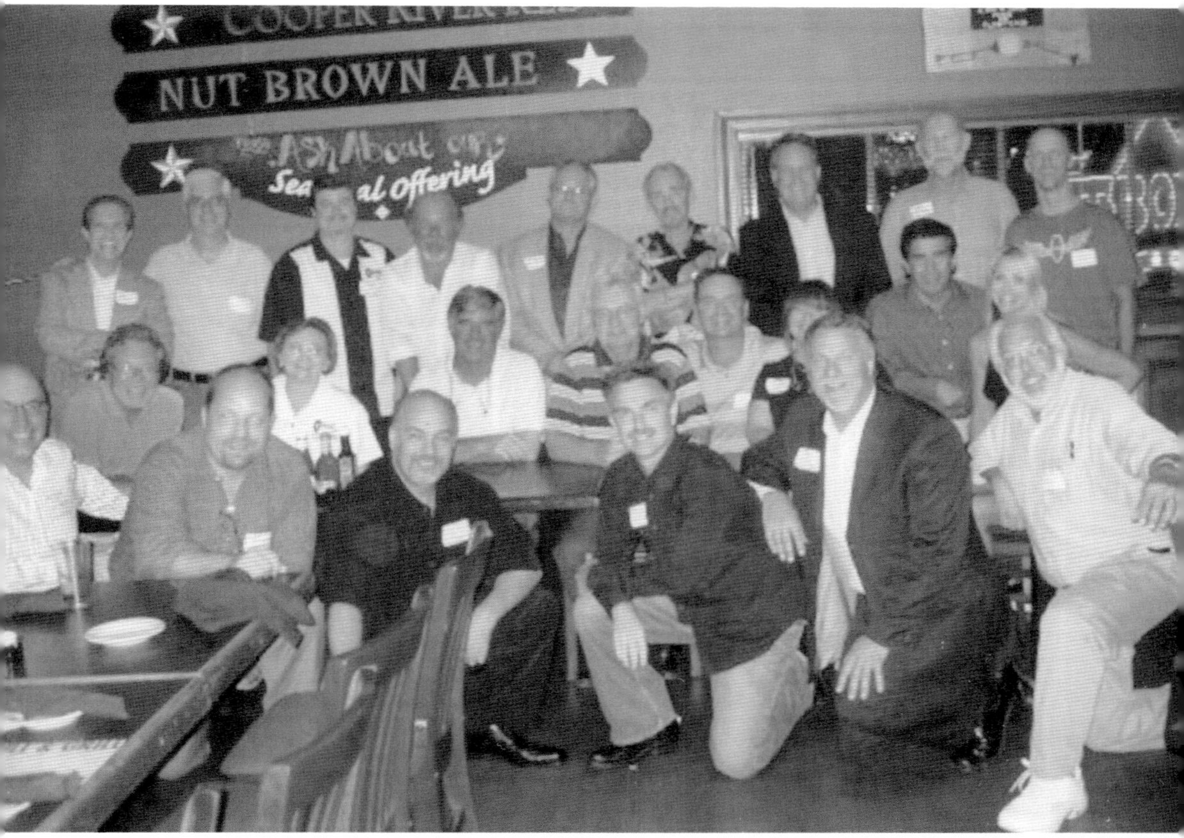

WKZQ/QRock

From its automated beginnings, under the direction of Bill Hennecy, WKZQ became the station to listen to in the 1980s and 1990s. They added live DJs, did on-site newscasts, and changed the music to top 40. If someone wanted to know what was going on in Myrtle Beach, they tuned into WKZQ 101.7 on the FM dial. QRock was awarded *Billboard Magazine*'s Station of the Year Award and won several Brandon Station of the Year Awards. Pictured here at a QRock Reunion in 2009 are only a few of the radio personalities that residents will remember, including, from left to right, (first row) John Van Pelt, Scott Summers, Shotgun Jeff Stone, Banana Jack Murphy, J. Patrick Milan, and Ken Heinlein; (second row) Al Ervin, Linda Franklin Moore, Bill Hennecy, Tom Rogers, John Kilgo, Chris Thomas, Johnny D. Summer, and Summer James; (third row) Chris Williams, Al G., Mike Willis, Mixin' Dixon, Tom Walters, Freakin' Deacon Dawson, Bob Scarborough, John Dixon, and Joe Hutchins. (Courtesy Janice McDonald.)

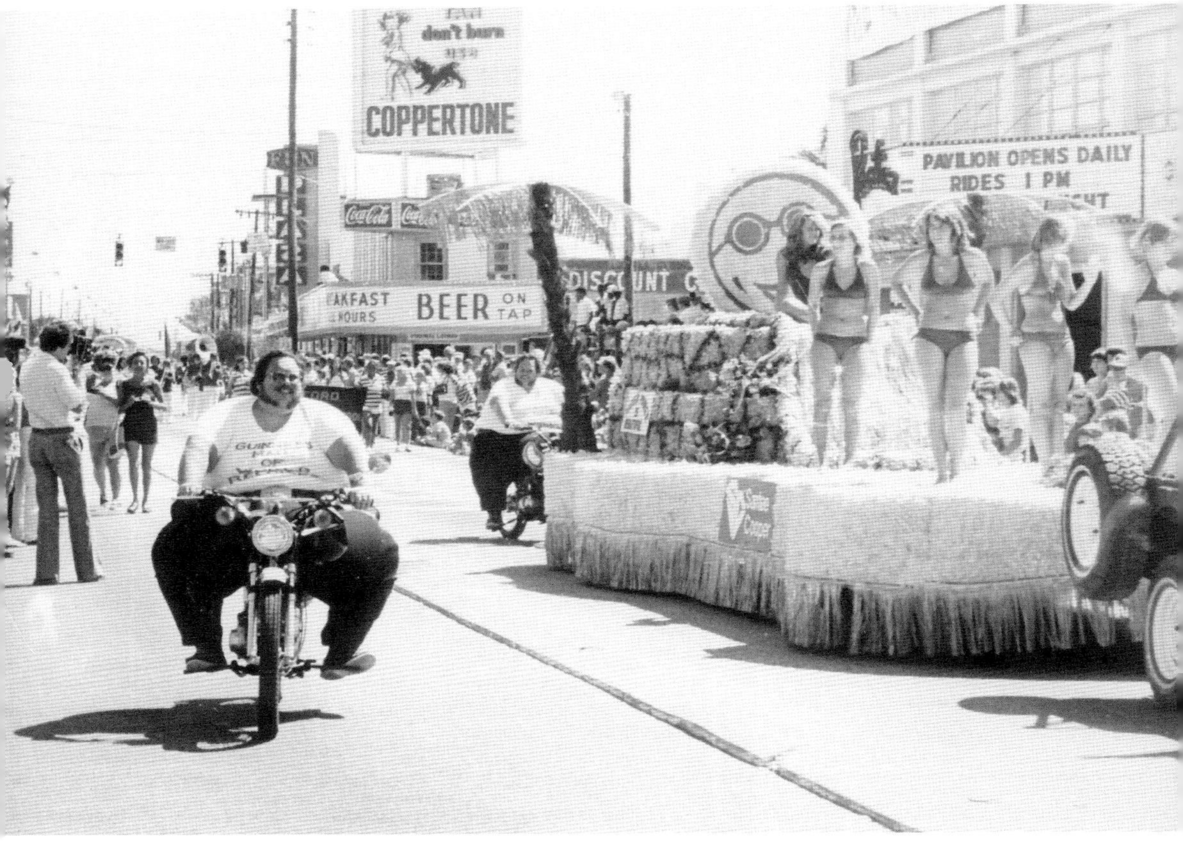

Benny and Billy McCrary

Guinness World Record–holders as the world's heaviest twins, Benny and Billy weighed in at 814 and 784 pounds respectively at the height of their career. They formed a wrestling and comedy team after high school, calling themselves the McGuire Twins. During the summer months of the 1970s, they could be found sitting outside Ripley's Believe It or Not signing autographs and having their pictures taken with the tourists or at one of the ever popular all-you-can-eat restaurants in town. Always smiling, they would ride around town on their signature mopeds, waving and speaking to everyone they would meet. Billy died on July 15, 1979, due to what was believed to be the result of a recent motorcycle accident, and Benny died on March 30, 2001, from heart failure. (Courtesy MBCC.)

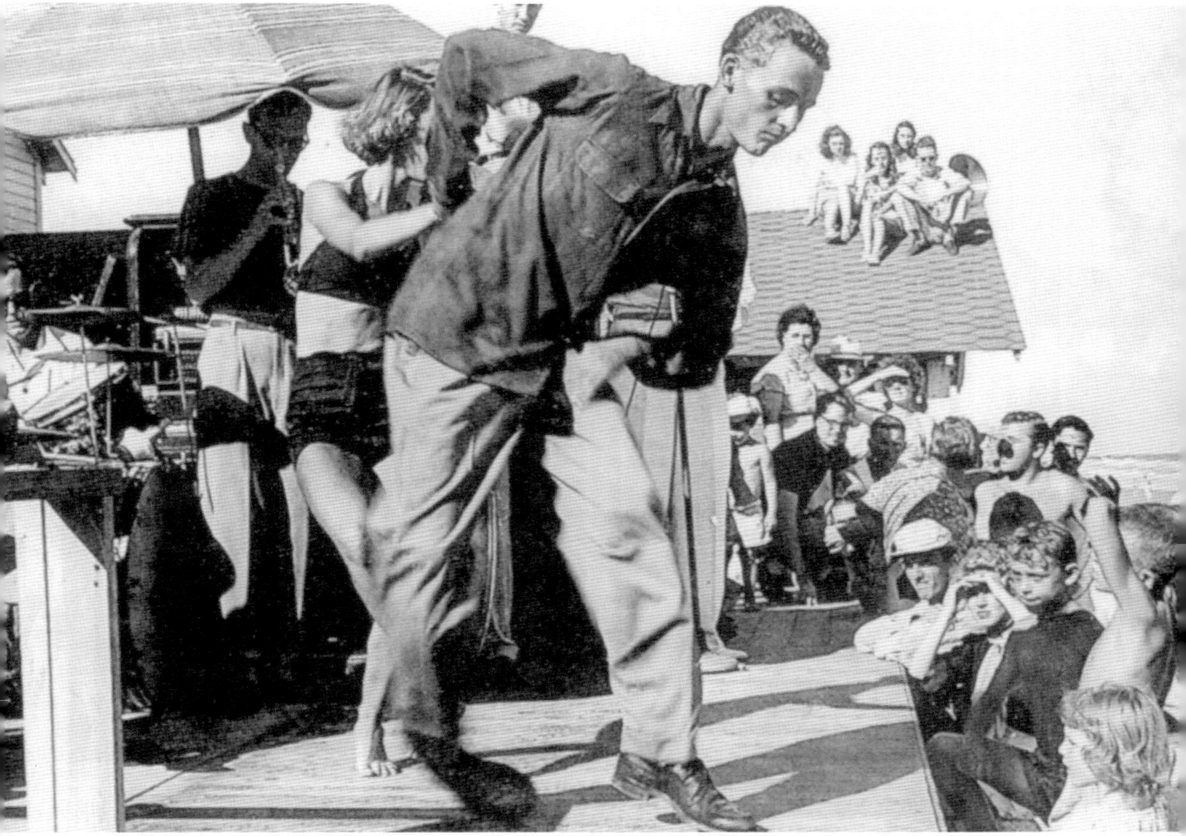

Leon "Rubber Legs" Williams
Leon, an original founding father of the Society of Stranders, was inducted into the Shaggers Hall of Fame in 1983. Known for his particular style of shagging where he would cross his legs, rock back and forth, and move down into a squat, he was nicknamed Rubber Legs. He loved to dance and devoted most of his spare time to dancing, practicing, and promoting shag. He also started the Old Timers Shag Club. While they are based on the north end of town, Williams could be seen dancing at the local clubs and participating in competitions at places like the Myrtle Beach Pavilion. He married Dolores and they had two children, Rudy and Joyette. He passed away on December 25, 2012, and his memorial service was held at one of his favorite spots, the OD Beach Club, a few days later. (Courtesy Frank Beachum.)

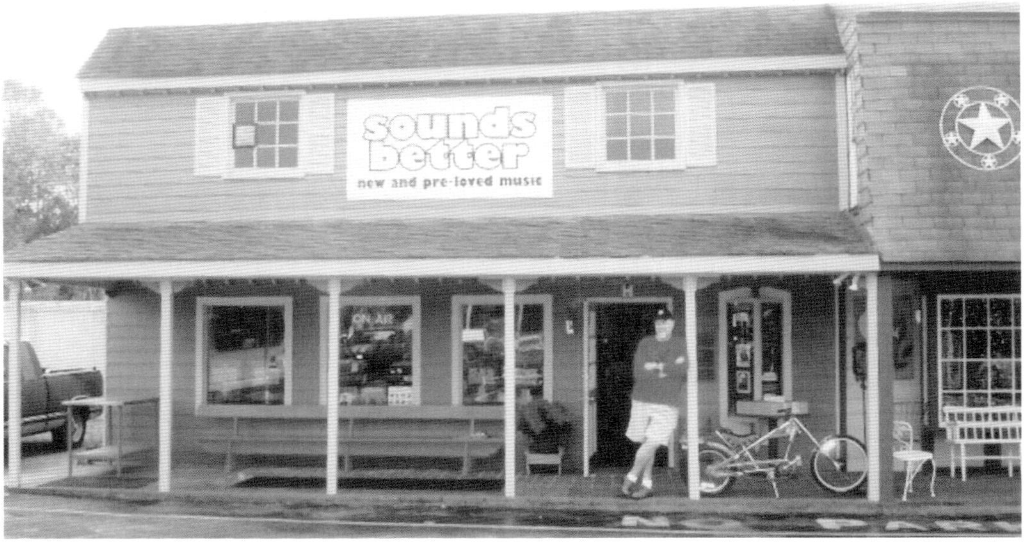

Jeffery Lloyd Roberts

When one thinks of music, one thinks of Jeff Roberts. He operated three stores in the area, starting with the Record Bar at the mall in the 1970s, to Sounds Familiar on Thirty-Eighth from 1979 to 2003, and Sounds Better at the Hidden Village. Jeff remembered everything: from the last piece of music someone purchased to minute details of musical history that he would recall instantly. He had the biggest heart, a huge smile, and always stood out in a crowd, and not just because he was six feet eight inches. Along with Sam Hannaford, he cofounded South by Southeast, a festival put on each year to bring unknown talent to the Grand Strand, using the proceeds to purchase musical instruments and award scholarships to low-income students. On January 11, 2010, at the age of 55, the "Minister of Music" passed away of a heart attack.

Jeff is seen below at the QRock reunion with (from left to right) John Mixin' Dixon, Jeff, Bob Scarborough, and his son Hunter. (Above, courtesy Wendy Roberts; below, Janice McDonald.)

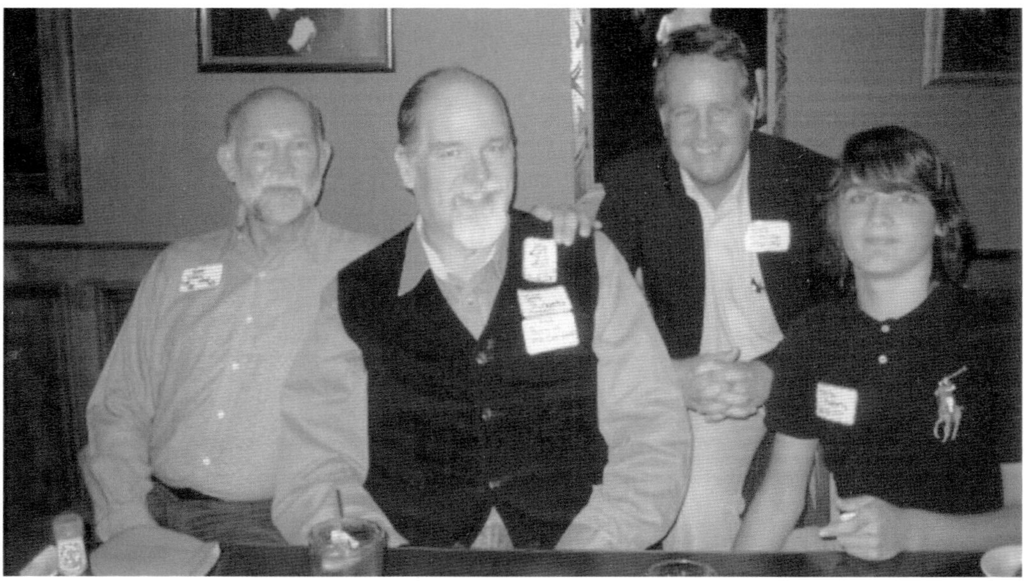

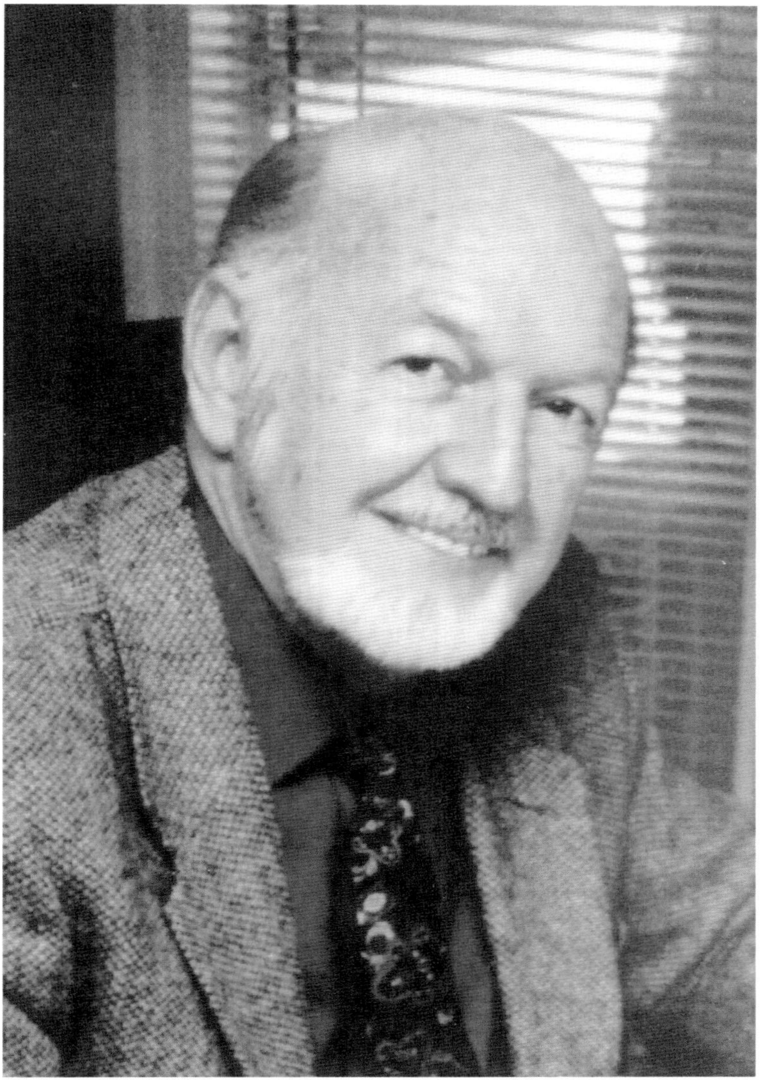

Jack Thompson
Born in Greenville, he escaped to Myrtle Beach as soon he could at the age of 13 when he and some friends hitchhiked across the state. They landed at the Pavilion, where within the hour Jack got his first job. Now, over 55 years later, he is still taking pictures. Over the years, Thompson became a beloved photo historian, taking hundreds of thousands of shots, documenting the history of Myrtle Beach as no one else. A compassionate and generous man, he has shared these pictures with historians, reliving the past, the happy times, and the sad times, for which the residents are grateful. His coffee table book *Memories of Myrtle Beach* showcases some of his pictures, taking readers down memory lane from when Myrtle Beach was young. Passionate about history, as chairman of the Myrtle Beach All Aboard Committee, Jack and a group of faithful friends saved the now 76-year-old train depot. The committee cleaned up the grounds, raised funds, and restored the beautiful and now functional depot. The building is now used for events, and the occasional train will come into the station when special rides are scheduled. His current studio is located on Highway 17 and Main Street across from the old Pavilion where it all began. (Courtesy Jack Thompson.)

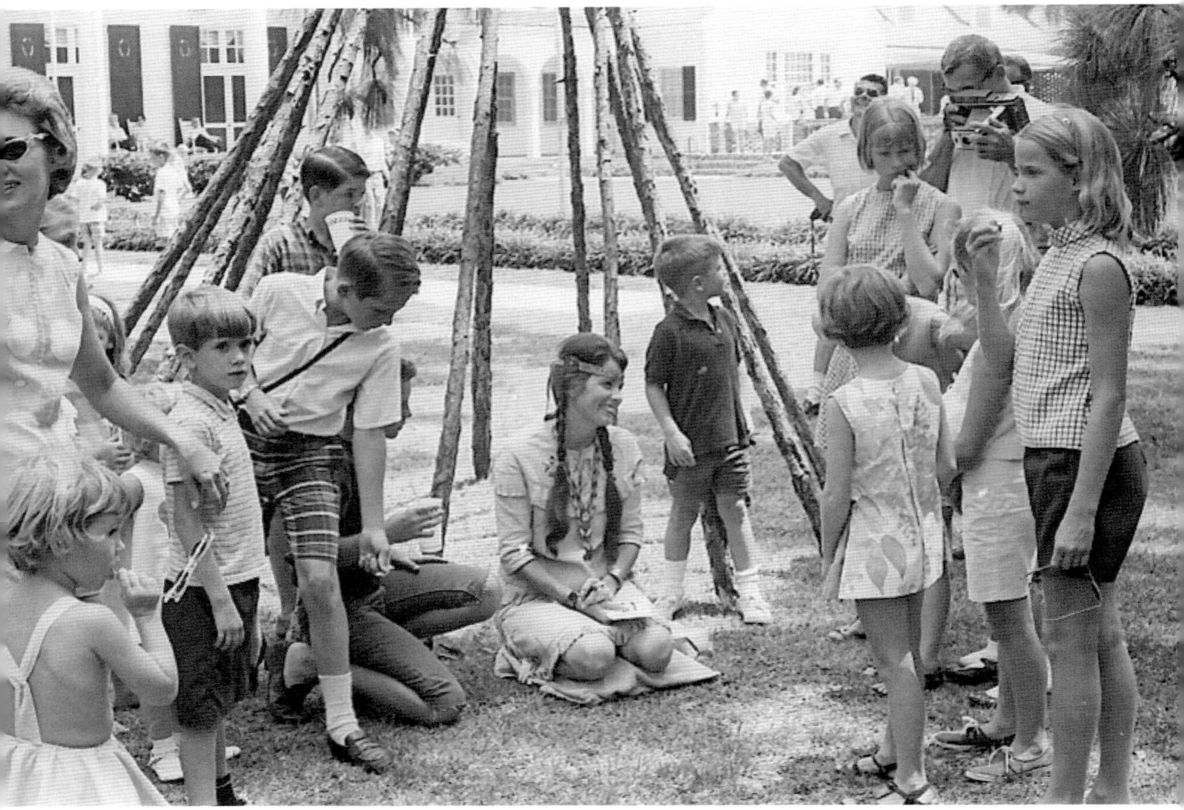

Lorraine "Happy Raine" Evans

In a show that premiered in April 1960 on WCSC Channel 5 in Charleston, Lorraine Evans began a children's show called *Happy Raine*. With limited channels, this was one of the first children's shows the children of Myrtle Beach had seen, and they were immediately smitten. Some even talked their parents into traveling to Charleston to be on the show. Imagine their delight when she came to Myrtle Beach and spent the day with them, as shown here, at Pine Lakes Country Club. Happy Raine is still remembered today with great fondness by the many adults who grew up watching her. (Courtesy MBCC.)

CHAPTER THREE

Business Leaders and Professionals

"New Town" was the name that was first bestowed upon Myrtle Beach. How fitting it was. A new town, full of possibilities, and the people came to find out what it was all about. In 1900, a contest was held and the name was changed to Myrtle Beach. People came to this new town, this Myrtle Beach. They bought lots and built houses. They opened restaurants and movie theaters. They saw the need for a bank, a bakery, and gas stations. Roads, sewage, and schools were needed. Mayors were elected, a newspaper was started, maps were drawn, children were born, a hospital was built, and still more people came. Guesthouses were opened and a hurricane came and blew it all away. It was time to rebuild anyway. The locals came together and cleaned up and rebuilt. They built better hotels, a better boardwalk, and sturdier buildings. Still, the people came.

This area is filled with people from all over the world like Holland, Greece, India, England, Austria, Russia, Germany, Italy, and Turkey. These people first came looking for paradise, and they found it here. They stayed—they raised their families here and made it their own. Myrtle Beach is still a small city but with a big heart. It opens itself to visitors—welcoming them every year. Still, people come by the millions. Burroughs was right: Myrtle Beach became a world-class resort.

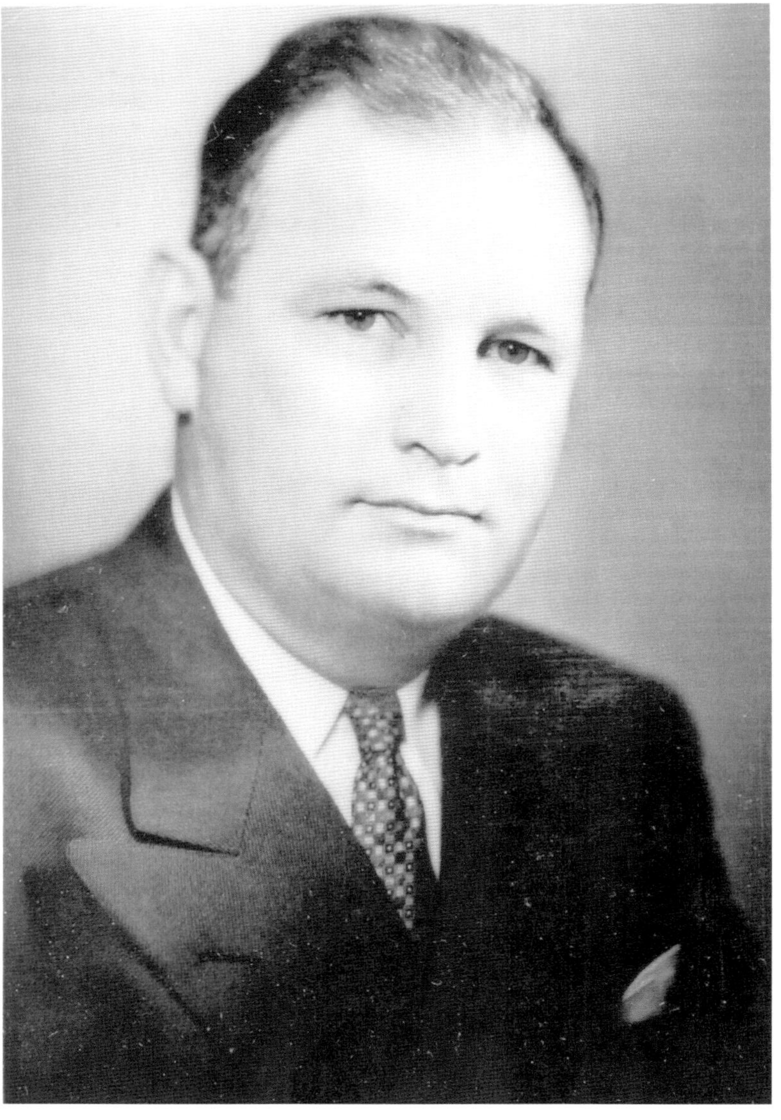

George W. Trask Jr.

His father, George Trask Sr., was a pioneer in shipping vegetables commercially up to the northern markets and was the first person to ship lettuce long distance. Living in Wilmington, George Sr. decided to purchase land in Myrtle Beach to extend his farms and George Jr. moved here to run the business G.W. Trask and Sons. The large farm was off of Tenth Avenue North, and they grew a variety of produce including lettuce, radishes, cucumbers, and beans on over 200 acres. Because of their need for ice (they used it to pack the vegetables for shipment) George Jr. built the first icehouse, Crystal Ice Company, which supplied the guesthouses and other locals with ice. George was a quiet man always looking out for people, seeing their needs, and helping them with those needs whatever they were. If a fisherman needed a new net, George would go buy some fish from him. He was a founding member of the Dunes Golf and Beach Club, a charter member of the Rotary Club, and on the school board. He was on the city council, the board to get a hospital built, and the building committee to build the first sanctuary of the First Presbyterian Church. (Courtesy Ruth Trask Gore.)

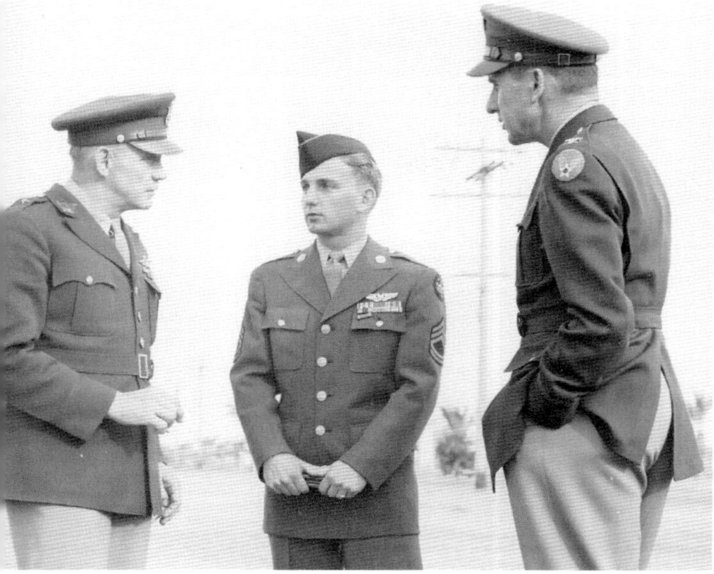

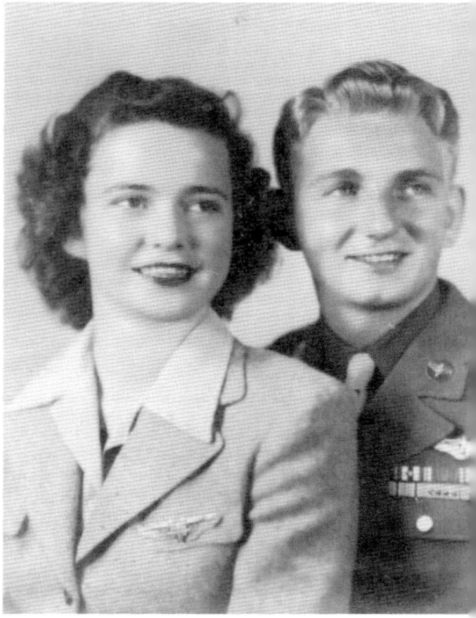

J.J. "Johnnie" Able Jr.

Above left, the commanding general of the 37th Flying Wing presents the Distinguished Service Cross to Tech Sergeant Able in ceremonies at Williams Field. Johnnie grew up reading true stories of heroes, and became one himself. A true patriot, he enlisted 10 days after Pearl Harbor and became part of a group known as the Eager Beavers. They took on missions no one else wanted in their modified B-17, called OLD 666. While on one such flight, they were attempting to get photographs of the ground forces in order to plan a ground attack, when the Japanese attacked them. Their plane was shot up and several men were severely wounded, including the pilot. Able jumped into the pilot's seat and was able to clear the area and fly away from the attack, bringing the plane, crew, and photographs back to base safely, even though he did not have a pilot's license. For his many acts of bravery, he received over 20 awards including the second highest award available, the Distinguished Flying Cross. He was honorably discharged after his second reenlistment when he was wounded in action. Johnnie came home, finished college on the GI Bill, moved back to Myrtle Beach, and became one of the most beloved attorneys in town. He offered his services pro bono to those who needed it, helping many sort out their legal affairs and purchase homes that they might not have been able to otherwise. He married Joyce Worrell and had two daughters, Robin and Carol Ann—known as "Candy." (Courtesy Robin Able Chapman.)

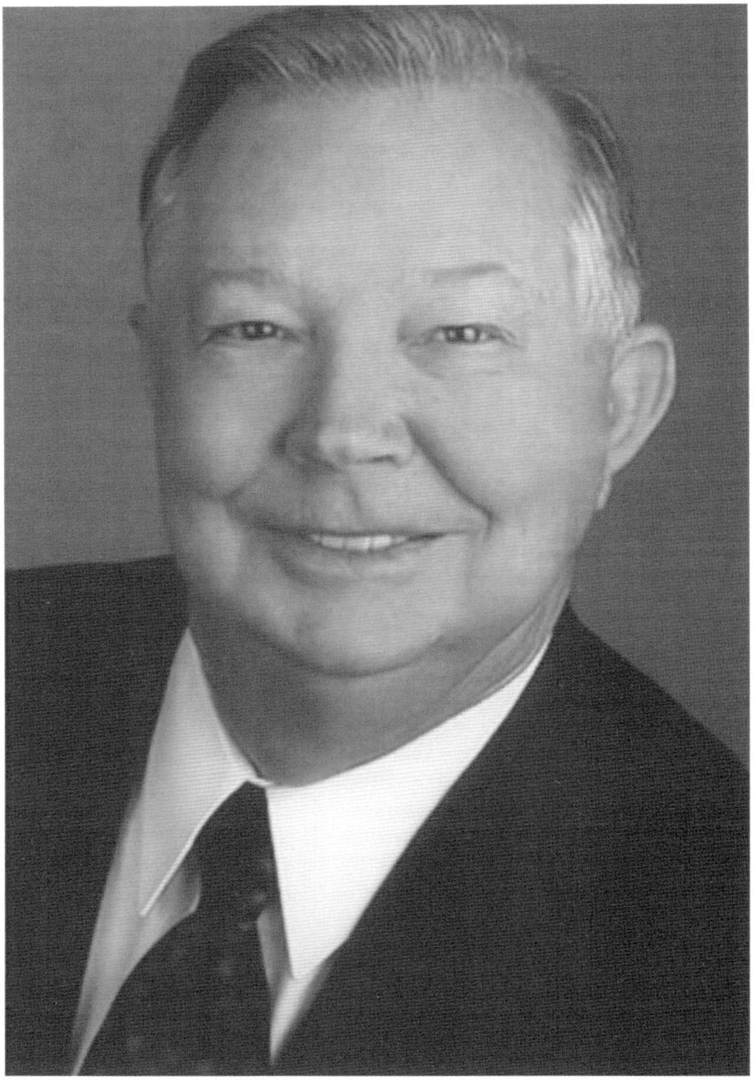

Robert Howell "Bob" Brooks

A native of Loris, Bob graduated from Clemson with a dairy degree. Later he moved to Atlanta, developed a non-dairy coffee creamer, and in 1966, founded Naturally Fresh Foods. Today, Naturally Fresh preservative-free refrigerated dressings are found in grocery stores all over the country. In 1986, he purchased a small restaurant concept called Hooters. Now a multinational chain with over 430 locations in 46 states and 20 countries, they are known for their fresh dressings, fresh wings, and fresh waitresses. Under the Hooters name, he launched a magazine, a pro golf tour, a stock car racing series, a credit card, a casino, and—probably the best known—Hooters Air. Bob also gave back to his communities. His alma mater Clemson has the Brooks Center for the Performing Arts building and the Brooks Motorsports Institute in honor of his son Mark who died in a tragic plane crash. In 2003, CCU named its new football facility Brooks Stadium in honor of its largest supporter. Deciding to slow down a little, Brooks named his son Coby president and CEO of Hooters of America and spent most of his time here. At the time of his death, he was survived by his wife Tami Springs Brooks, daughter Boni Belle, and son Coby. (Courtesy MBCC.)

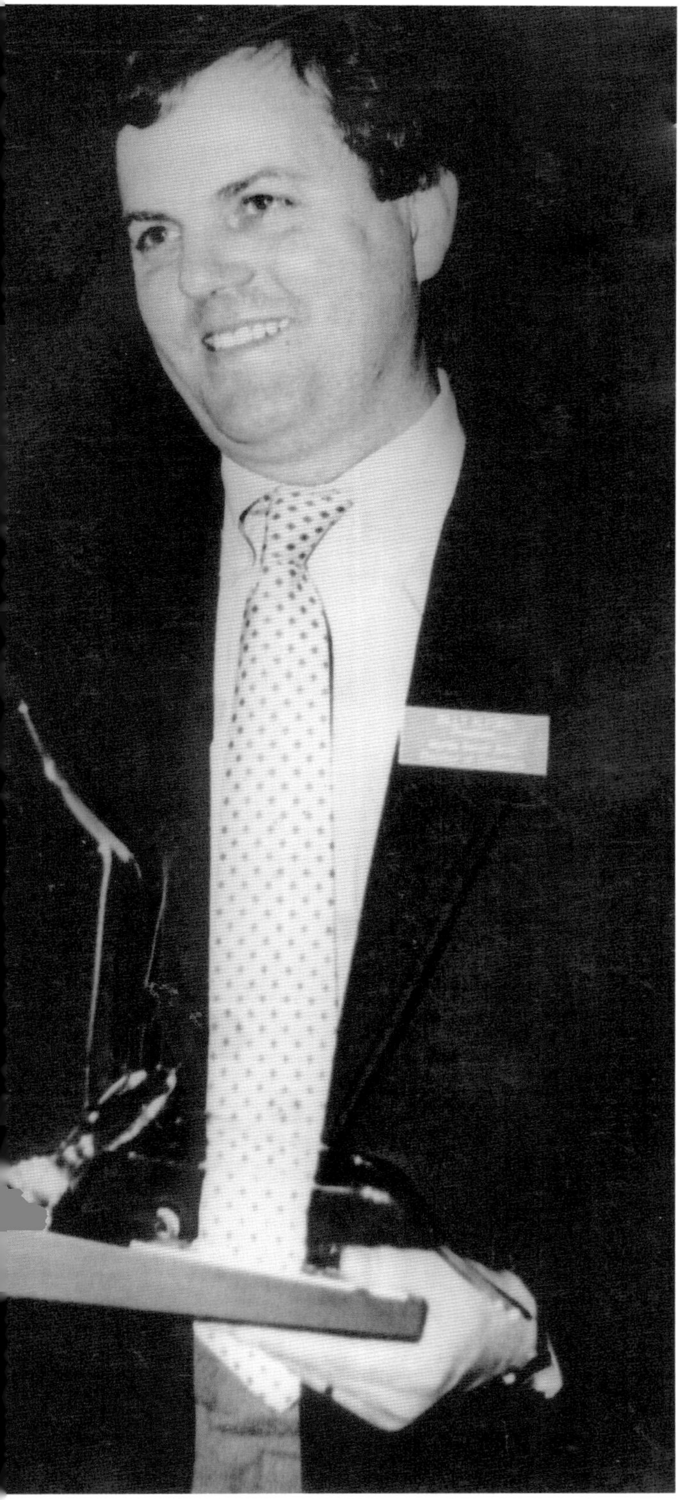

William H. "Billy" Alford
Billy's family moved here from Conway when he was 12. As locals like to say, "I got here as fast as I could." Billy is married to Dawn and has two children, Natalie and Wells. Along with Danny Isaac, he founded A&I Fire and Water Restoration Company here in Myrtle Beach. He has strived to contribute to the community, and has won several awards for his endeavors including the Citizen of the Year Award in 1985, the South Carolina Jaycees Outstanding Young American, Coastal Carolina's 1992 Alumnus of the Year, Conway American Legion Outstanding Community Service Award, the 1992 Distinguished Service Award from the South Carolina Department of Highways and Transportation, the Order of the Palmetto in 2001, and in 2003, the Ann DeBock Leadership Award for outstanding leadership and service. Known not only as a mover and shaker but also a doer, he has spearheaded efforts to fund the Carolina Bays Parkway and the Conway Bypass (the bridge bears his name), Coastal Carolina University's independence from USC, and bringing the Beach Music Hall of Fame to CCU. Keeping busy, he has served on many boards including CCU, the South Carolina Highway Commission, the Myrtle Beach Regional Economic Development Corporation, and the North Eastern Strategic Alliance organization. (Courtesy MBCC.)

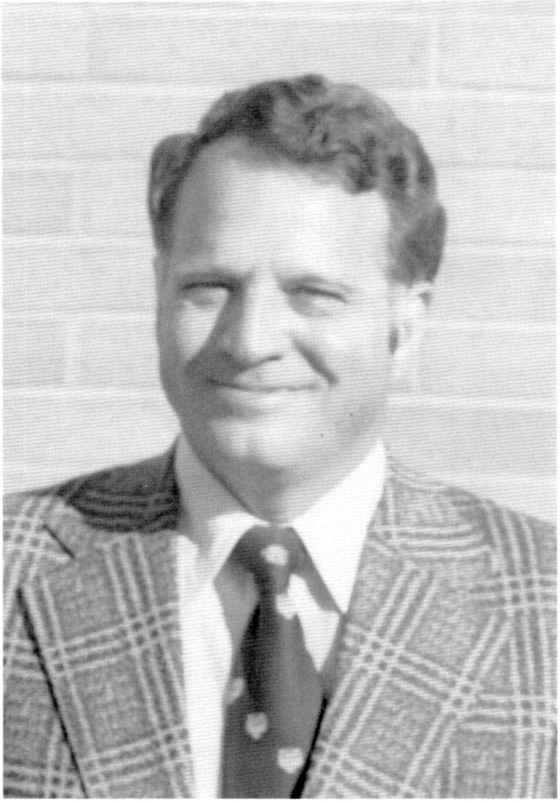

George Jacob Bishop III

After earning a degree in ceramic engineering at Clemson University in 1952, he worked in Columbia for several years. George and his family moved to Myrtle Beach in 1965. He opened Waccamaw Clay Products, producing a rare earth-toned brick that can be seen on many homes and businesses in the area. In 1977 he opened Waccamaw Pottery, known for its outlet-priced pottery and household items. Within a few years he opened Outlet Waccamaw and had franchises in the southeast a few years later. Serving on the Myrtle Beach City Council and other boards, he was known as a keen businessman and above all a Christian, and he wanted everyone to know that he loved God and wanted them to know God as well. (Courtesy MBCC.)

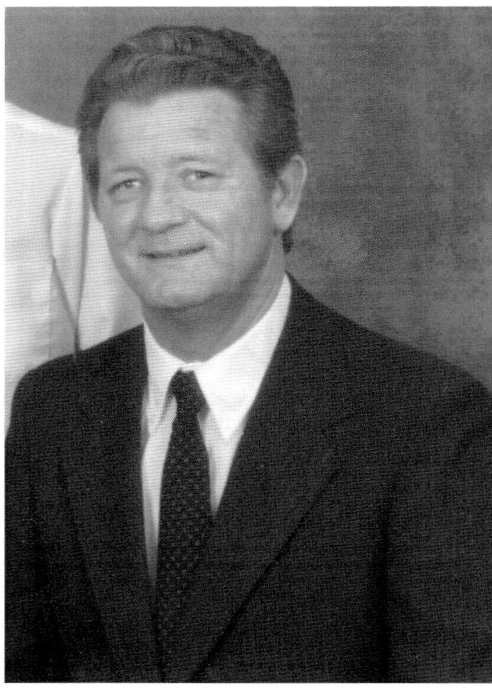

C. Ray Caudle

Born in Pilot Mountain, North Carolina, Caudle moved to Myrtle Beach in 1965, where he soon opened up Ray Caudle's Office Supply in the downtown area. A favorite among locals, he was a mainstay in the business community for many years. As president, Ray was very active with the Exchange Club, Rotary Club, Jaycee's, and the Men's Club at the First United Methodist Church. He was also on the board of directors of the chamber of commerce and the MLC Shrine Club. Best remembered for his wry sense of humor and ready joke, Ray died in 2010 at the age of 76. (Courtesy Caudle family.)

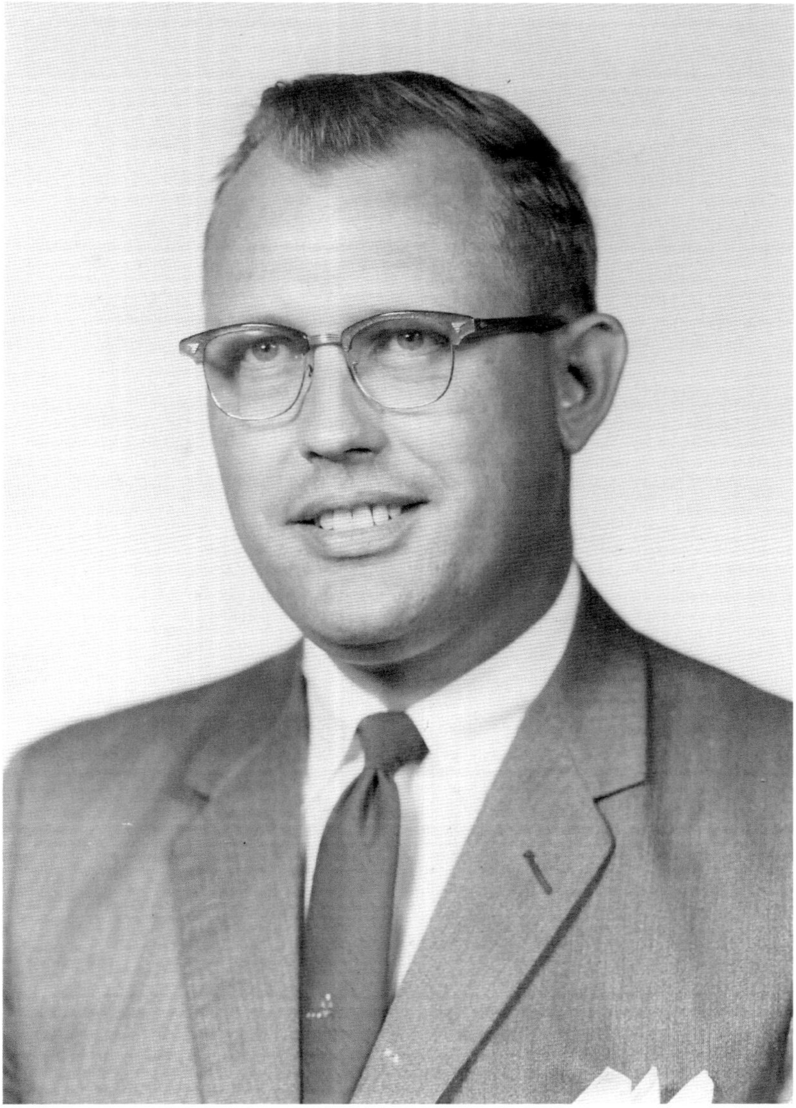

Archie Shaw Dargan Jr.
With a degree in mechanical engineering he received from Clemson in 1949, Archie founded Dargan Construction Co. of Myrtle Beach in 1953. A southern gentleman of faith and generosity, he believed in giving back to the community where he made his home and raised his family. He supported area colleges, universities, and churches and was active on many boards and civic organizations. Because of his contributions, he received many awards including Rotarian of the Year, Service to Mankind (Sertoma Club), the Community Award of Merit from Coastal Carolina University, Citizen of the Year from the Chamber of Commerce, and the Silver Beaver Award from the Boy Scouts. His legacy can be seen up and down the strand in many of the high-rise hotels and buildings like the Dixie Stampede, the Carolina Opry, Georgetown Hospital, Myrtle Beach Manor Nursing Home, Horry-Georgetown Technical College, and Coastal Carolina University. Always up for a challenge, he was an investor in many businesses such as Myrtle Beach National, Coastal Crane, and the Caravelle Resort. Archie died at the age of 86 in 2011. (Courtesy of MBCC.)

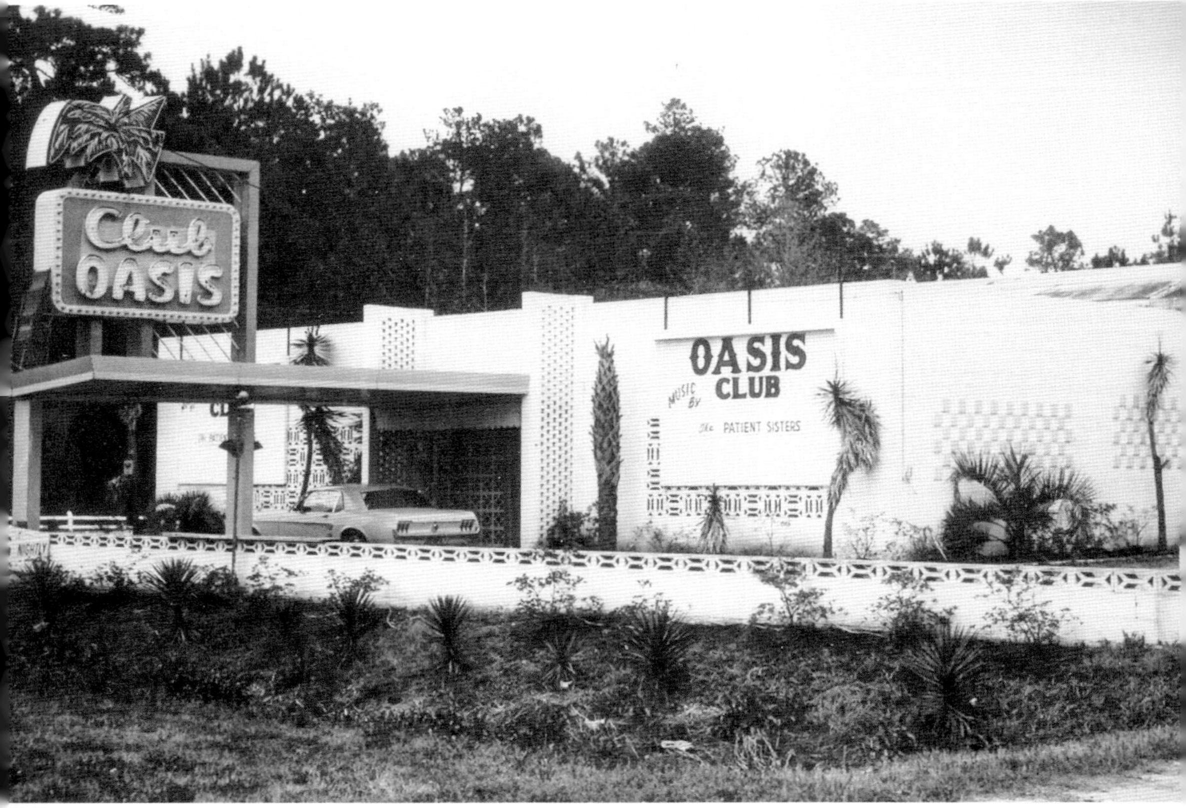

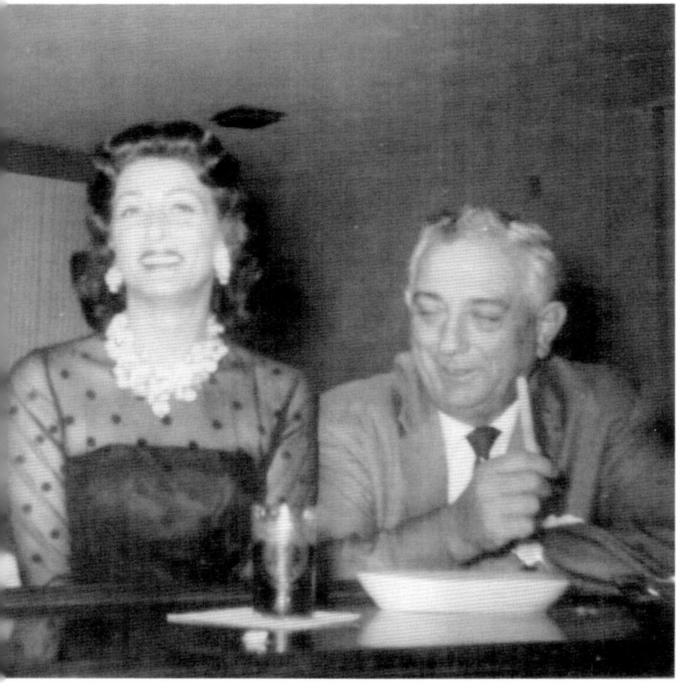

Ira "Cooter" Jennings
The Hub Drive-In, Sloppy Joe's, and The Bowery are just a few of the businesses he was involved in along the Grand Strand, either owning, co-owning, or operating them. Located just past the city limits was his Oasis Club on Highway 501. the club's building had previously been the Seminole Indian Village, which featured alligator wresting. The Oasis had the first piano bar and burlesque dancers in the area in the 1960s. Jazz piano, beach, and other popular music could be heard there most nights, and locals and tourists alike could be found on the dance floor. Cooter was also involved in the Brookgreen Room and Marine Patio at the Ocean Forest Hotel. He died November 29, 1979, at the age of 76 from heart problems. He and his wife Rebecca had five children: Rex, Jay, Randy, Sandra, and Darlene. (Courtesy Randy Jennings.)

Truman Ellenwood Moore Sr.

He came to Myrtle Beach and partnered with his brother Jeff at Moore Construction to build high-end buildings. They built the Chapin Memorial Library, the third Myrtle Beach Pavilion in 1949, and the Meher Spiritual Center. They also built many residential homes including James Bryan Sr.'s house and both of Gerard Tempesta's homes. A truly great artist, Truman was a 1923 graduate of the Chicago Art Institute. In later years he began working with wood, feeling the grains and seeing the possibilities in a piece of wood that most people will never see—he became a fine wood sculptor. (Courtesy MBCC.)

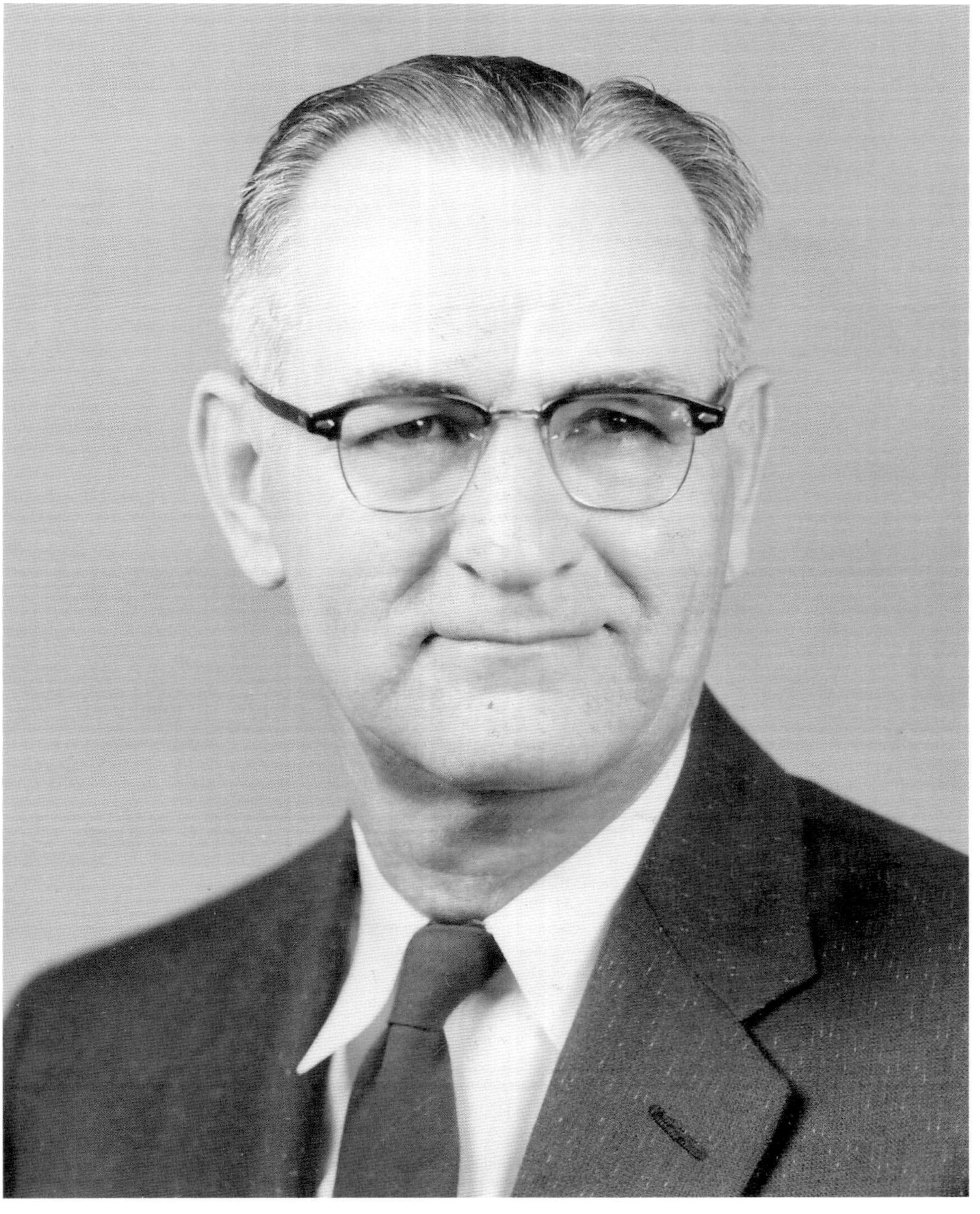

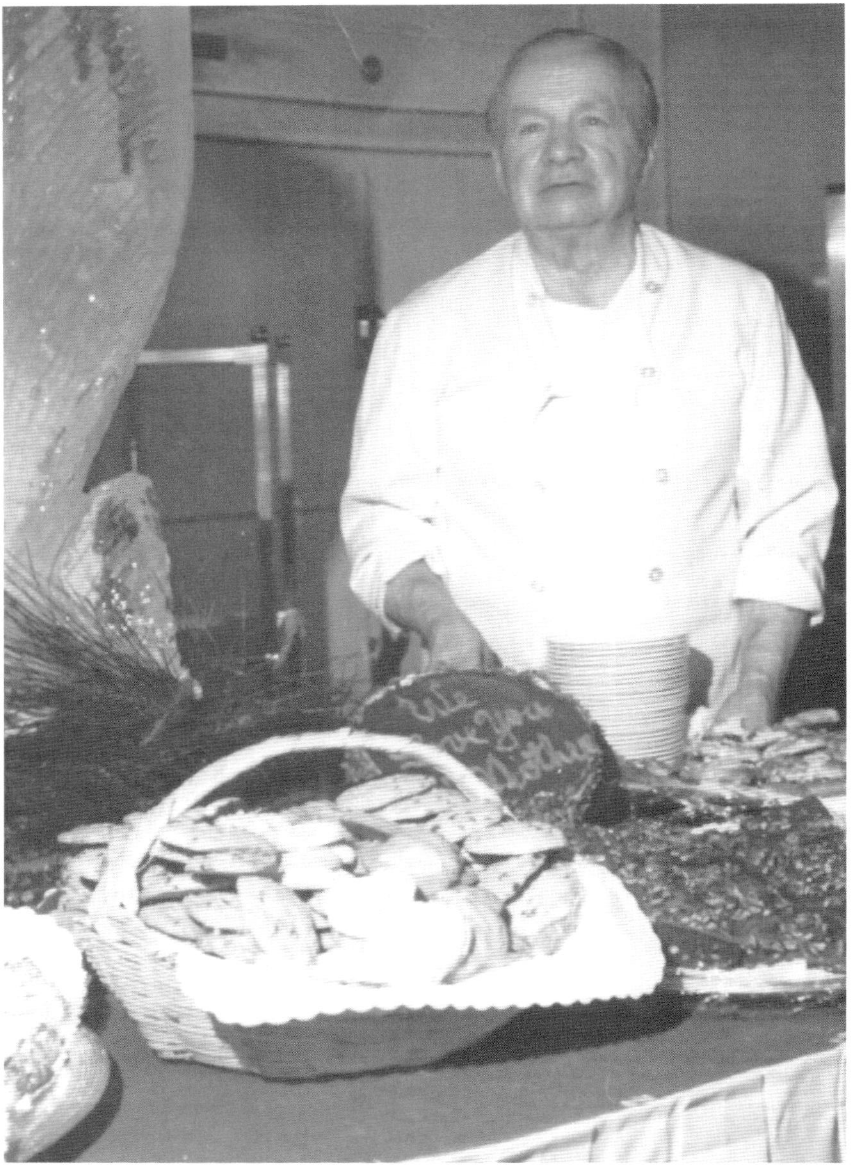

John H. "John the Baker" or "Pops" Schiller

John the Baker opened the first bakery in 1946. Before coming to America he was an apprentice baker, served in the military, was a prisoner of war, and a stow-away. All of this made him who he was, known for his positive attitude and easy smiles. Like many immigrants to this country, he was a hard worker. He would work seven days a week. The bakery was open six days, and he would go to church on Sunday and then over to the bakery to clean and prepare for Monday. Pops loved his "paradise," (Myrtle Beach) and was always ready and willing to help anyone, even sponsoring people from his native Austria to come to America, including his mother and one of his sisters. He searched for years for his second sister, finally finding her in a nursing home in the 1970s, in what was then Czechoslovakia. Even at the age of 90, the government would not let her leave the country. Retired, John the Baker made the trip several times to see her before she died. (Courtesy Ruthie Schiller Kearns.)

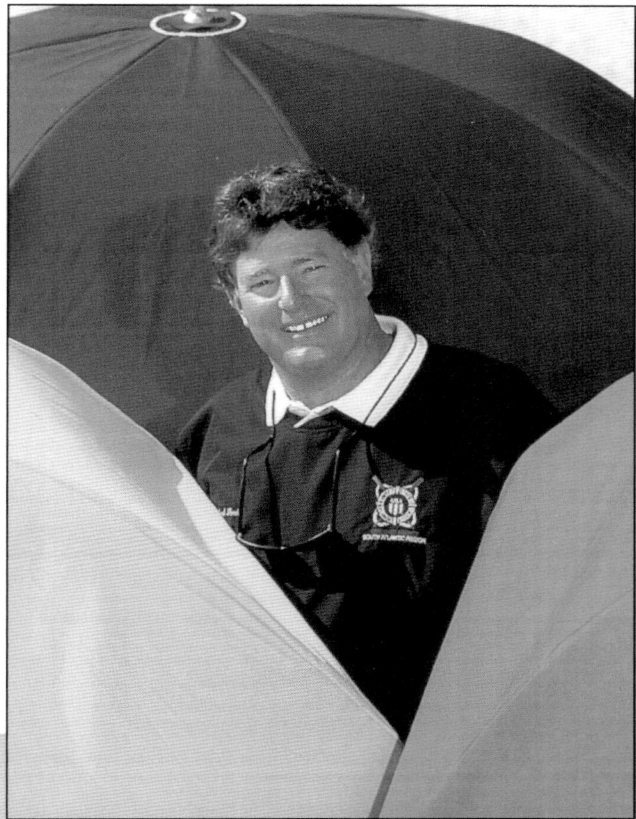

George Lack
George moved to Myrtle Beach in 1956 and began living the dream when, at 17, he began lifeguarding and was always on the beach. The dream continued when he bought the beach concession service he was working for and renamed it Lacks Beach Service. He has worked hard over the years toward public awareness of beach erosion, storm drainage, and public access to the beach, while keeping the beach beautiful, safe, and open to everyone. With Lacks Outdoor Furniture, Lack expanded the business to include umbrellas, chairs, and cabanas when he could not find the high quality furniture needed to handle the salt, sun, and constant use on the beach. This gave his once seasonal employees year-round employment. (Courtesy Debra Lack.)

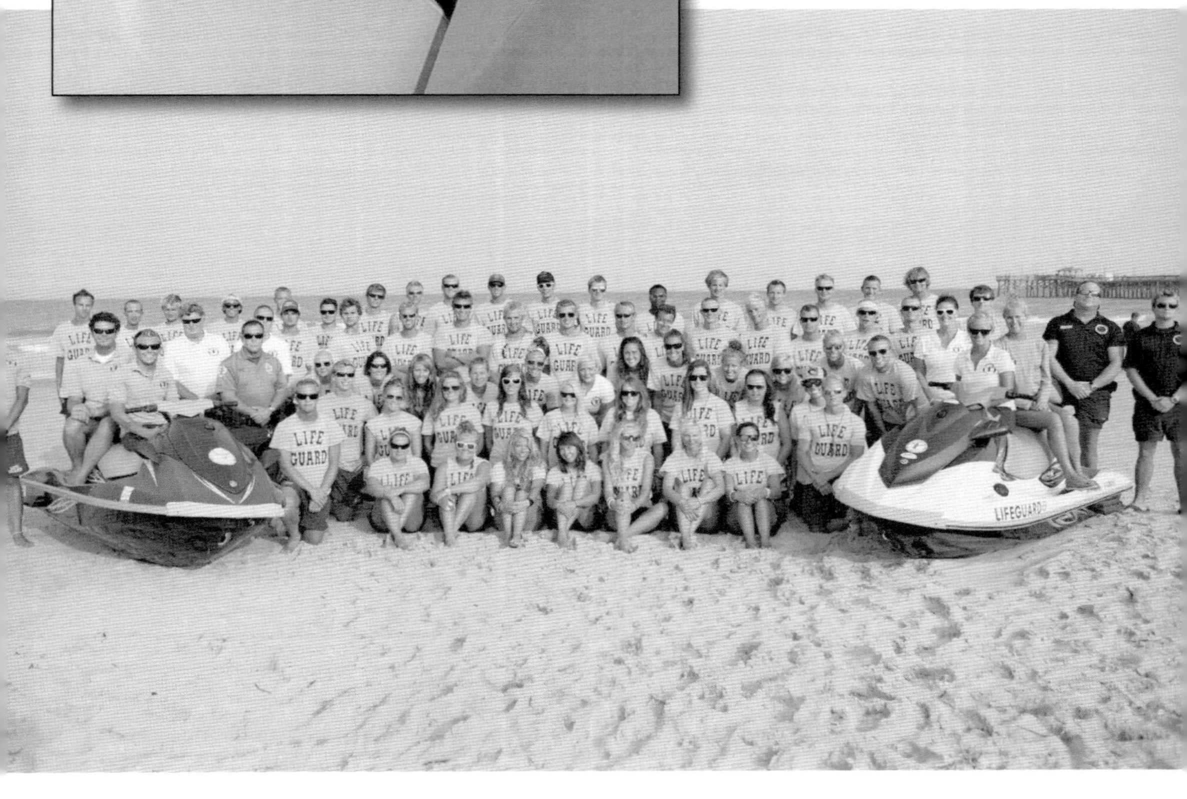

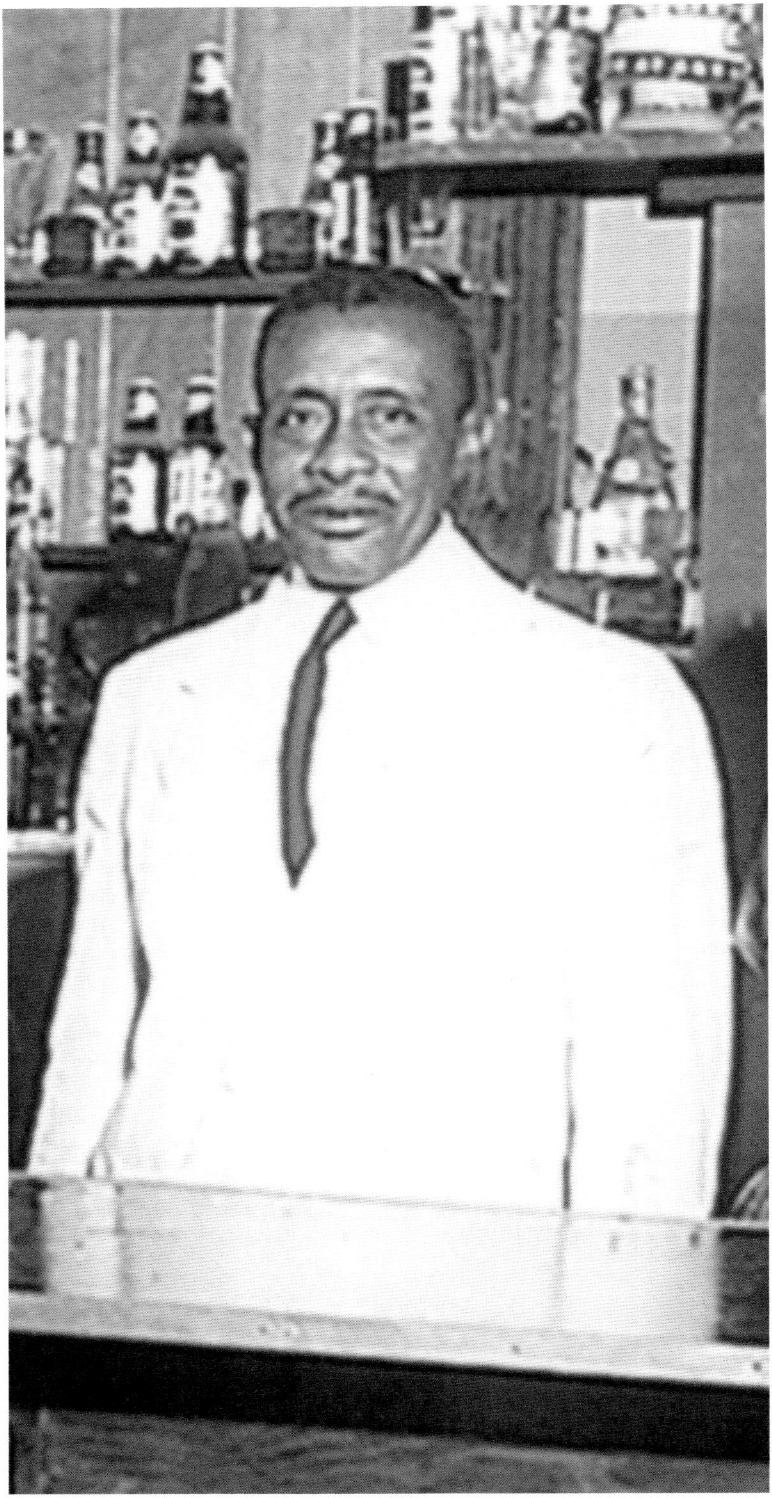

Charlie Fitzgerald
Charlie was the owner of Charlie's Place in Whispering Pines over on Carver Street where everyone would come to dance in the 1940s. Known for being a stopover for famous and soon-to-be-famous music acts, dancing was the order of business. It was also the site of a shootout staged by the Klu Klux Klan on August 26, 1950. The Klan assembled, drove over to Charlie's Place, abducted Fitzgerald, and proceeded to fire over 500 shots into his place of business. One person, a Klansman, was killed. Charlie was beat up, knifed, and left in the street. Thankfully, he survived and reopened his business a little later. Things were not quite the same after that, and he and his wife left the area a few years later. A piece of history, the buildings now sit abandoned. (Courtesy Jack Thompson.)

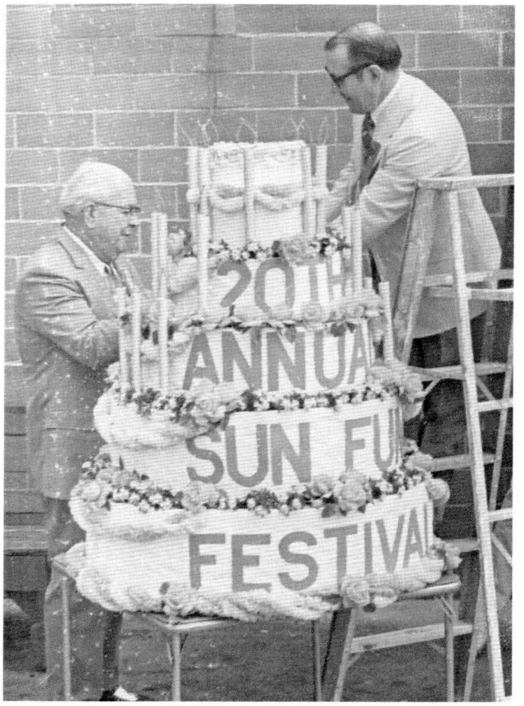

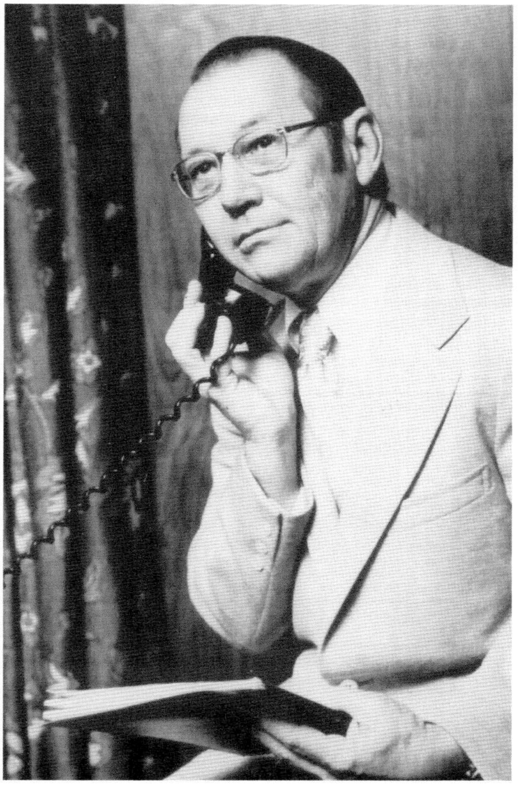

Mark Garner
Mark Garner was a newspaper owner and editor. He was known for his fairness in business and his love of Myrtle Beach. He was the mayor for multiple terms, constantly vigilant in promoting the image of a family beach. He worked with business owners, the chamber of commerce, and locals to make Myrtle Beach all that it could be. Even after retirement from the hustle and bustle of the newspaper business, Garner was always available. People could find him in his little office over on Broadway beside the old *Sun News*, still working at promoting the city and helping others in any way he could, ready to sit down and talk for a while if you needed advice or listen if you just needed an ear. No matter what he did or what award he won, he always said he was just a newspaperman. (Both, courtesy Jack Thompson.)

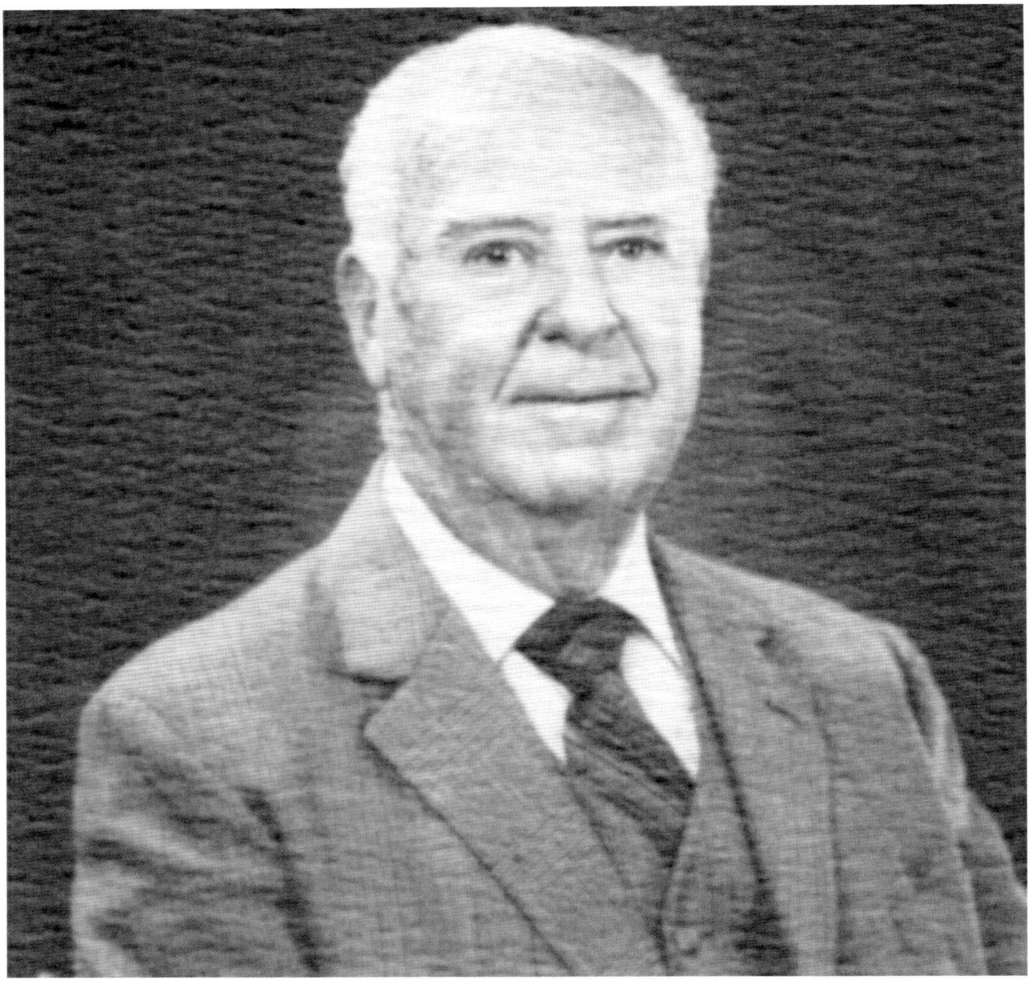

John S. Divine

Divine was born in 1899 and came to Myrtle Beach in 1934, where he became one of the first merchants. His tackle business eventually expanded and turned into Divine's Sporting Goods Store. He was a charter member of Coastal Federal Savings and Loan Association and an original board member. John was one of the organizers of the first American Legion post here, a charter member of the Civitan Club (serving as the first president), and on the city council in 1954. (Courtesy Ruthie Schiller Kearns.)

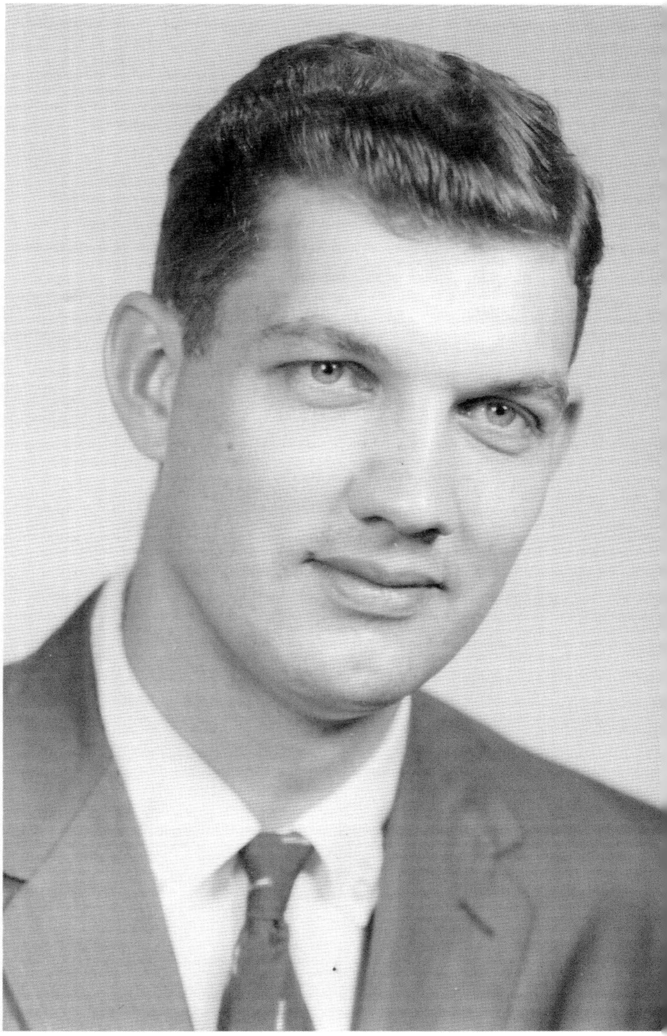

Clay Brittain Jr.

Originally from North Carolina, the patriarch of the Brittain clan began his career in the local tourist industry when he went into business with his uncle Steven Craig Chapman, who built the Chesterfield Inn. In 1962, they bought a small guest house called Howard's Manor and opened a seafood restaurant called The Sea Captain's House. This restaurant is still in business today and has been added on to over the years, but upon close inspection visitors can still see the original vacation hideaway that the Taylor family built in the 1930s. The Sea Captain's House is known for its she-crab soup. Clay's son David began his career at the restaurant. When David died unexpectedly in 2011, the community lost a great friend and the family lost a beloved son.

Clay became the owner of the Chesterfield Inn in 1965, which he managed until 1991. One of the great community visionaries, Clay was one of the founders of Myrtle Beach National when it began in 1971. It is now the largest golf course management company in the Southeast. Clay served as the president until he retired in 2006.

A firm supporter of education, in 1993, Clay, along with Craig Wall Jr. and CCU business dean Bill Baxley, created the Wall Fellows program at CCU. In 1995 he was named an honorary founder of Coastal Carolina University, and in 2001 the Clay Brittain Jr. Center for Resort Tourism at CCU was named in his honor for his work in establishing the professional golf management degree there. Over the years, he has received many awards and honors for his unending service to the community, tourism, and the golf industry.

While known as a mentor and community leader, his priority has always been his faith and his family. These are qualities his wife, Pat, shares and that they passed on to their children, David, Clay III, Matthew, and Ann, and continue to pass on to their grandchildren. (Courtesy MBCC.)

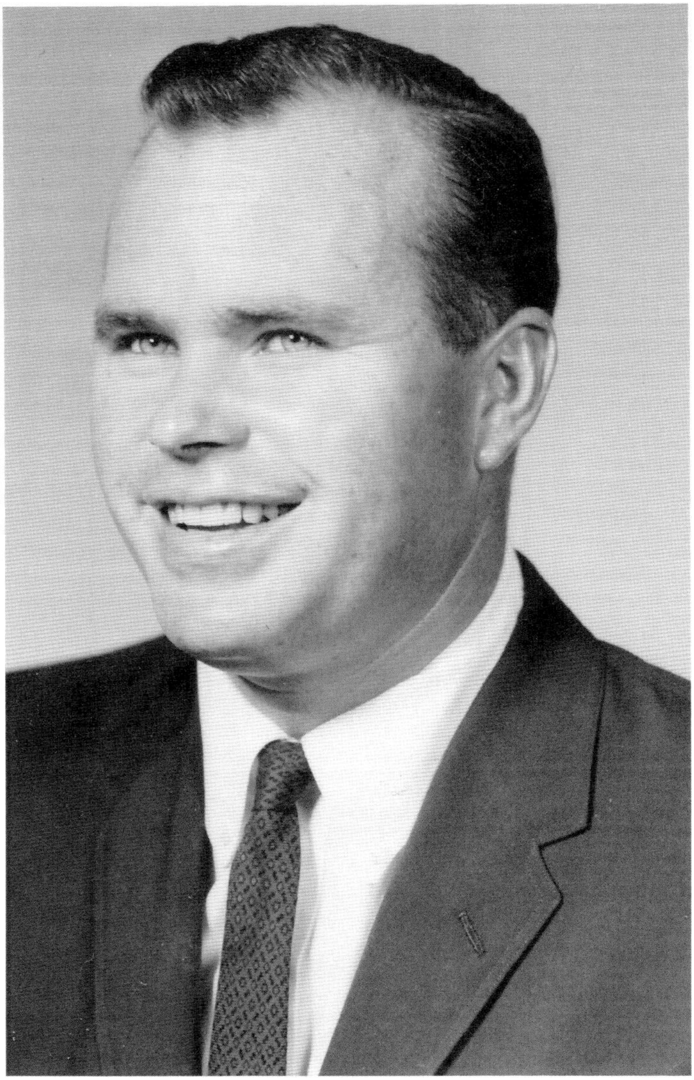

Cecil Brandon

Cecil opened Brandon Advertising in 1959 and was known for making postcards of area guesthouses. These cards are treasured memories of a bygone era. His son Scott runs the business today. As one of the founders of the Golf Holiday in 1963, which became the Myrtle Beach Golf Holiday in 1967, Cecil Brandon has been a part of Myrtle Beach for many years. He was president of Myrtle Beach Golf Holiday until he retired in 1997. He has been honored with many awards including the Coastal Academy Parent of the Year Award in 1981, the South Carolina Tourism Award in 1982, the Myrtle Beach Citizen of the Year Award in 1994, and the Jason Ammons Free Enterprise Award in 1995. In 1996, he was awarded the Order of the Palmetto, the South Carolina Tourism Ambassador of the Year Award, and the Habitat for Humanity Award. In 1997 he also received the Palmetto Patriot Award, and in 2005, he was named one of South Carolina Golf's 100 most influential people and inducted into the Carolinas Golf Hall of Fame. When the Myrtle Beach Golf Hall of Fame was created, he was one of the six charter members inducted in 2009. Cecil is a man who envisioned the future of golf, and through a lot of hard work set about making it a reality. (Courtesy MBCC.)

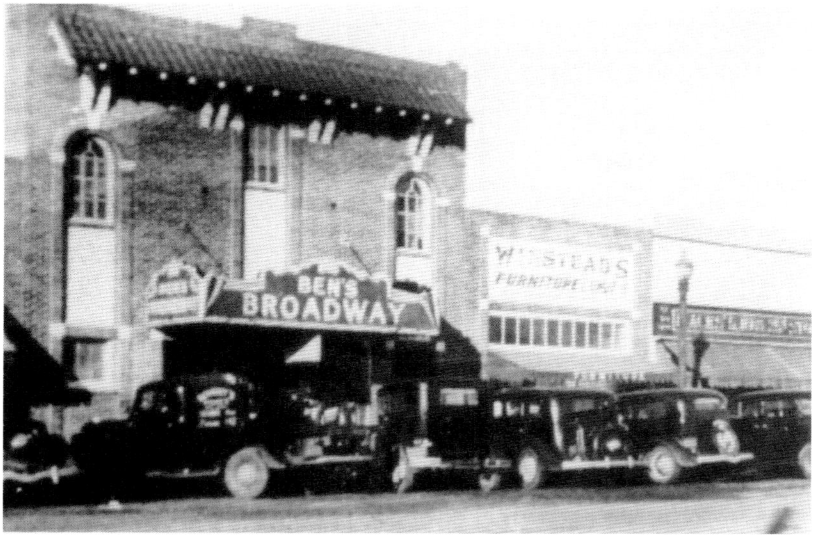

Bunyon Bailey Benfield

B.B. Benfield was born in 1891. He came to Myrtle Beach from Dillon in 1935. As a businessman, he saw the need for the first movie house and built one a couple years later—the Broadway Theatre on Main Street. For many reasons, everyone was excited when the theater opened. Prior to its opening, those with cars would travel the long dirt road to Georgetown to see a movie, making a day of it. At that time, some people had never seen a movie, and now they could walk down the street to see one. Benfield brought a much needed and new form of entertainment to Myrtle Beach. He also opened the Gloria Theatre a few years later. The Broadway closed in 1959 and reopened as the Cinema Theatre and would show movies only on the weekends. B.B., as his peers knew him, was on the first city council of Myrtle Beach. He was also a member of the First Baptist Church of Myrtle Beach. He was appointed by Carl C. Pridgen as a member of the original board of the First National Bank of Myrtle Beach. When the First National Bank of Myrtle Beach merged with the South Carolina National Bank, Benfield was retained as a member of the advisory board of directors until his death in 1972. He is pictured below with his wife, Clara. (Above, courtesy CML; below, Mary Catherine Hardee.)

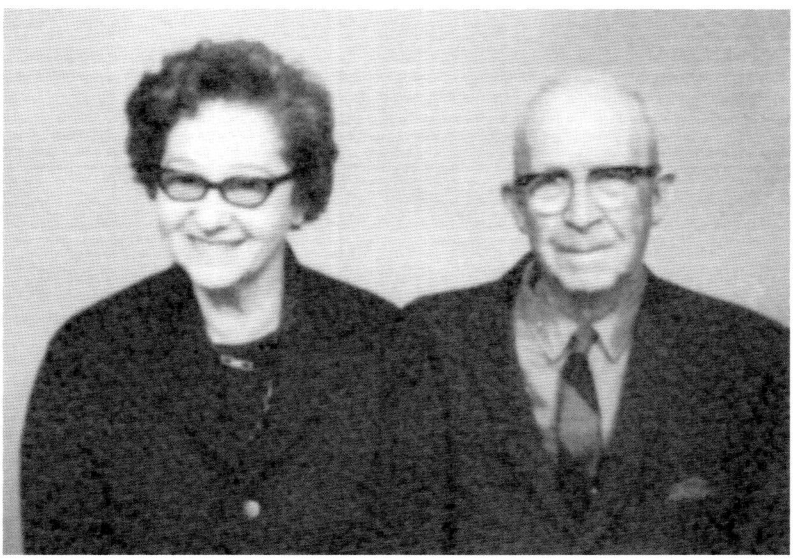

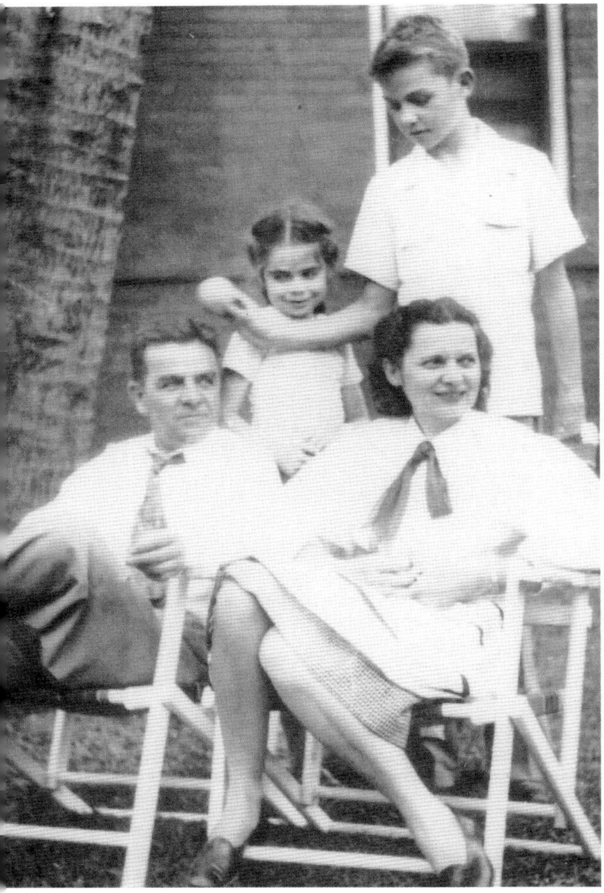

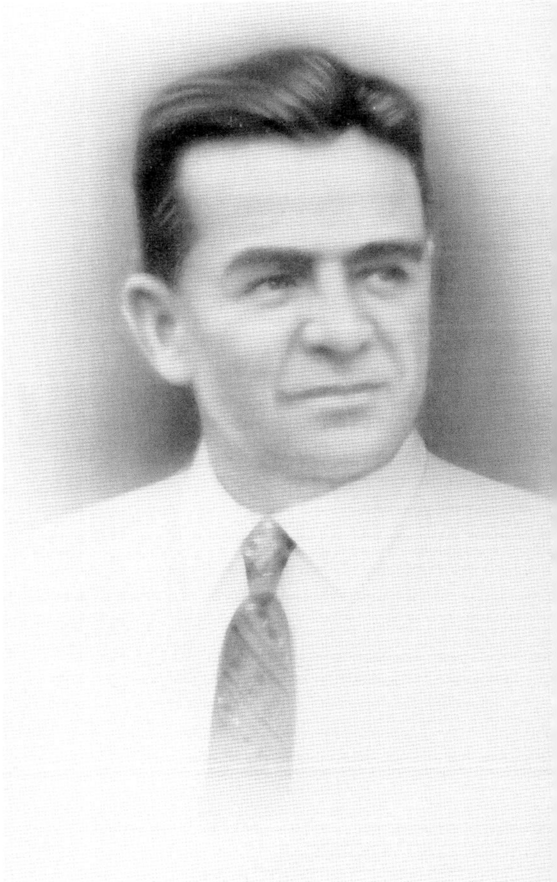

James Edward Bryan Jr.
Very active in the community and interested in the shape of the future, Bryan was a member of the steering committee to discuss incorporation of the town. He was a member of the Myrtle Beach Schools board of trustees, the City of Myrtle Beach Zoning Commission, The Rotary Club, and the Elks. After his father's death, he was named president of Chapin Company and the general manager of Myrtle Beach Farms in 1938, positions he held until his untimely death in 1955. He was honored with several awards including the Myrtle Beach Chamber of Commerce Man of the Year Award in 1954. Always planning and thinking of ways to make Myrtle Beach better for residents and visitors alike, he was instrumental in giving land for many projects including the Dunes Golf and Beach Club and to the City of Myrtle Beach for its first park and library, named the Chapin Memorial Park and Chapin Memorial Library in honor of Simeon B. Chapin. Bryan married Sarah Eugenia Gordon in 1931 and they had two children, Poddy and Sallie. (Courtesy Sarah Bryan.)

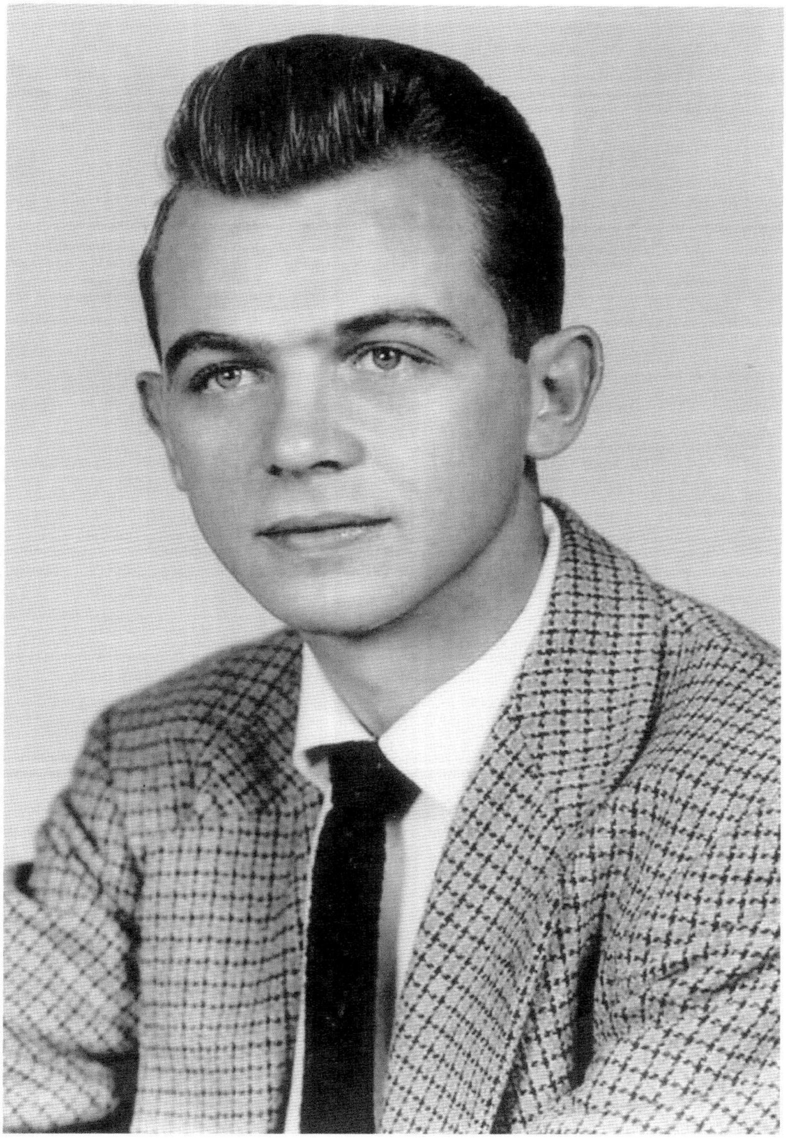

James Edward "Poddy" Bryan III
Poddy, as he was affectionately called by family and friends, is remembered primarily for another take on golf: miniature golf. He, along with Al Tirrell, built the first miniature golf course, The Jungle Golf, in the late 1960s. The next course was Around the World in 18 Holes. It was filled with igloos, mountains, and lakes. They captured the imagination of residents and tourists alike, so much so that they were asked to build them in other states, including Virginia. Poddy and Clements built the first driving range where Myrtle Square Mall was later located. He and Lloyd Chinnes had a company to manage the miniature golf courses in the area. They also built the Swash Boat rides and waterslides. One of his last creations, Atlanticus, located behind the old Chapin Company, still operates today. When Poddy went off to school, he majored in English literature and became a professor. He married and they had four children, John "Andy," William F., Laura Caroline, and Sarah Luisa. He is fondly remembered around town for his imagination and creativity. (Courtesy Sarah Bryan.)

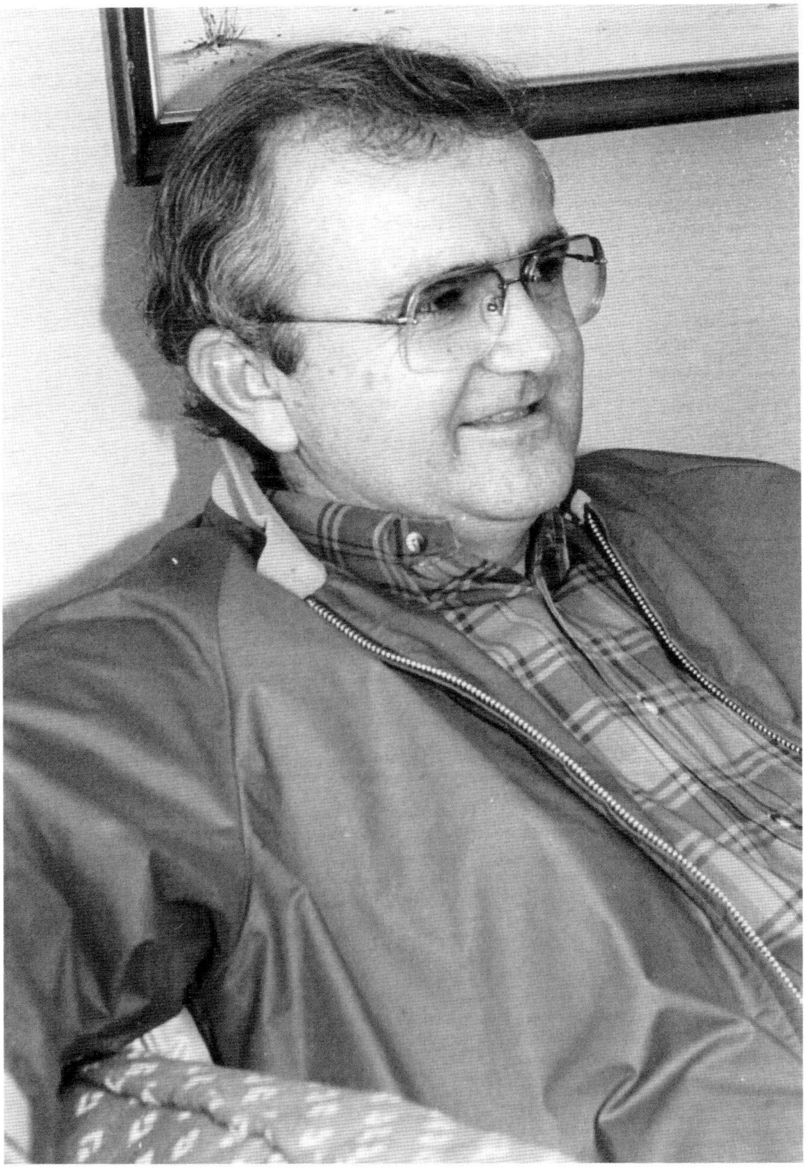

Vernon Brake

The Brakes have been busy since their move here in 1960. Vernon opened the Firestone dealership and shortly thereafter the family leased the Cottonwood Motel, which his wife Georgie Ann ran until 1980. Their hotel was one of the first to offer the golf package. In 1970, along with partners, Vernon bought The Breakers Hotel, which he managed until 2004. In 1972, they tore down the old building and built a four-story "high-rise," added heat to the rooms, and expanded the golf packages. Soon, Myrtle Beach Golf Holiday was born and Vernon was a part of it. The season expanded to February–October, and eventually Myrtle Beach became a year-round destination. Named Hotelier of the Year in 2002, Vernon Brake is also a past board member of the Myrtle Beach Chamber of Commerce. He is part of the Myrtle Beach National Corporation and serves on the board of directors. A man of integrity and wisdom, he is considered by his peers as a person to listen to when he speaks. (Courtesy MBCC.)

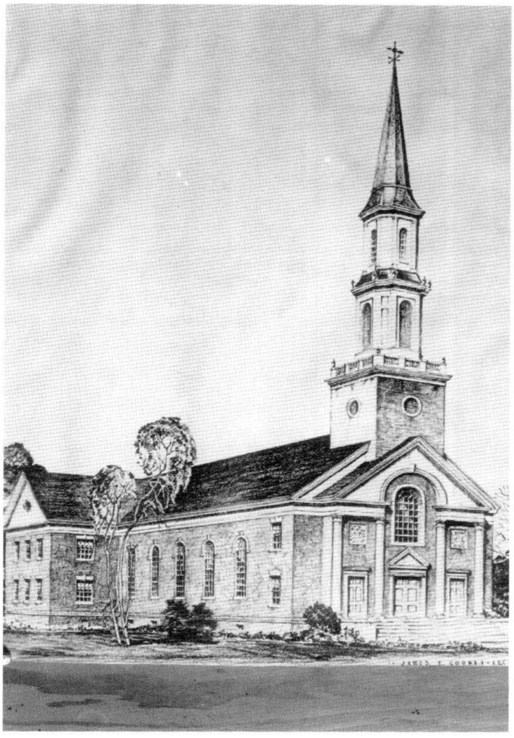

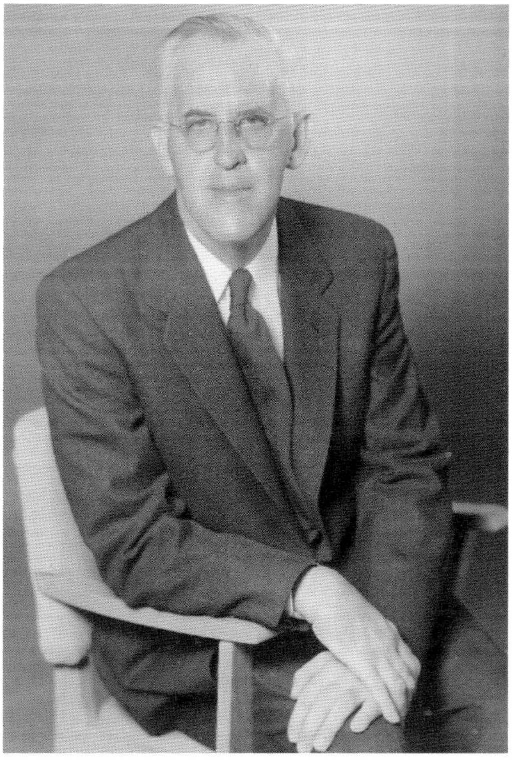

James Edward Cooney
Since there was not an architect between Wilmington, North Carolina, and Charleston, South Carolina, and after much encouragement from the locals, James moved with his wife Florentine and first daughter, Barbara, to Myrtle Beach in 1938. Their second daughter, Janice, was born here several years later. As the first architect in the area, he is remembered for the design of many of the historic buildings, some of which still stand, although many have been lost forever. He designed the Chapin Memorial Library in 1949; the first city hospital, Ocean View Memorial Hospital, which opened in 1958; the first convent, St. Andrews Convent in 1958; and the first city hall—Myrtle Beach City Hall. Also designed by Cooney were the Myrtle Beach High School on Sixteenth Avenue North, the Dunes Village development in 1955, the Church of St. James in 1961, the Chapel of Lady of Rosary in Kingstree, the Singing Surf Motel, the First Baptist Church of Myrtle Beach, and the last Myrtle Beach Pavilion. He designed countless residences, office buildings, churches, and hotels throughout the Grand Strand. Very active in the community, he was a member of the Elks Lodge, the Myrtle Wood Golf Club, the Rotary Club, and the Racing Association of Myrtle Beach. (Courtesy Janice Cooney.)

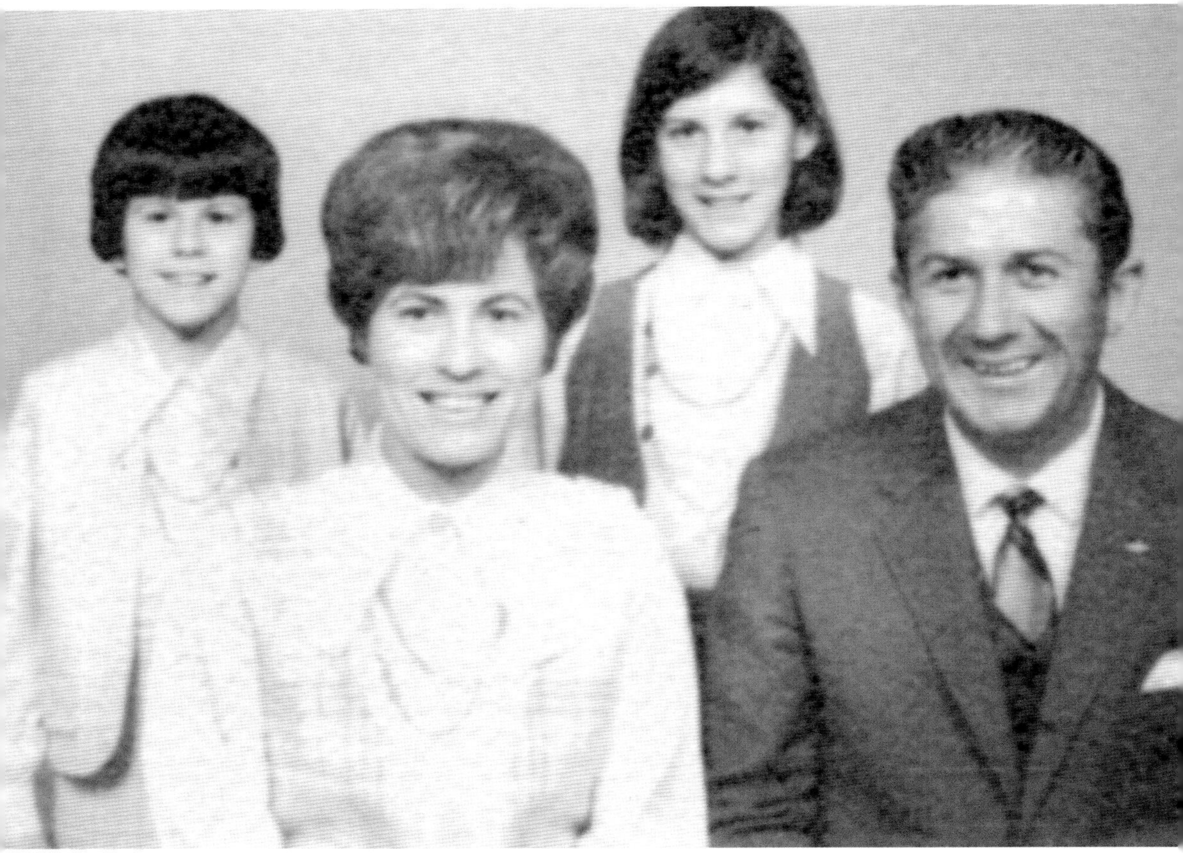

Ted Clifton Collins

Collins was appointed municipal court judge in 1988 and served until his unexpected death in 2000. Being well respected, on March 13, 2001, the city council named the law enforcement center in his honor. The proclamation at the ceremony read "Ted Collins was well known for his compassion, humor, friendliness, warmth and personality, traits that won the respect of others and served him well in politics and on the bench." (Courtesy Mary Catherine Hardee.)

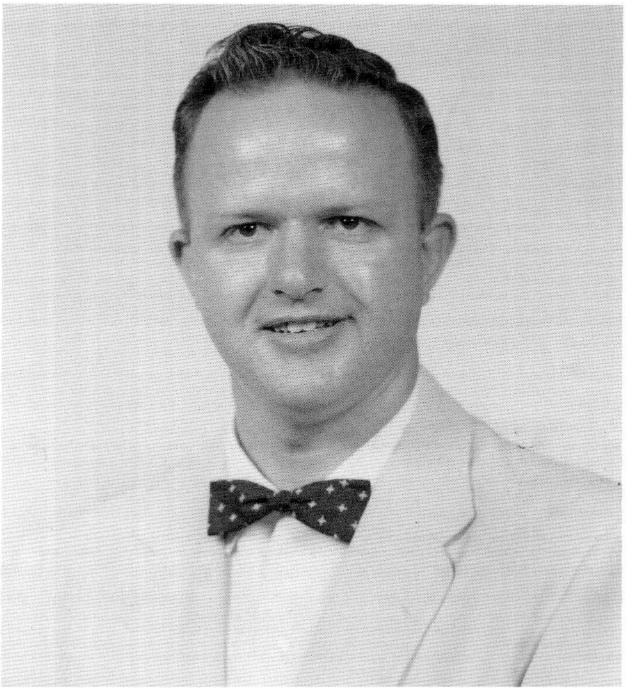

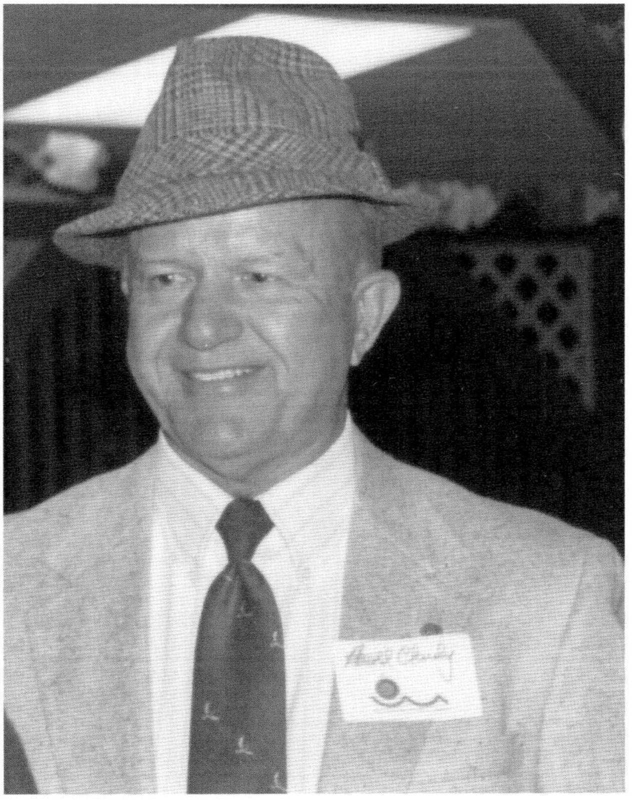

Harold Dean Clardy
Clardy began working for Chapin Company in 1943 and became president of Myrtle Beach Farms in 1975. He served on many boards over the years including Coastal Federal, the chamber of commerce, and the Merchants Association. Always active in civic affairs and the community, he was also involved with the Convention Center Committee, the Hi Newcomer, Horry County Red Cross, American Legion, and the Lions Club. He passed away at the age of 84 in 2012. (Courtesy MBCC.)

Julius Lambert "Lambo" Schwartz

Known for his leadership, hard work, and love of others, Lambo, a Rotary member since 1946, followed the Rotary motto "Service above Self" and was an exemplary role model. After he moved his family to Myrtle Beach, Lambo bought the Nu-Way Laundry and Royal Cleaners in 1962, which his family still operates today.

Julius Lambert Schwartz, CEO of the Nu-Way Laundry and Royal Cleaners and the state director of Rotary Club International, was best known for his interest in promoting positive growth in the city. He was the driving force behind The Myrtle Beach Convention Center and the reason that Dan D'Antoni's Beach Ball Classic moved to the Myrtle Beach Convention Center as he (along with John Rhodes) catapulted the yearly basketball tournament from an 8-team to a 16-team event. The wastewater treatment facility was named for him because of his work that began when he first came to this area. He was chairman of the Grand Strand Water and Sewer Authority for 15 years and a member until his death.

He and his wife Mary Jane had seven children: Mark, Ann, Michael, Jay, Sydney, Sonia, and Janie. Described as the best friend anyone could have ever had, he left behind a world full of them when he died. He suffered a heart attack while playing his favorite game, golf, at the Dunes Golf and Beach Club in 1993. (Courtesy Schwartz family.)

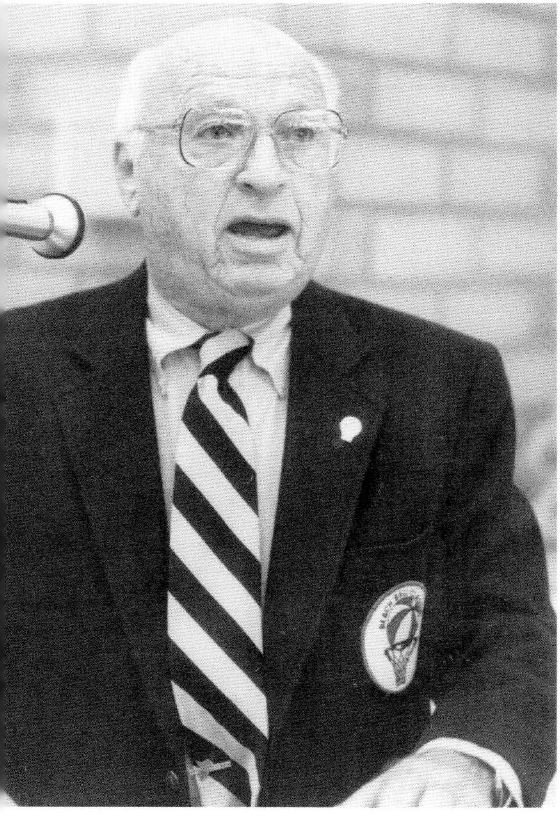

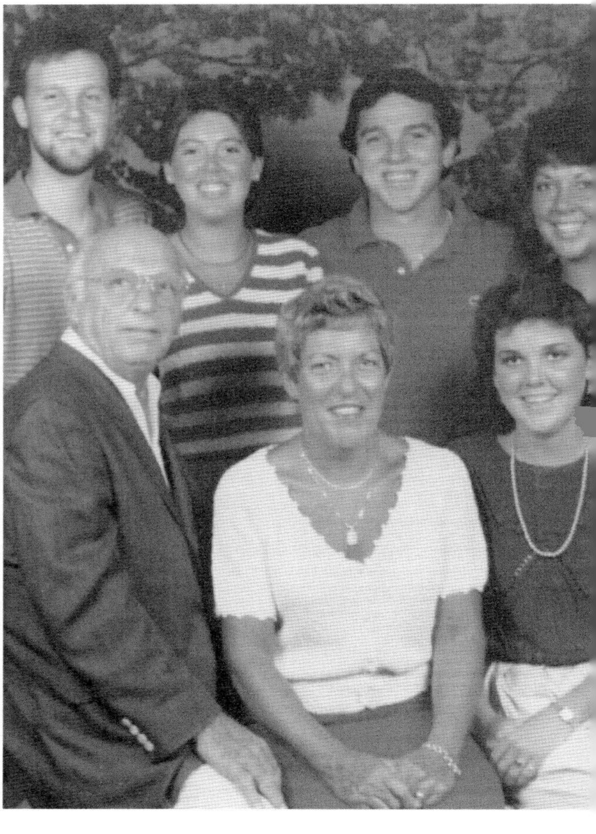

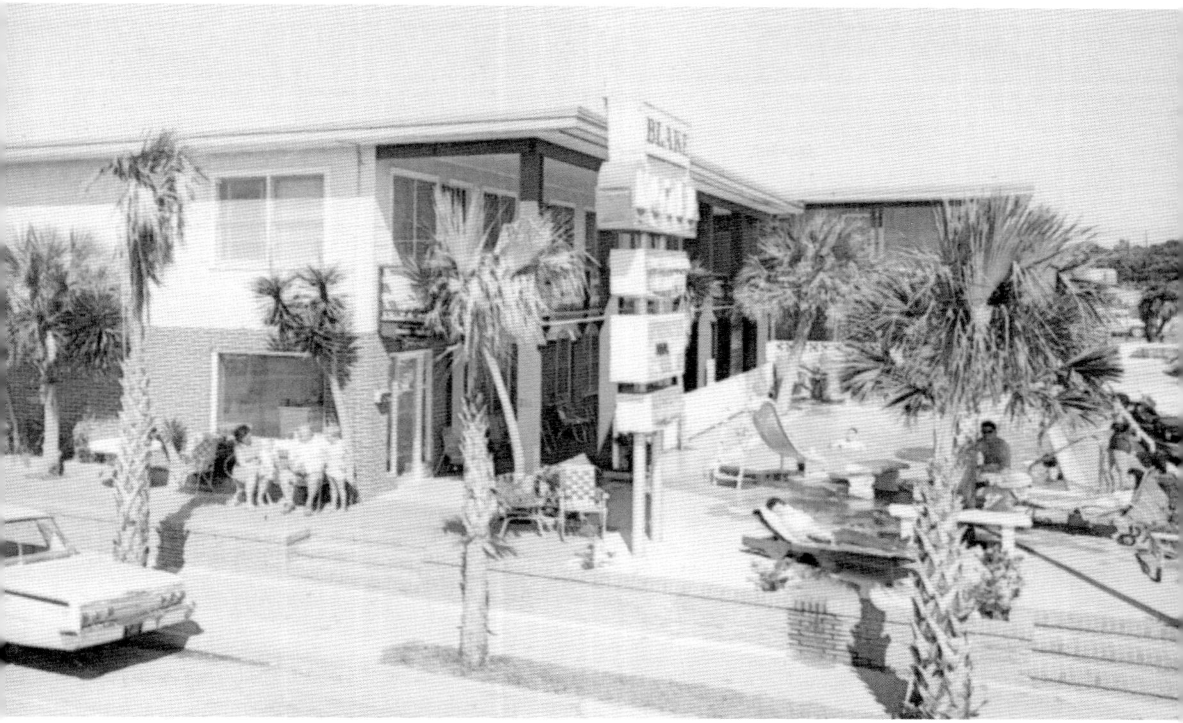

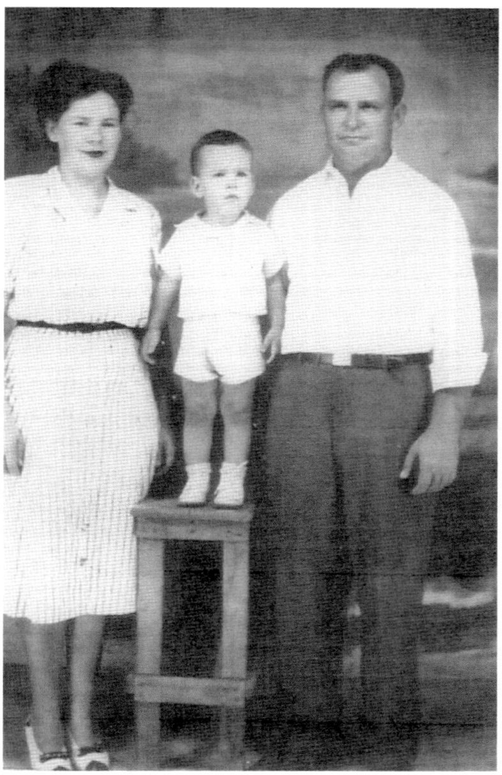

Acie Verion Sr. and Nelda Blake
Nelda and Acie built the Blake Motel in 1960. Like many mom and pop motels built in the years after Hurricane Hazel, it was a family affair and they raised four children at the hotel. While Acie was a brick mason, Nelda usually managed the hotel and he would join in when he was home. Acie was a World War II veteran and they were both members of the First Baptist Church of Myrtle Beach. Mr. Blake died in 1978, but it is still possible to ride by and see Miss Nelda, sitting on the porch of the motel, enjoying the view and welcoming her guests. (Courtesy Virginia Blake Oyster.)

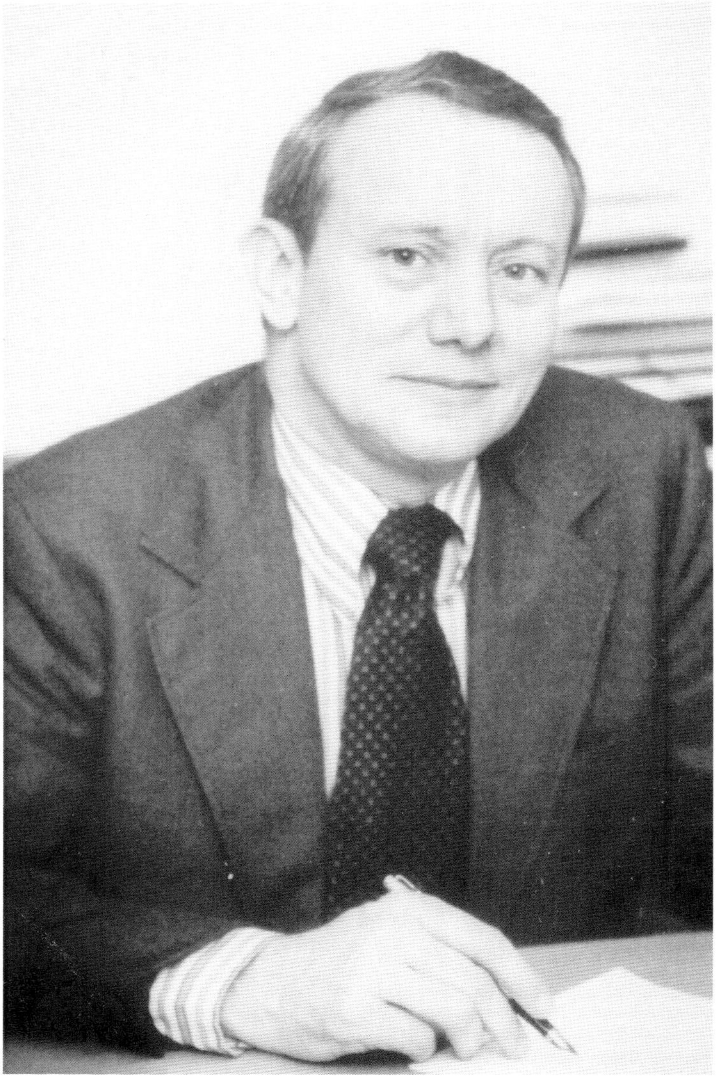

Fred Brinkman

At first glance, Fred looked unassuming, but when one looks back it is possible to see that gale-force wind that carried him into building the foundation of South Carolina tourism as it is today. He was head of our chamber of commerce from 1956–1964 and again from 1970–1973. He left the area to take a position as director of the South Carolina Department of Parks, Recreation, and Tourism, which he held until he retired in 1991. In 1992, he helped form the Council of Myrtle Beach Organizations, which lobbied for the area business community. Through COMBO, the city received needed funds for roads, beach nourishment, and tax rebates for large tourism developments. Fred was cofounder of the South Carolina Hall of Fame, and in 1992, he received the state's highest honor, the Order of the Palmetto. The South Carolina Governors Conference on Tourism and Travel has established the Fred Brinkman Award for outstanding tourism leadership in the state. There is also the Fred Brinkman Award, given to a South Carolina Gamecock baseball player who provides inspiration to his fellow teammates, coaches, and fans and a Fred Brinkman Scholarship Award for students in the tourism industry through the South Carolina Association of Tourism Regions. (Courtesy Jack Thompson.)

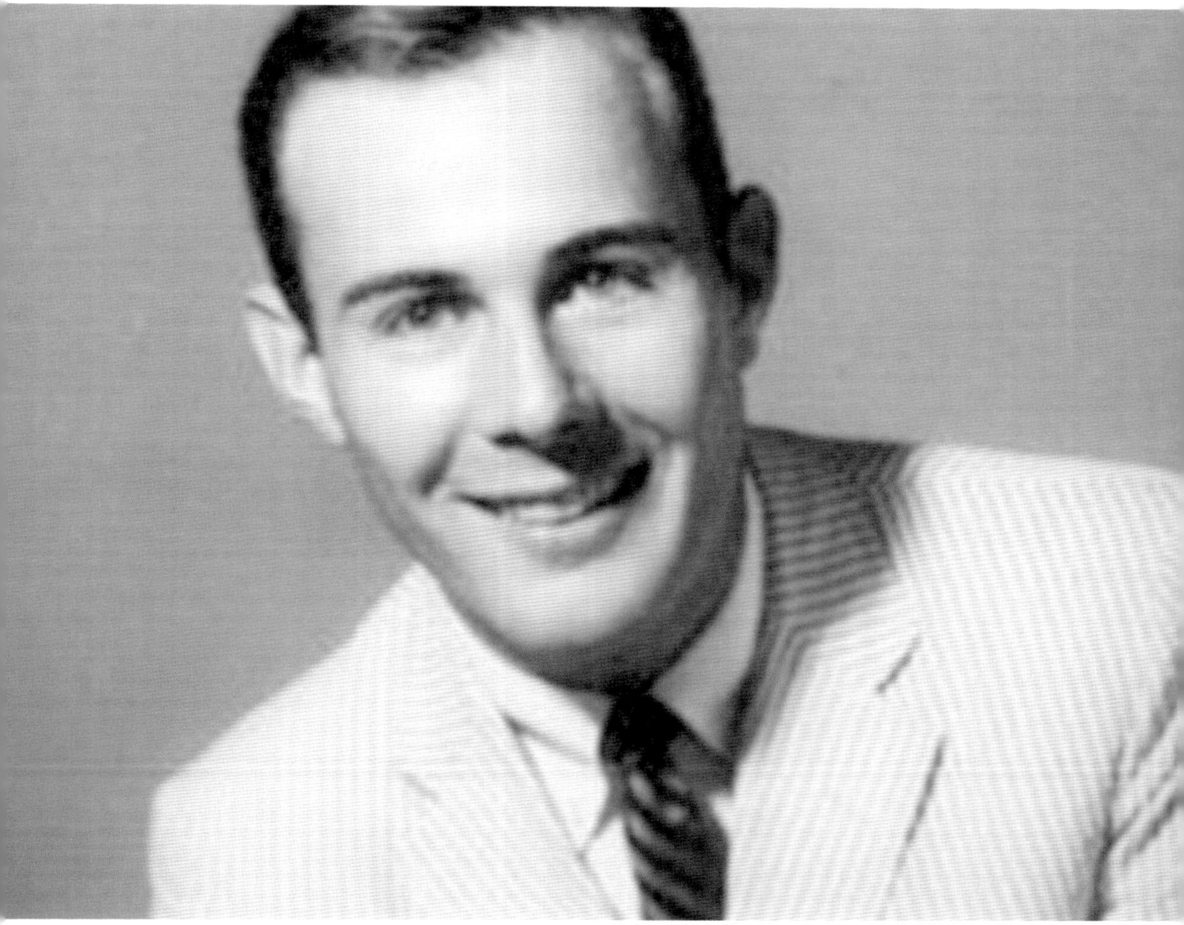

Cornelius Jason "Neil" Ammons

Neil was an optimistic, hard-working businessman who loved his community. Not widely known until after his death, he sponsored the Hearing Horry History historical interviews that Dr. Carl Compton worked so diligently on. Residents have him to thank for over 30 interviews of natives of the area, most of whom are now gone, but their legacy and his live on through these tapes. He was also well known for his orange hotel, The Sea Mist Resort, which his father Jason began in 1954. He owned many properties in the area including the Family Kingdom Amusement Park, which he bought in 1992 (the park opened in 1966 as Grand Strand Amusement Park). Neal died in 2009, but his family still runs the businesses. (Courtesy MBCC.)

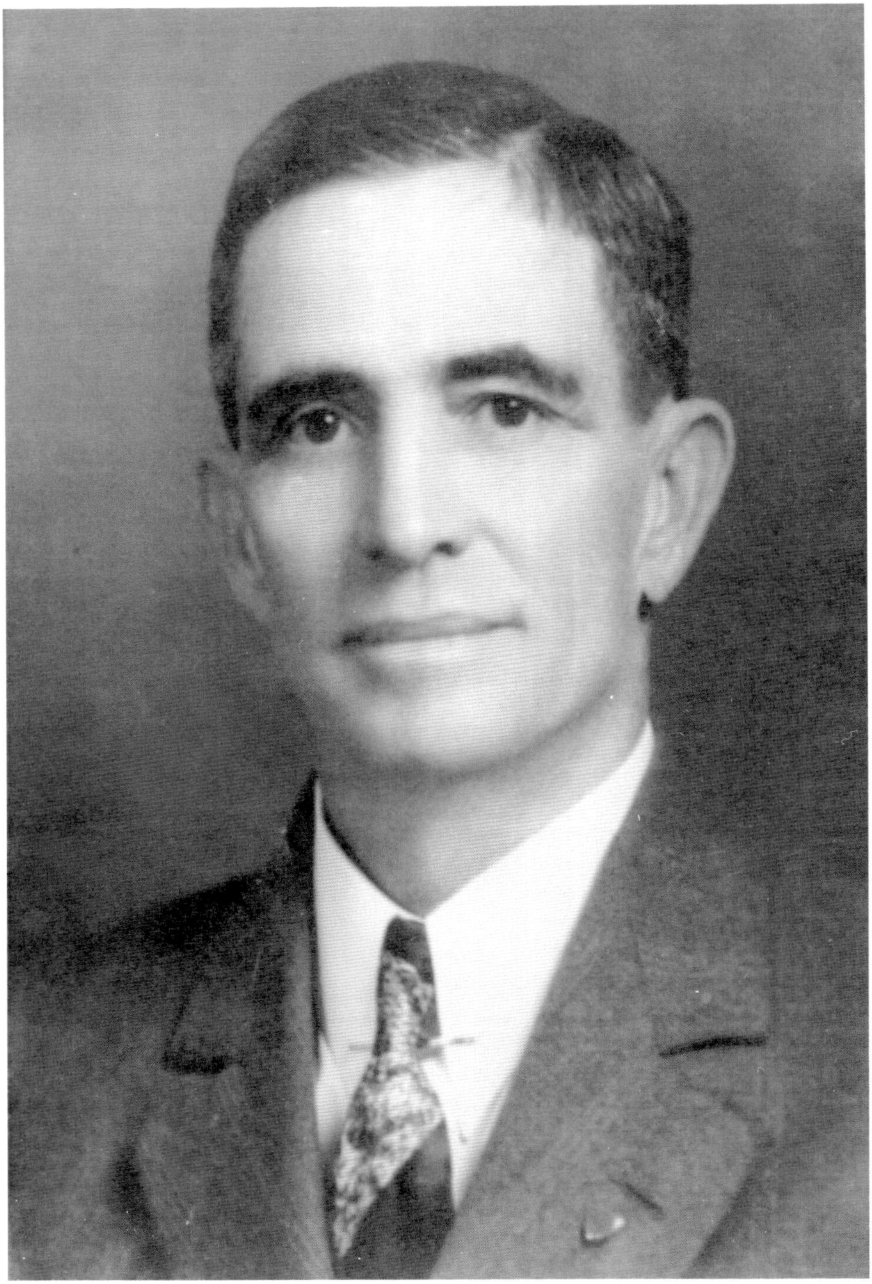

Nicholas Colin Hughes Jr., RCE

A registered civil engineer, Nicholas Hughes came to this area in 1929 to first draw the maps of Brookgreen Gardens, in Murrells Inlet. After being offered several jobs, he decided in 1931 to settle here with his wife and two daughters. His daughter Tempe was born the same year that Brookgreen opened. One of his first commissions was to draw the original maps for Myrtle Beach Farms. These became the maps for the Town of Myrtle Beach when it incorporated in 1938. Among other projects, he also drew the plans for the original Second Avenue Pier owned by St. Julien Springs. (Courtesy Tempe Hughes Oehler.)

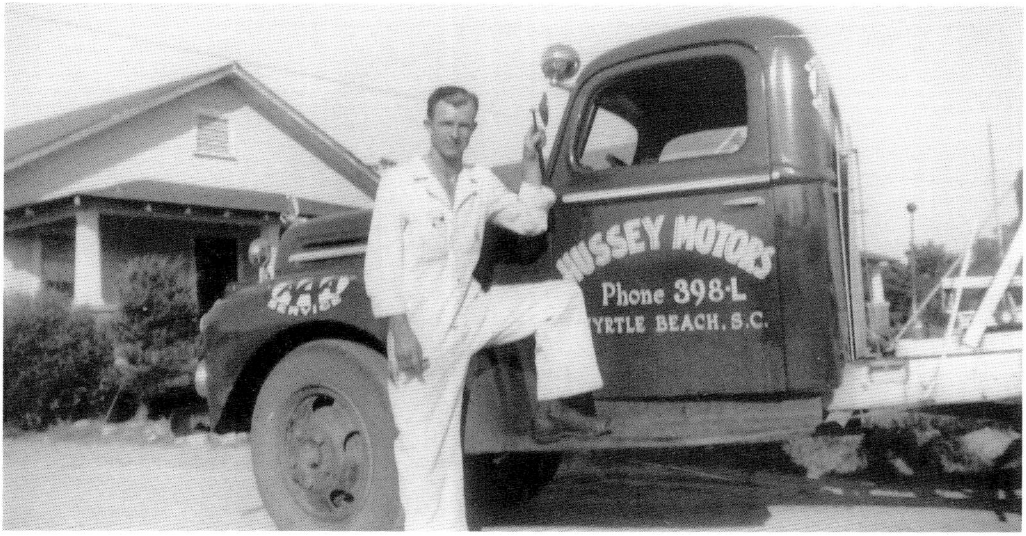

Richard Hussey

After his graduation from high school, Hussey moved to Myrtle Beach in 1940 and went to work for his older brother at Ocean Motor Company. Over the next few years, he met his future wife Pearline. They married, and then he joined the Navy and went to war. After he was discharged in 1945, he returned to his lovely wife and went back to work for his brother. In 1950, Richard opened his own place and named it Hussey Motors. He invested in a heavy-duty wrecker and spent as much time hauling people out of the sand as he did fixing cars. Once, he even pulled a small airplane that had to make an emergency landing out of the surf. When the Myrtle Beach Speedway in downtown Myrtle Beach (once Washington Race Track) closed due to increased traffic and noise complaints, Richard joined six others to buy land for a race track they named Rambi (an acronym for Racing Association of Myrtle Beach Inc.) Raceway. To raise money to build the track, they opened it up to stockholders. Within a week, they had sold over 200 shares. The racetrack opened during the Sun Fun Festival on June 7, 1958, on Highway 501. It is now known as Myrtle Beach Speedway. The photograph above shows Richard with his well-used wrecker. He is pictured below at right with his No. 14 racecar. (Courtesy Mike Hussey.)

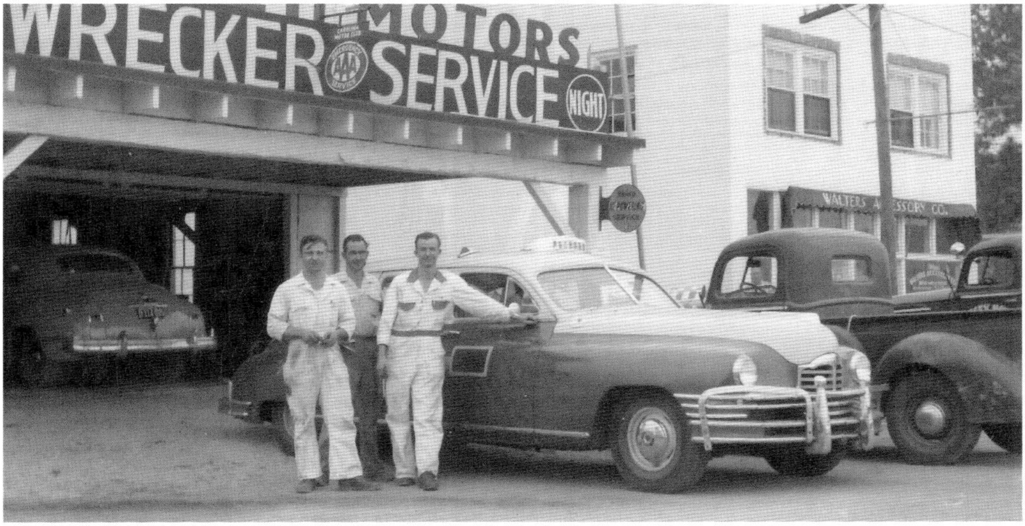

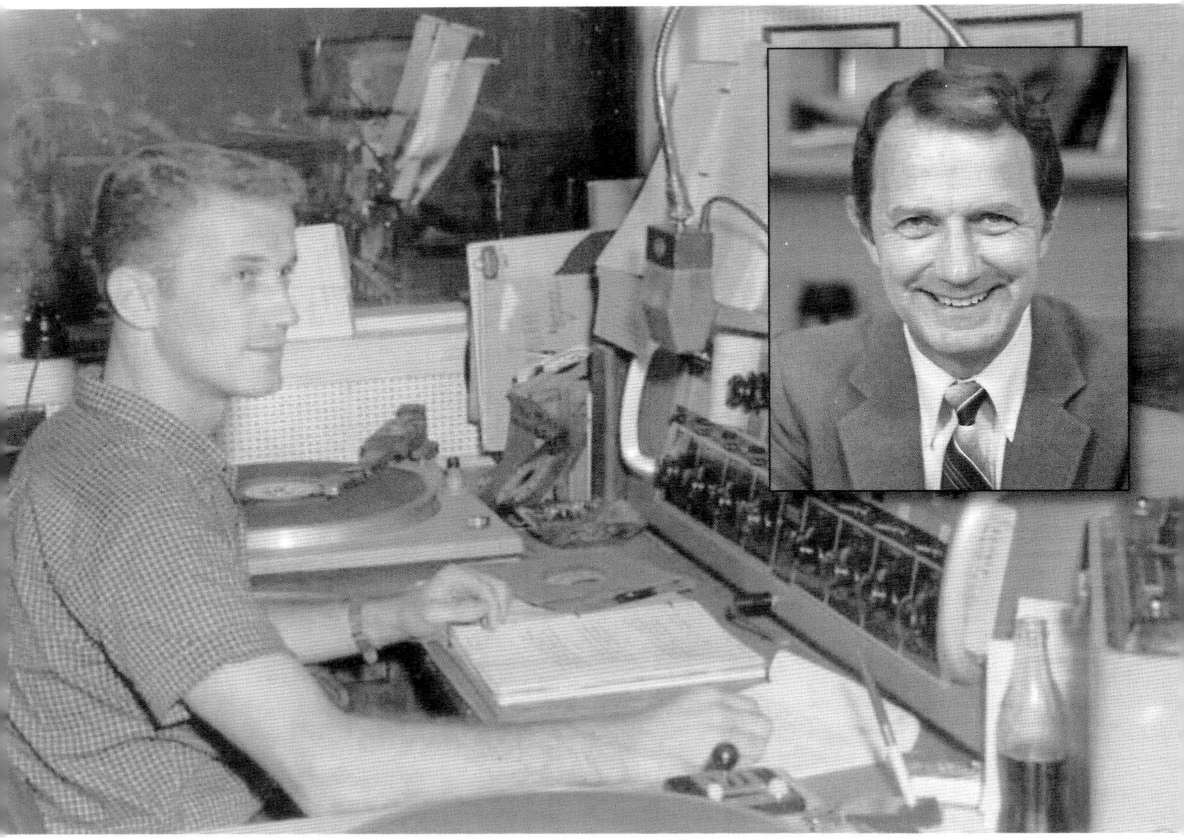

Ashby Ward

Ashby went into radio right out of high school. As a DJ in 1954 during Hurricane Hazel, he covered the storm from the WMYB control room, riding out the storm there with just the station manager Harry Hyman and Walt Tabler, the chief engineer. They read the announcements throughout the night and next day, keeping everyone abreast of the news of the storm and the aftermath. Over the next few years, he spent time with several regional television stations in South Carolina, some of them as the news anchor and some as host of *Captain Ashby's Playhouse*, a popular children's program. He was the director of public affairs for South Carolina Technical College System before he came into his dream job with the Myrtle Beach Area Chamber of Commerce in 1974 as the CEO. Over 30 years, he was a huge driving force of growth in Myrtle Beach. He received many awards for his civic and community contributions including South Carolina's highest civilian honor, the Order of the Palmetto. He was presented an honorary doctorate in commerce from the South Carolina senate in 1995. The chamber's visitor center on Oak Street is named in his honor in recognition of his hard work in promoting tourism along the Grand Strand. (Courtesy MBCC.)

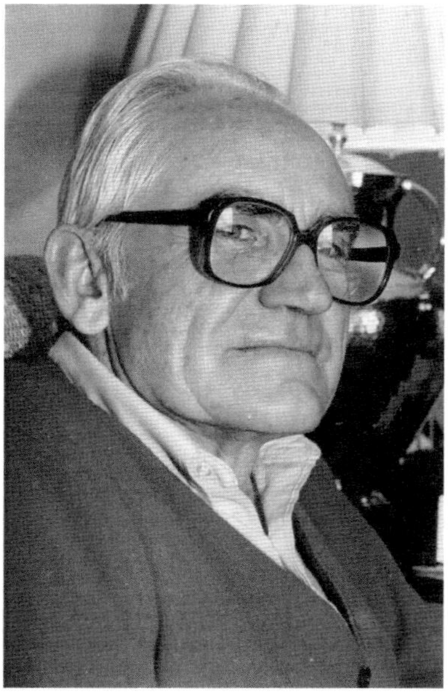

Zeb Thomas

Zeb and his family began operating the Dayton House Hotel shortly after he moved to Myrtle Beach in 1960. From a small 13-room, mom-and-pop hotel, it has grown to the over-300-room resort that it is today. Always devoting time to the community and growth of Myrtle Beach, he is a past president of the chamber, and of the Hospitality Association. He was a founding stockholder of the Anchor Bank and was chairman of its board of directors. Zeb received the first Ashby Ward Pioneer of the Year Award in 2004 for his efforts and contributions to tourism and building the city into the first-class destination that it is today. In 2005, a resolution was passed to name the Intracoastal Waterway Bridge on Robert Grissom Parkway the Zeb M. Thomas Sr. Bridge. He earned other awards over the years, including the Chamber Citizen of the Year in 1978 and the Order of the Palmetto in 1995. He was a Mason and member of the Lions Club. Zeb will be remembered as a hard worker with sound judgment, and putting God, family, and community first. (Courtesy MBCC.)

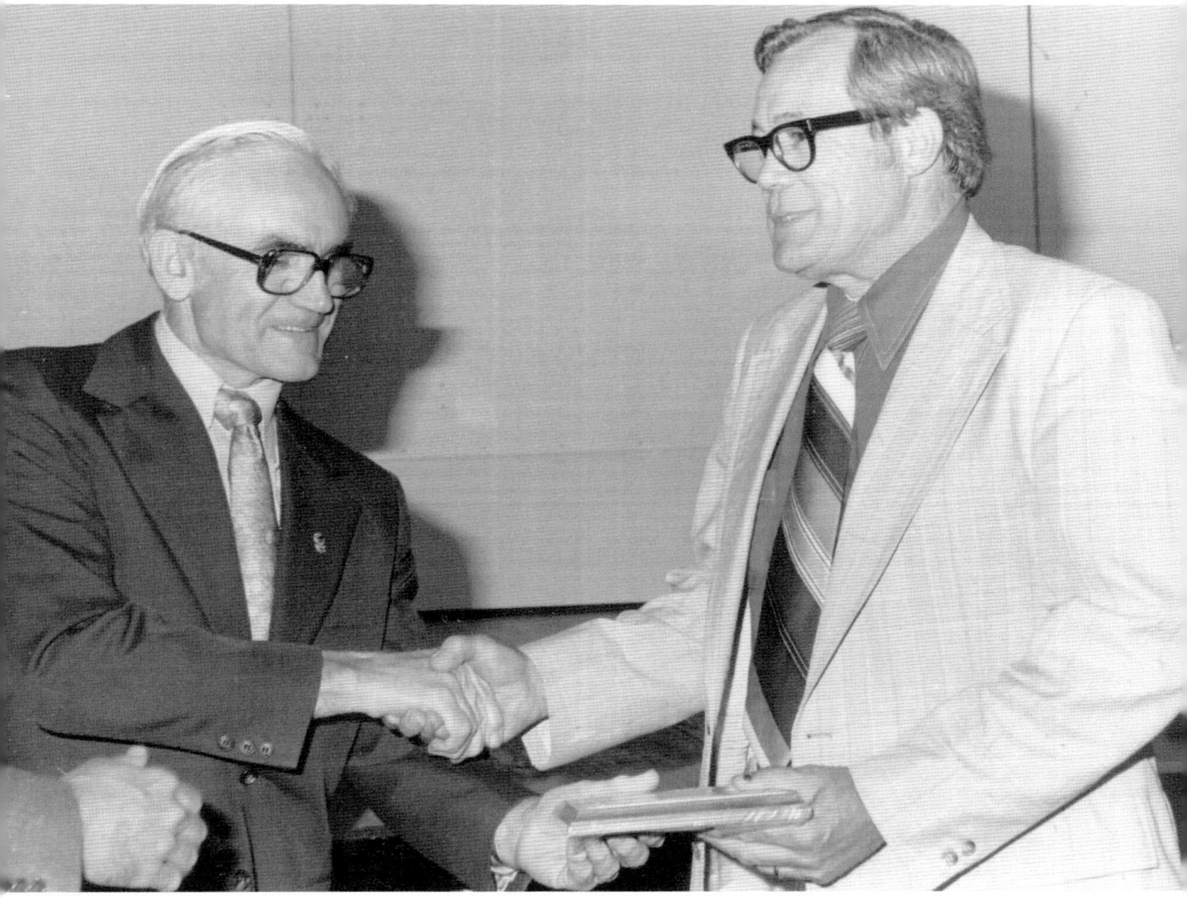

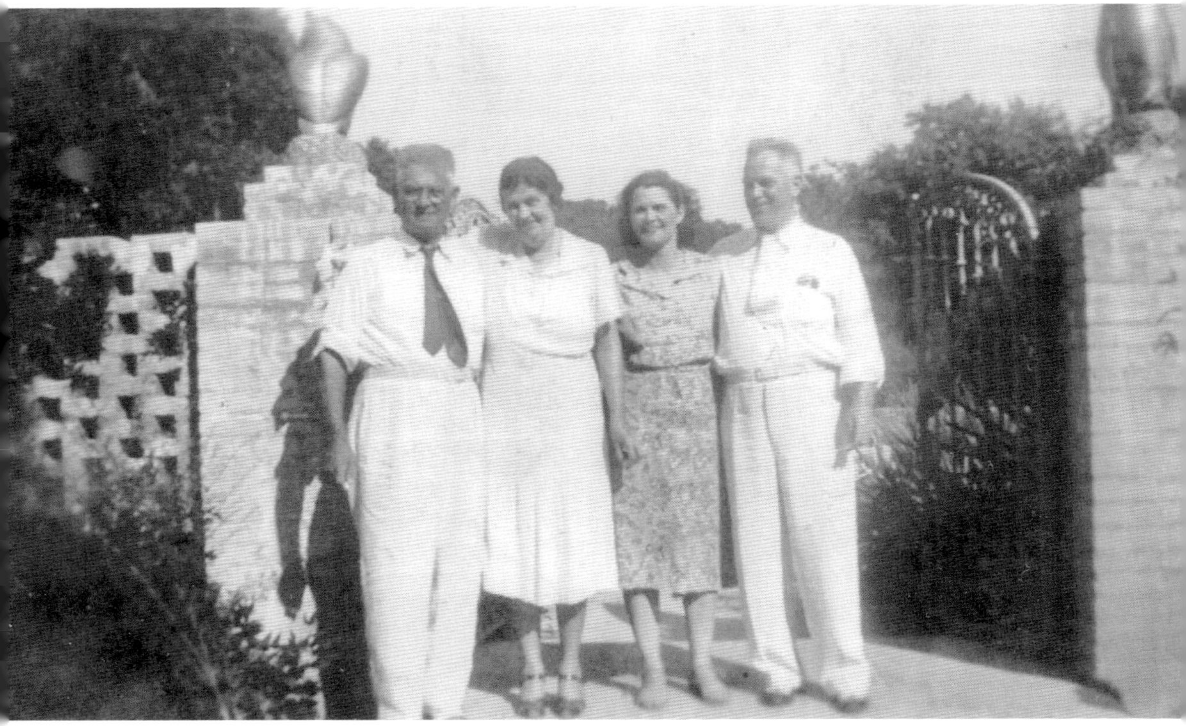

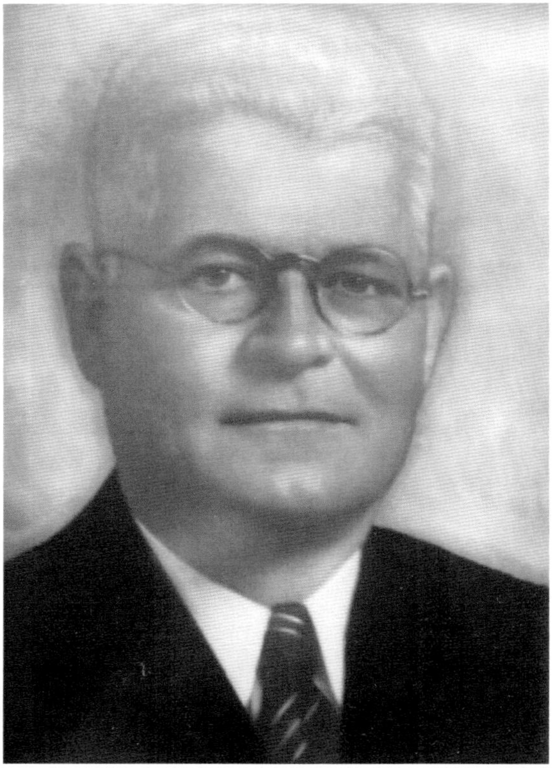

Dr. Wilford Leroy Harrelson Sr.
In 1927, Wilford and Harriet moved here and opened up the first drug store on Main Street, Delta Drug. They had two children, Roy Jr. and Mary Elizabeth. Wilford was elected the first mayor of Myrtle Beach on August 25, 1937. With a newly formed town government, Mayor Harrelson was very instrumental in creating many of the services that are still in place today. Land was purchased for an airport, the town police force was established, and the first jailhouse was built. The town also began paving the dirt and coquina streets as well as installing sidewalks and a sewage system. The Myrtle Beach International Airport was originally named the Harrelson Municipal Airport, and today everyone must drive Harrelson Boulevard to travel to the airport. (Courtesy Cal Harrelson.)

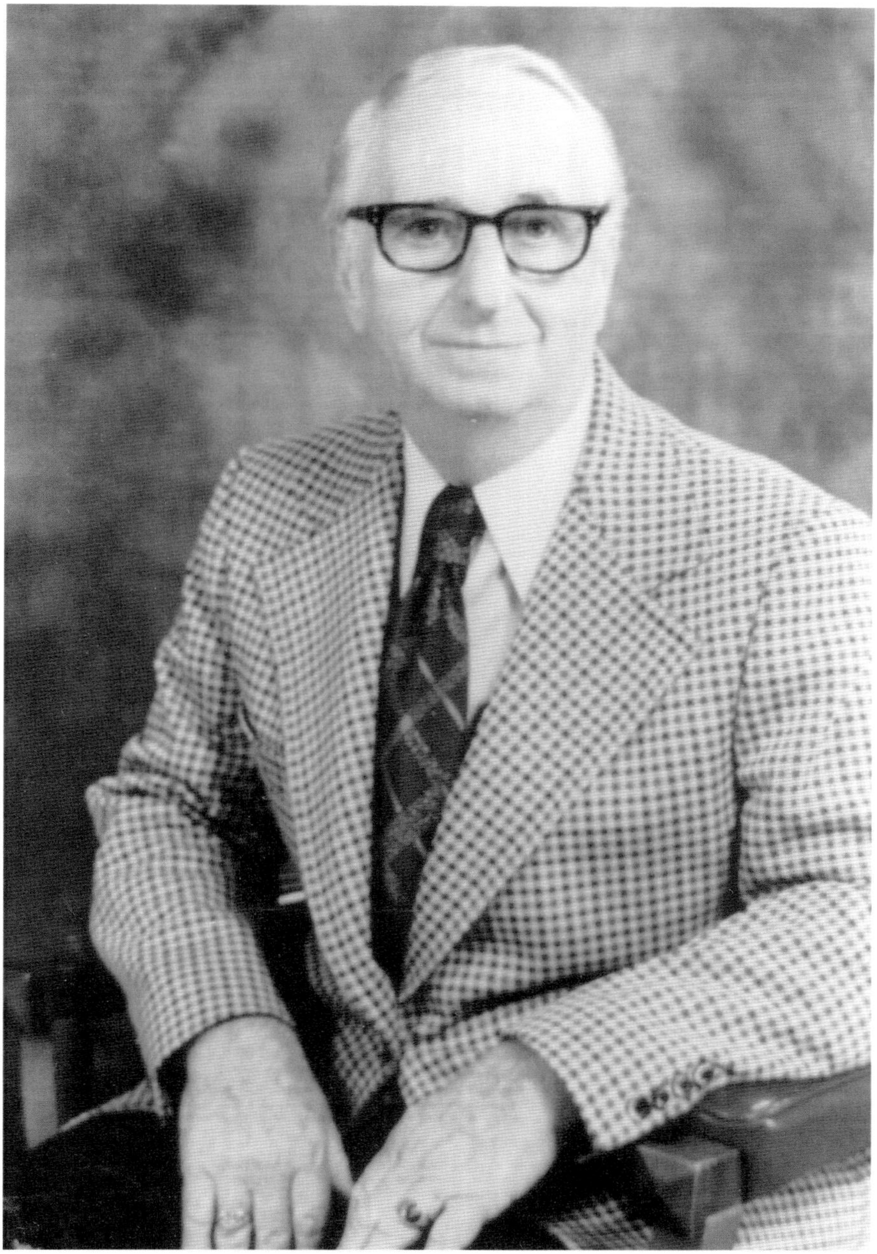

Arnold Edward "A.E." Beachum

Originally from North Carolina, Beachum moved to Myrtle Beach in 1937. He was employed with Mack's Dime Stores and was district manager when he retired in 1973. People always knew when he was in the store, not because of the distinct clacking his shoes made on the wooden floors but because of his whistling. He was a great businessman, and trained many who are still in the retail business today. A member of the Myrtle Beach Civitan Club since 1938, he served as club president for two terms. He joined the Coastal Federal Board in 1966, where he served as a director for many years. He and his wife, the former Julia Gertrude Niven, had two children. He died in 1993 at the age of 82. (Courtesy MBCC.)

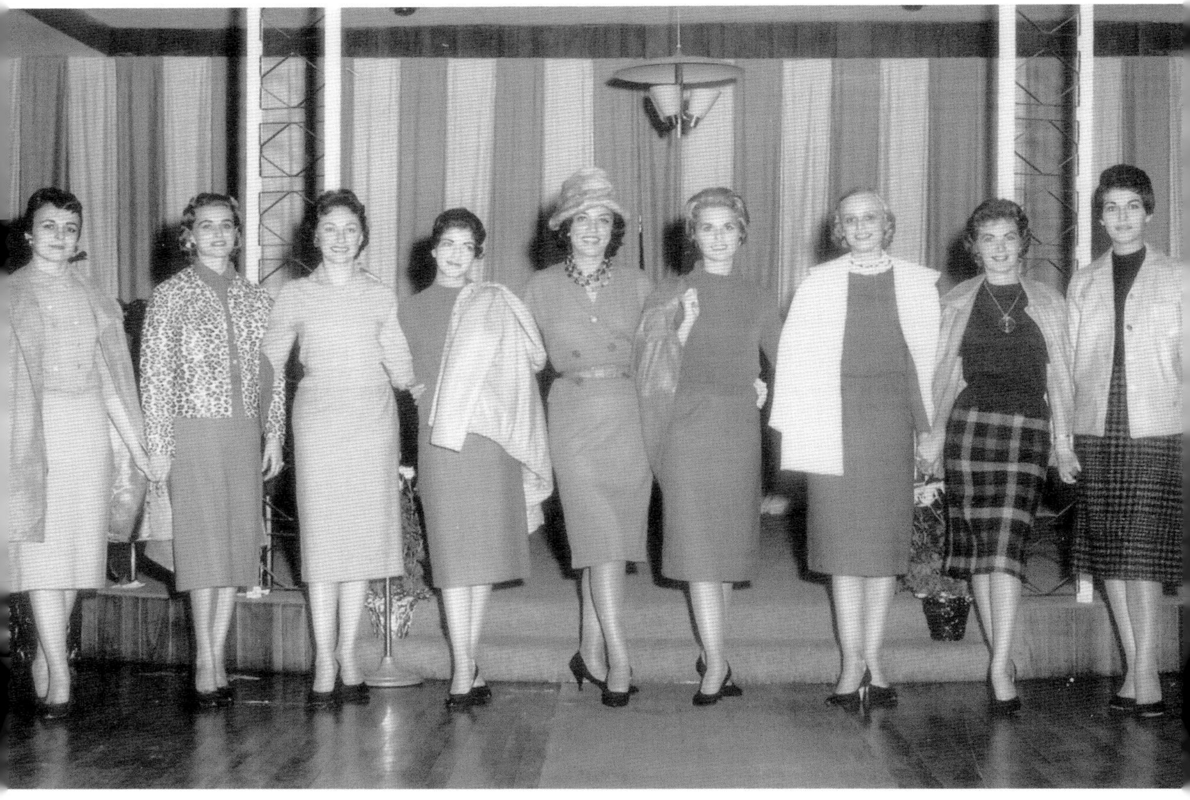

Helen Mates

Helen Mates moved to Myrtle Beach with her parents and siblings in 1939. She married Walter Mates, and together they opened the Helen Mates Shop. Most people remember it as being the place to shop for the latest women's and young women's fashions, but when it originally opened in 1947, it was a children's clothing store. Helen is remembered for her great taste in fashion, keeping up with the latest trends, and her flare for presentation. The fashion shows she produced around town were always met with excitement and were well attended. The women were filled with anticipation to see the new styles of the season. Always active in the community, she was a fashion consultant to the Myrtle Beach Playhouse, the summer stock theater at the Ocean Forest Hotel. She provided the wardrobe for many New York stage actors of the day, including Zasu Pitts, Veronica Lake, and Sylvia Sidney. When the Miss South Carolina pageant was held at the Myrtle Beach Pavilion during the Sun Fun Festival, she was the fashion consultant to the winner, donating wardrobe and gowns for the September competition in Atlantic City.

Helen served as the National Gifts Committee co-chair and city director of St. Jude Children's Hospital for children with life-threatening leukemia after meeting another Lebanese American, actor and comedian Danny Thomas, and learning of his vision to help these children. She had numerous fundraisers in Myrtle Beach, donating thousands of dollars over the years to the foundation.

Helen and Walter had four children: Carolyn, Beth, Walter, and Russ. (Courtesy Jack Thompson.)

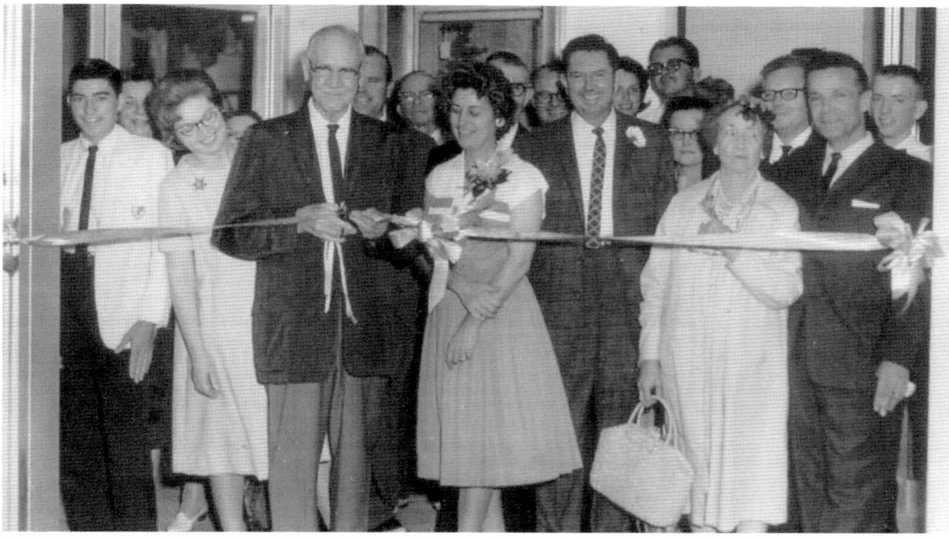

Justin Whitaker Plyler Sr. and the Gay Dolphin Gift Cove

When the original Gay Dolphin Gift Cove opened its doors in 1946, it was a small tourist gift shop, filled with several thousand enticing gift items. After Hurricane Hazel destroyed the building in 1954, the owners Justin and Eloise Plyler rebuilt the oceanfront building that has withstood every hurricane since. Over the years, the store grew to include a six-story glass tower and at one time an annex across the street. The Plylers also had an amusement park with children's rides and a wildlife show. Now run by their son Buzz Plyler, the Gay Dolphin has over 70,000 items ranging from seashells and jewelry to candles and gag gifts—fun for all ages with a maze of shopping coves to entertain people for hours. At one time the tallest building in Myrtle Beach, tourists and locals alike would climb the circular steel steps to the top of the tower to see the view for miles. Always committed to improving the city for tourists and residents, Justin was chairman of the first Sun Fun Festival in 1952, president of the Jaycees and the chamber, and a former chairman of the Myrtle Beach Zoning Board. He was also a founding member of Anchor Bank.

The current boardwalk extends past the Gay Dolphin north to Plyler Park, named after Justin Plyler Sr. It was dedicated at the Sun Fun Festival in 2005. Buzz carries on his family legacy, traveling the world to stock his store with gifts, much to the delight of his shoppers. (Courtesy MBCC.)

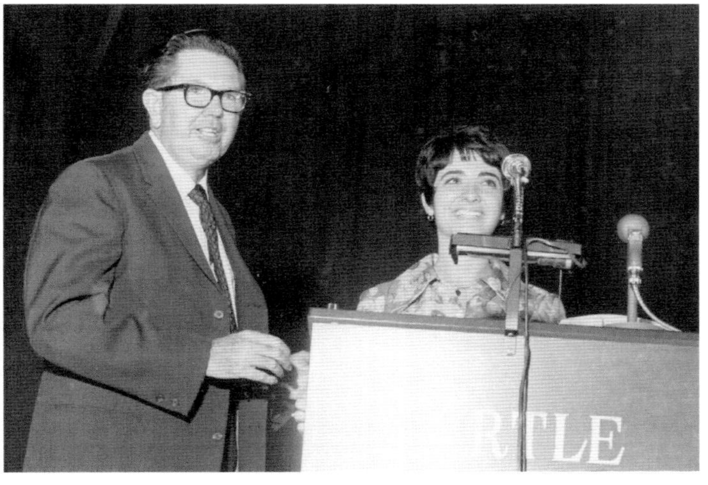

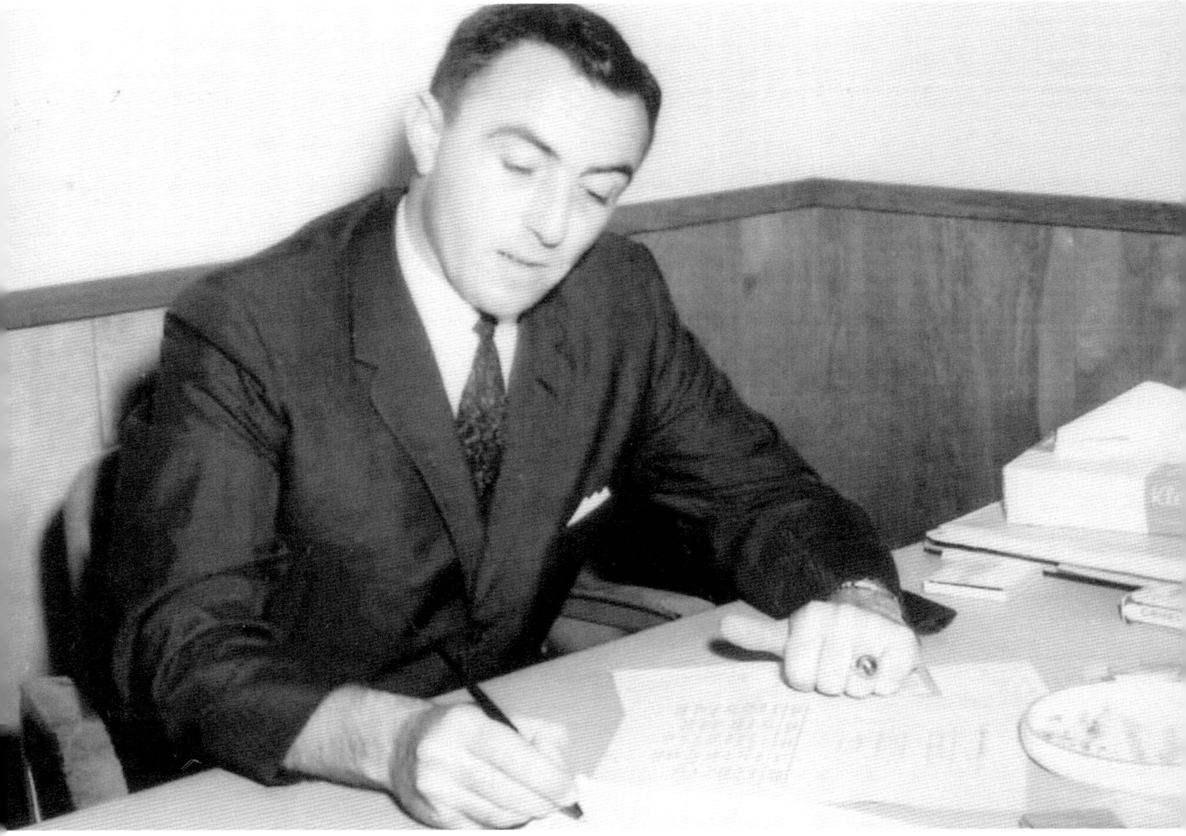

Fred Burton

Fred came to Myrtle Beach from St. Petersburg, Florida, in 1965 to head up the Myrtle Beach Chamber of Commerce. During his tenure, the Georgetown chamber and the Myrtle Beach chamber voted to merge resources and they became the Greater Myrtle Beach Chamber of Commerce—serving from Little River to Historic Georgetown, effective January 1, 1969. (Courtesy MBCC.)

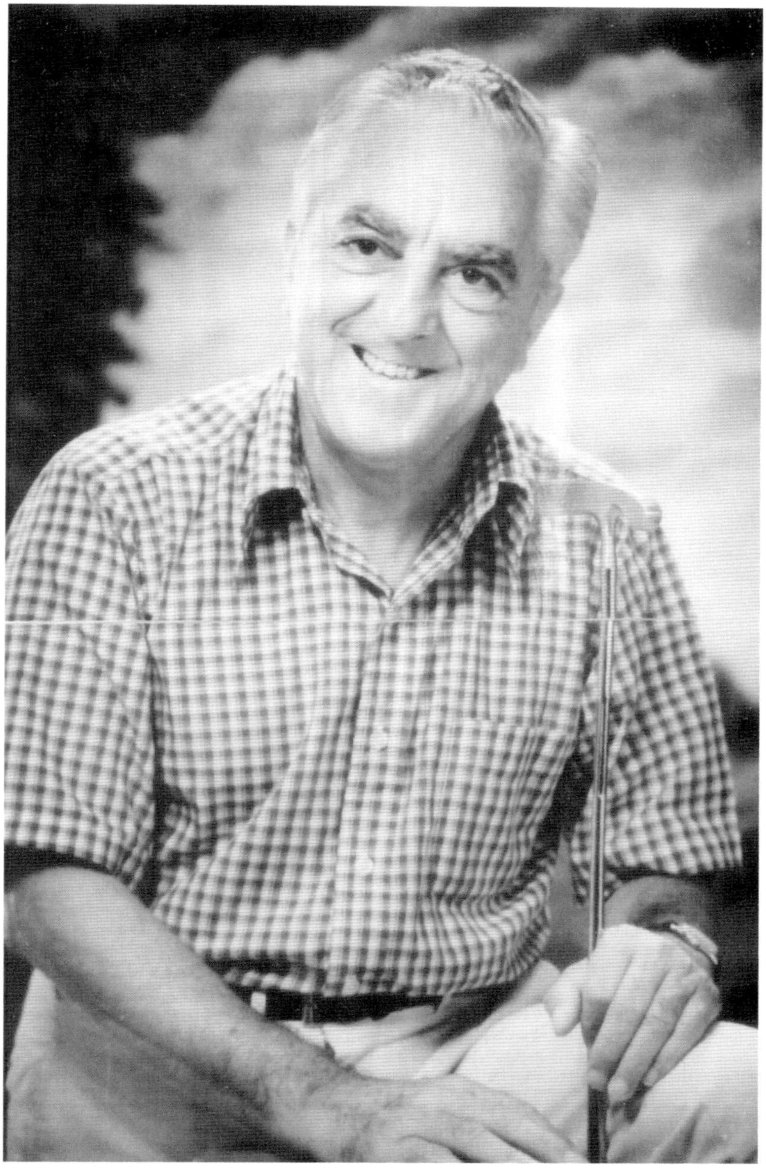

James J. "Jimmy" D'Angelo Sr.

Jimmy was the first golf pro at the area's first golf course, Ocean Forest Club (now the Pine Lakes International Country Club) and the first pro at the second golf course to be built in Myrtle Beach, the Dunes Golf and Beach Club. He was the pro there when it opened in 1949 until he retired in 1968. Before he came here, he was vice president of the PGA of America in 1942. He created the annual Golf Writers Association of America Tournament. After retirement, he worked with Myrtle Beach Golf Holiday as a teaching pro and consultant. He was known as the godfather of Myrtle Beach golf and helped make Myrtle Beach the "Golf Capital of the World." Jimmy was named Citizen of the Year in 1974, the same year he was proclaimed "Mr. Golf" by the city. In 1984, he was inducted into the Carolina PGA Hall of Fame and the South Carolina Hall of Fame in 1985. He died May 18, 2000, at the age of 90. In 2005, he was named one of South Carolina Golf's 10 most influential people. (Courtesy Jack Thompson.)

Fishing Is Great Along the Strand

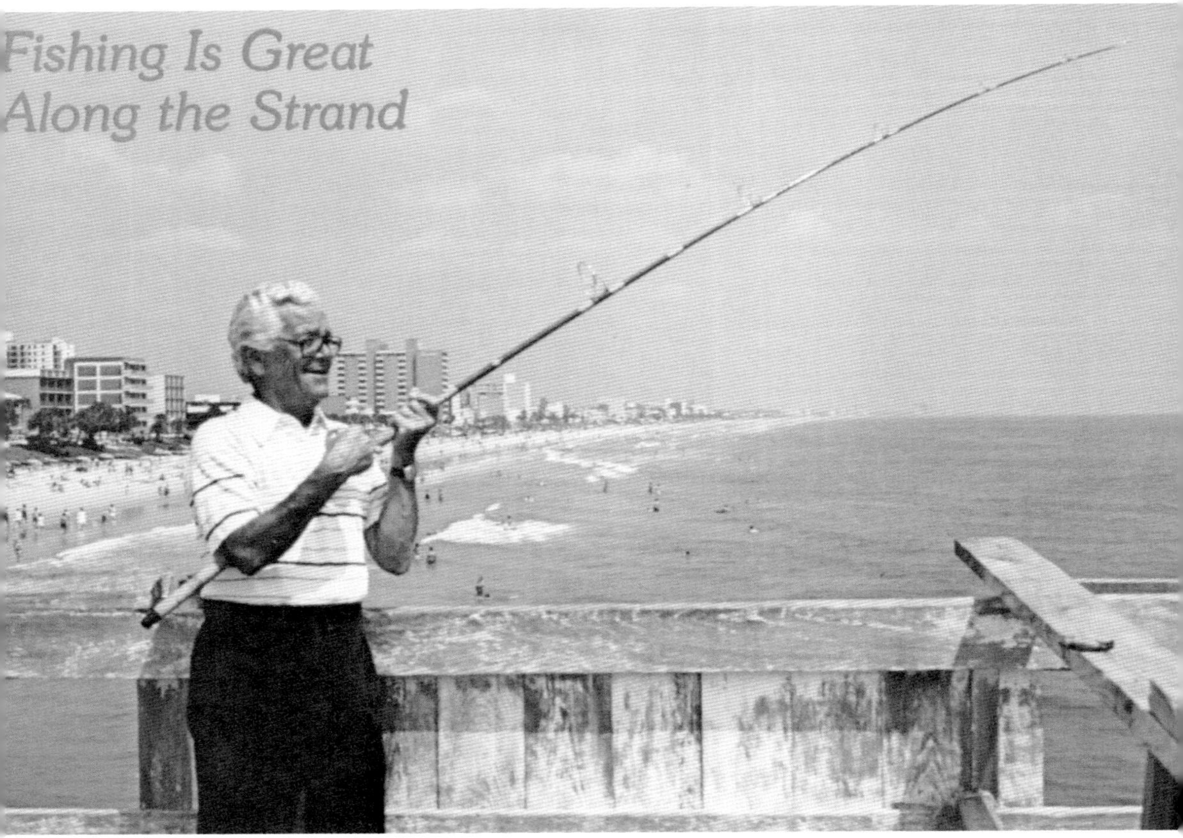

Christ Drosis

Born in Turkey, Christ immigrated to the United States in 1923 and settled in Pennsylvania, where he met his wife, Irene Antonaki. They had two children, Elaine and Dino. His good friend Alex Karetas contacted him and asked him to move to Myrtle Beach to run his restaurant, the 8th Avenue Grill. The family came in 1954, and he worked there for two years before purchasing the year-old Mammy's Kitchen—a small drive-in with five stools. It became the family business, with him in the kitchen and his wife in the front. The next year he built an extension, and Irene came up with the slogan "All roads lead to Mammy's Kitchen." A savvy businessman, he opened several restaurants over the years including Hickory House Drive-In, the Seafood House, Colony Restaurant, and Christy's. Always willing to help, he employed many Greek immigrants when they arrived, helping them to start their own restaurants after a few years, like Tommy Arakas and the National House of Pancakes. He retired in 1972 so that he could fish and spend more time with his family. Christ died in 2000, and Irene died in 2004. (Courtesy Elaine Karavan.)

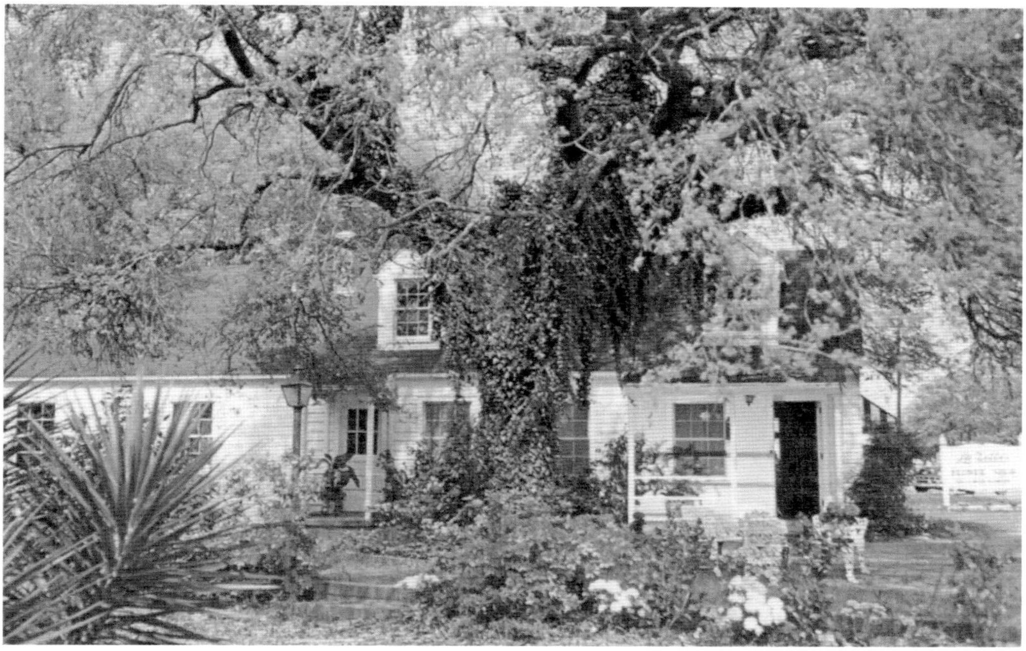

Lazelle Simmons DuBoise

Lazelle founded the first flower shop, called Lazelle's (above), in April 1946 at 101 Broadway when it was on the edge of town limits. In 1929 her parents, William and Lell, purchased the Pleasant Inn at 200 Broadway, which was built in 1927. Her mother ran it as a boardinghouse, and it is now listed in the National Register of Historic Places. Her father was the first Horry County magistrate for Myrtle Beach. Lazelle married O.C. and together they had three children, Lyticia, Ann, and Theta. She was an active member of the South Carolina Florists Association and had a weekly column in the local paper, *The Sun News*, during the 1960s. She was born in April 1914 and died in March 1982. (Above, courtesy Lazelle's; right, MBCC.)

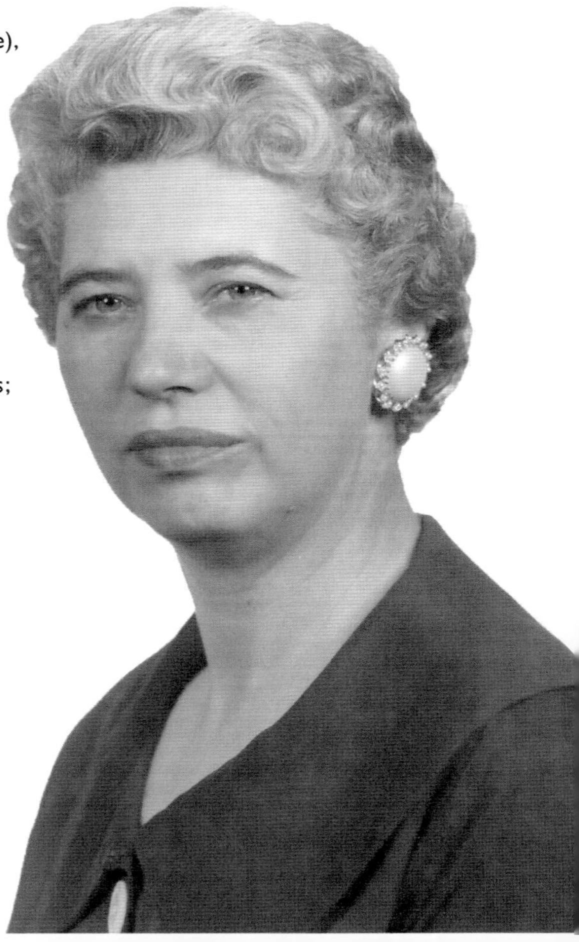

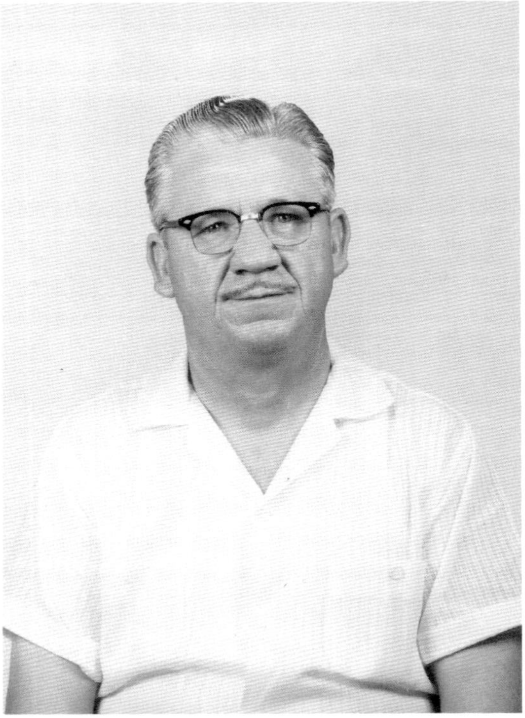

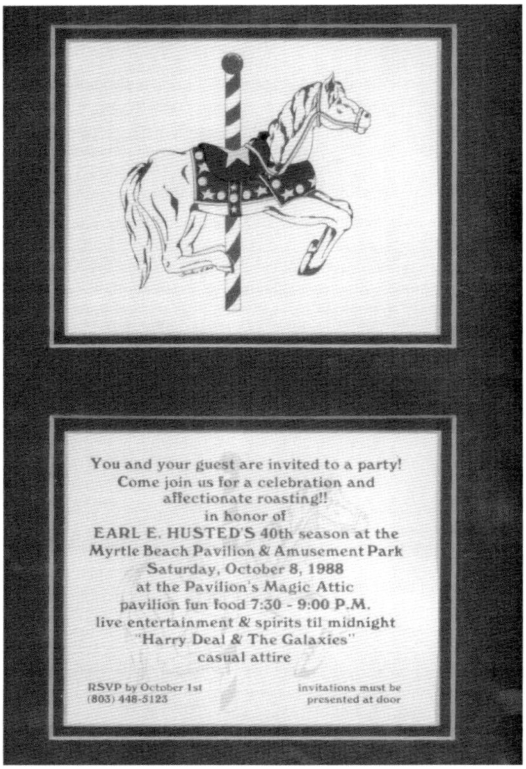

You and your guest are invited to a party!
Come join us for a celebration and
affectionate roasting!!
in honor of
EARL E. HUSTED'S 40th season at the
Myrtle Beach Pavilion & Amusement Park
Saturday, October 8, 1988
at the Pavilion's Magic Attic
pavilion fun food 7:30 - 9:00 P.M.
live entertainment & spirits til midnight
"Harry Deal & The Galaxies"
casual attire

RSVP by October 1st
(803) 448-5123

invitations must be
presented at door

Earl Husted

Edward Burroughs first met Earl when he and his brother Sherman brought their traveling carnival to Conway's annual Tobacco Festival in 1948. Burroughs and Chapin had an arcade, a few rides, and some food concessions at the Myrtle Beach Pavilion on Eighth Avenue North and needed someone to enlarge the operation and manage it. Earl signed on in 1948 and was the general manager until 1991. During Husted's tenure, the Pavilion went from a couple of rides to one of the top-rated amusement parks in the country. (Top, courtesy Jack Thompson; bottom, courtesy Deacon Dawson.)

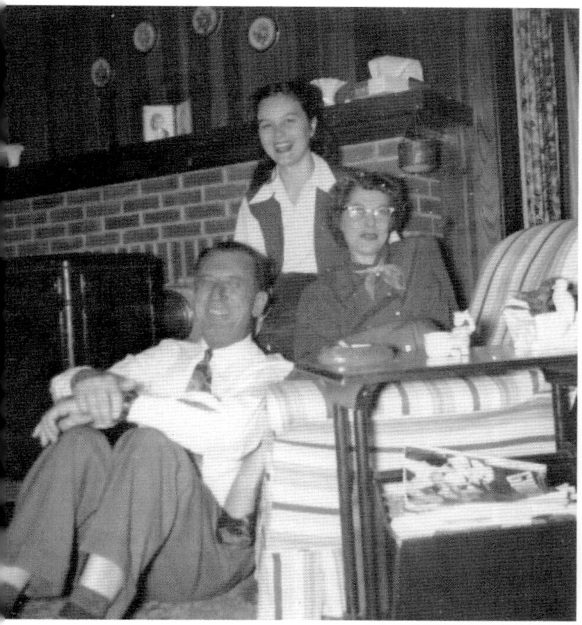

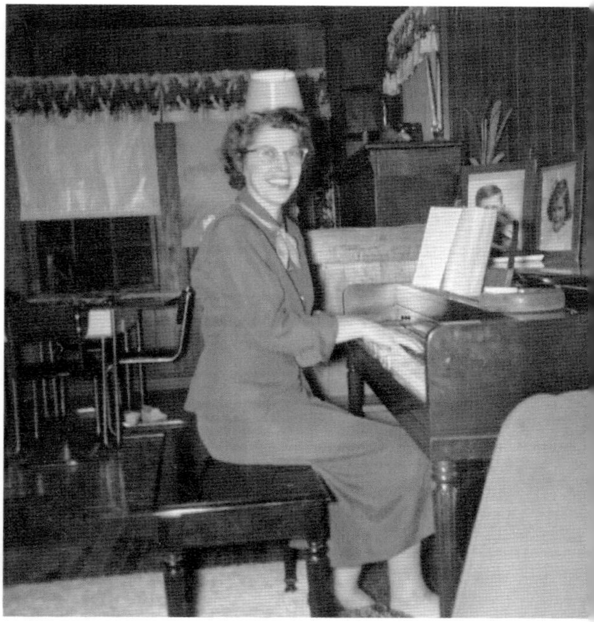

Edna Huggins

Edna first opened Victory Beauty Salon in the Colonial Drugs Shopping Center. She then moved it to the Chapin Shopping Center when they updated their building and added on to it. This location was also closer to her home at 500 Chester Street. Because this area did not have very many apartments in the 1940s and 1950s, many women made their homes into a boarding house, opening them up to people needing somewhere to stay long term. Jack Thompson and his brother stayed there while finishing school when they first moved here. The homes were perfect for people needing a room but also wanting that homey feel—meals were usually included. At left, she sits with Harvey (who worked with the Boston Braves and would come each year during spring training) and Mary Catherine in the middle (who was from Bayboro and worked at Aervox, which later became AVX). A vivacious and multitalented woman, Edna often played the piano, much to the enjoyment of her guests. (Courtesy Mary Catherine Hardee.)

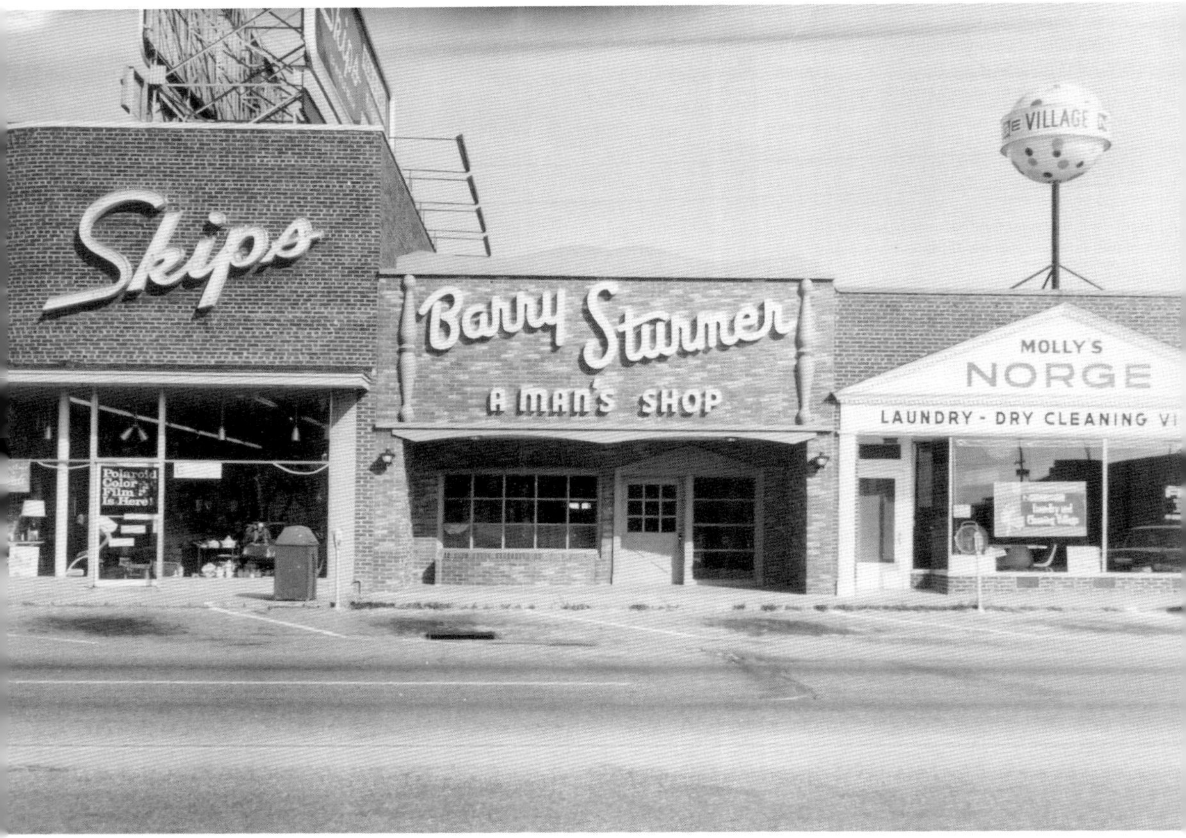

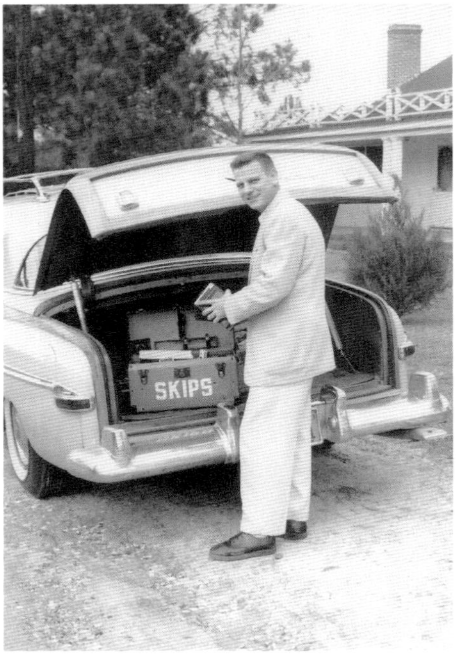

Dwight Lambe

Owner of Skips Camera and Gifts, he began the photographic history of Myrtle Beach when he moved here in 1946. He also owned the photo booth at the old Myrtle Beach Pavilion in the 1950s where Jack Thompson went looking for a job at 13. If a resident has a picture of themselves that was taken down at the pavilion in front of the city jail backdrop or the moon backdrop, chances are Dwight or Jack took the picture. An avid photographer, he took pictures of the guesthouses, the Sun Fun Festival, and all of the events going on in Myrtle Beach. Many families came to the studio to have their family portraits made. He loved this community, and when he was not taking pictures, he was acting as the chamber of commerce president from 1948 to 1949, a city councilman from 1960 to 1963, and the municipal judge from 1981 until he retired in 1993. He loved Myrtle Beach, and in 2002, in honor of their father, his sons Ron, Leland, Paul, and David donated over 9,000 negatives and photographs to the chamber. (Courtesy Jack Thompson.)

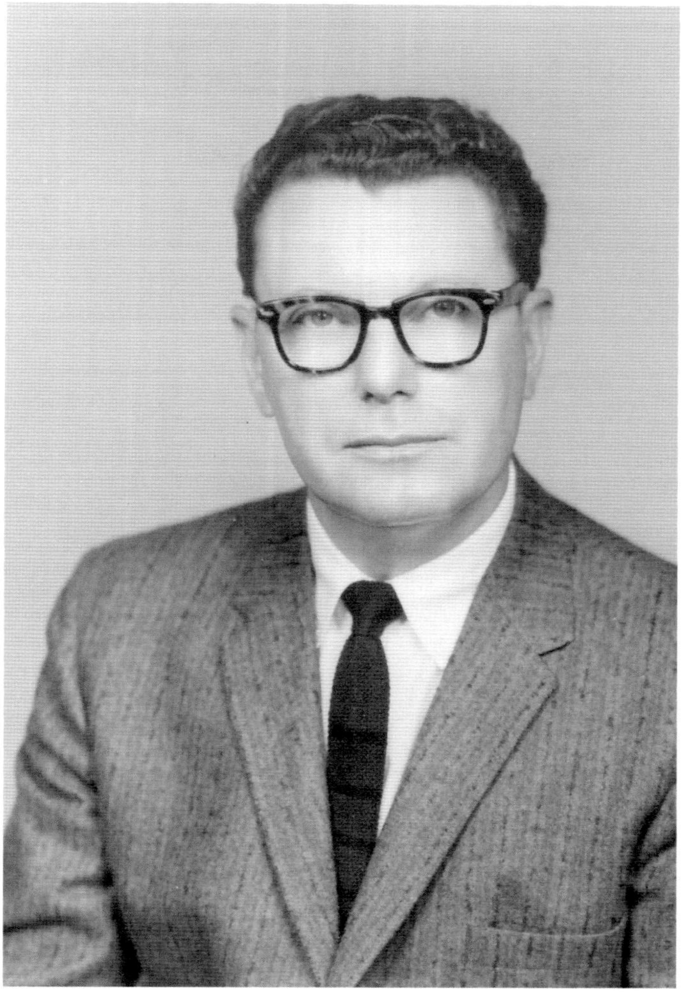

Emil Louis "Barry" Sturmer

Many people remember Barry for his tennis. In 1993, he organized the first Barry Sturmer All Pro Challenge at Kingston Plantation. For years, he wrote a tennis column for the local paper, *The Sun News*, and he spearheaded the development of the tennis center at the local high school.

Then there are those who remember Barry before he retired. Always creative, he approached life with style and panache. Early in his career, he worked in the theater in New York, wrote a play called *We're both Crazy*, and became one of the youngest off-Broadway playwrights at 16. He was a model, enlisted in the Army during World War II, and produced USO shows, and all of this before 1950. He came to Myrtle Beach with his wife, Marjorie, and opened up Barry Sturmer A Man's Shop, known for its stylish men's attire. Most men in this area had at least one sports coat from his store. He also managed the Myrtle Beach boxing team in the 1950s and was active in the community and in promoting tourism to this area. He was one of the organizers of the first Sun Fun Festival in 1952 and created the Human Checkerboard, a popular event during the festival. An idea man, he came up with the concept of Canadian American Days, a popular event that is still held every March by the chamber. Besides the first store, he also opened The Little Shop that featured children's wear and The Slack Shack for men. Barry was also involved in the Elks Club, Civitan's Club, the community playhouse, and the chamber of commerce. After a full life filled with love and laughter, Barry died at the age of 91 in 2005. (Courtesy MBCC.)

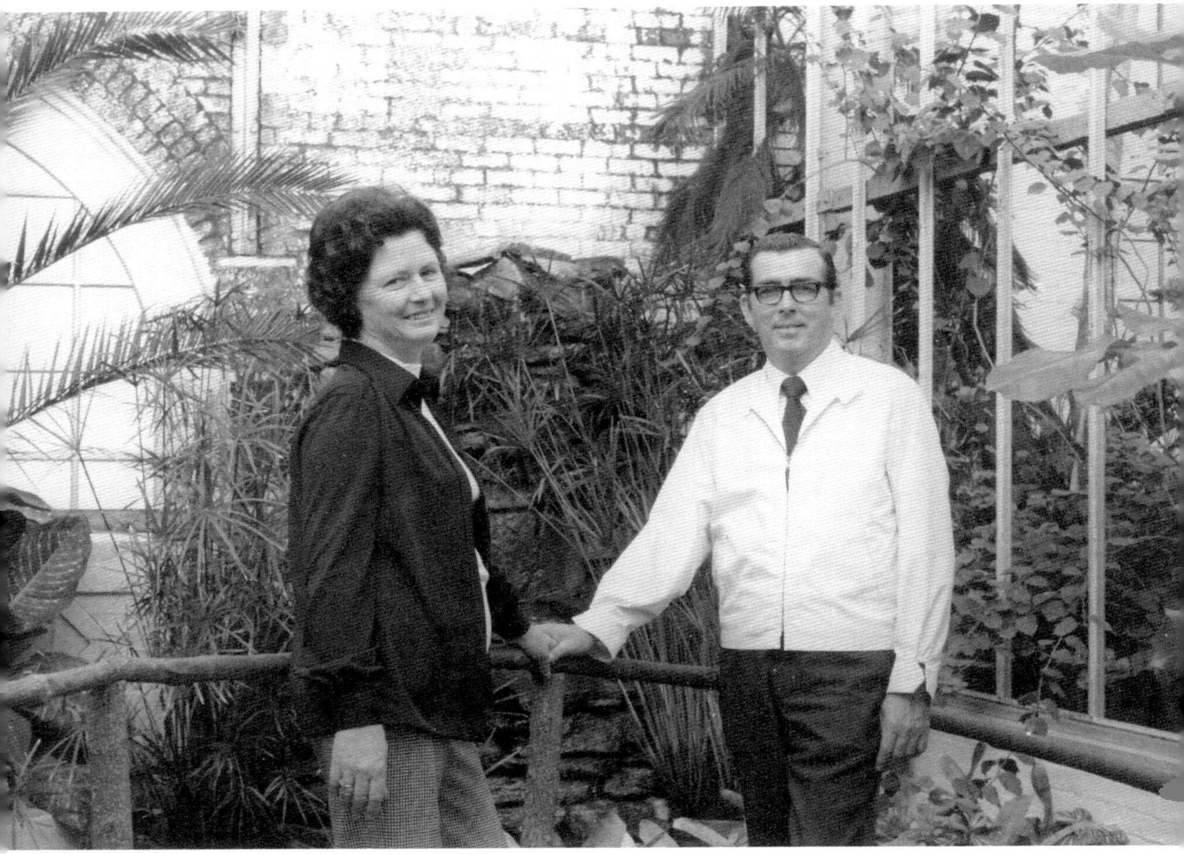

Luke West

Luke opened the Terminal Barber Shop in 1954 and was mostly a one-man operation until in the early 1970s Linwood Lewis became a partner in the shop with him. Prior to 1954, R.D. Vaughn had owned the shop. When Vaughn died, Luke—an employee there—decided to purchase the shop and changed its name. At the time, the Union Bus Terminal was located on the street adjacent to him. Luke gave a lot of haircuts and shaves over the years: from flat tops and Mohawks, to long sideburns and goatees, he has seen it all. Generations of families brought their children there for the dreaded first haircut, and some still carry the locks around or have them tucked into a jewelry box somewhere. No child, young or old, ever walked out without their piece of Bazooka bubble gum. West is pictured here with his wife, Mary. (Courtesy Patricia West Brocklesby.)

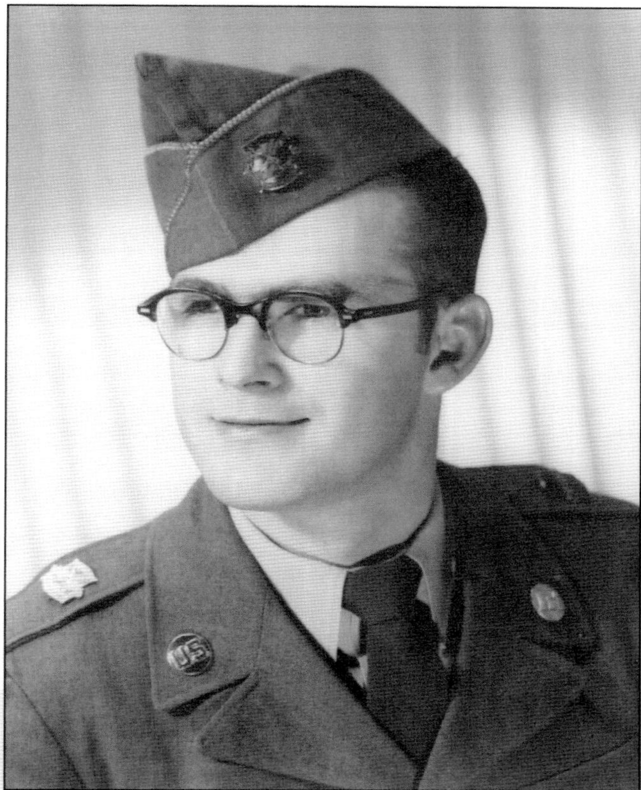

Wadeus West
Wadeus and his brother James owned the first cab company in Myrtle Beach, Veterans Cab Company. He was a land developer and, with several others, was instrumental in the early development of Surfside Beach. Very active with the Shriners and Masons and a member of the Myrtle Beach Lodge, he helped with the organization of the Socastee Masonic Lodge. He was also the brother of Luke West. (Courtesy Patricia West Brocklesby.)

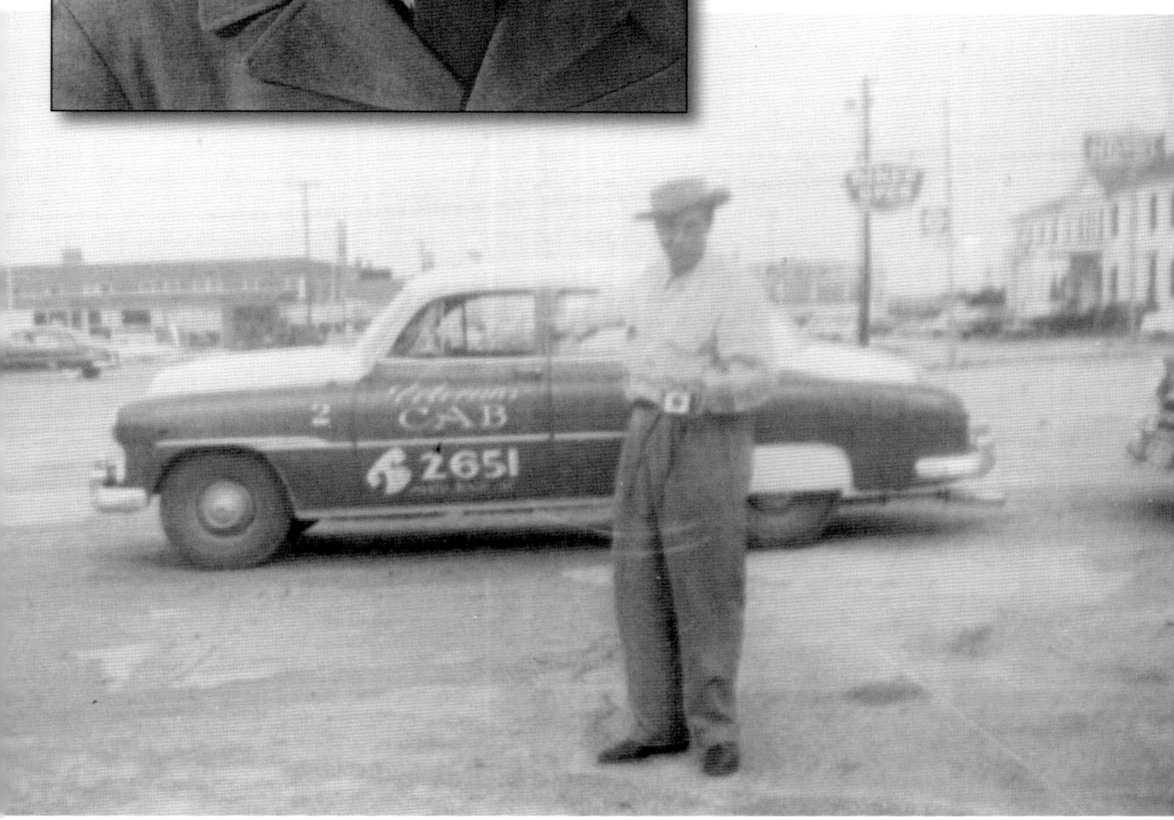

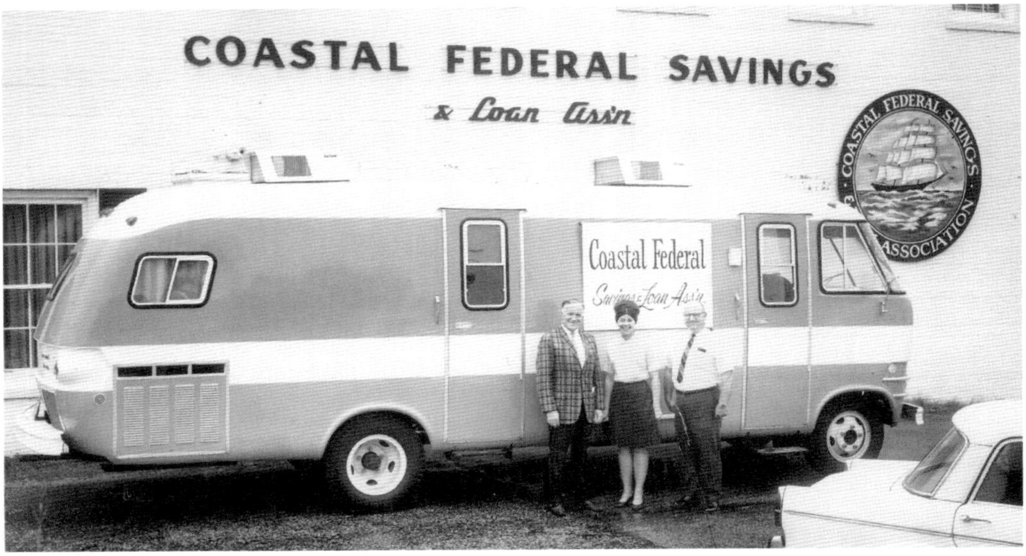

Coastal Federal Savings and Loan Association
The first bank in this area to have a drive-up window, Coastal Federal Savings and Loan Association opened its doors in the Colonial Building in October 1954. Coastal Federal was the only bank in the area to have a mobile unit. During his tenure, Gerbrand Poster saw the need for branches and purchased land for future building sites. To promote the bank and establish a client base, he purchased the mobile unit to travel the county, stopping on these sites so that customers would not have to travel all the way into Myrtle Beach. There were signs at each site in Surfside Beach, Murrells Inlet, North Myrtle Beach, and Little River posting the hours of operation. Branches were eventually built at each of these sites as well as others. (Courtesy Ruthie Schiller Kearns.)

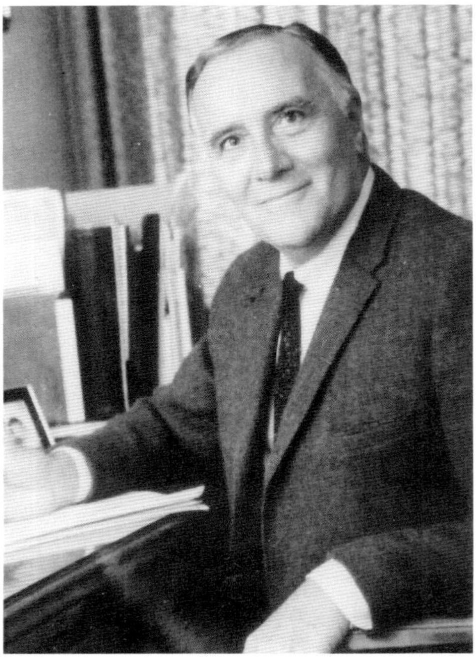

Gerbrand Poster Jr.
Poster immigrated to the United States from Holland in the 1940s, eventually settling in Myrtle Beach with his wife. He saw the needs of the city and was instrumental in laying the groundwork for USC–Coastal Carolina (now Coastal Carolina University), the Convention Center, and an airport. He stressed the need for a college here, explaining that if the locals went to school here, they would stay and build the community instead of leaving and establishing themselves elsewhere.

As a visionary, he realized the need for a savings and loan in Myrtle Beach, laid the groundwork, solicited local businessmen for start-up accounts, and handpicked the first board of directors for Coastal Federal Savings and Loan. To establish the business, when the bank first opened in 1954, Geri was the only employee for nine months while he built up the customer base. Poster was very hands-on, paying attention to details, and Coastal Federal soon became the hometown bank for locals. (Courtesy Jack Thompson.)

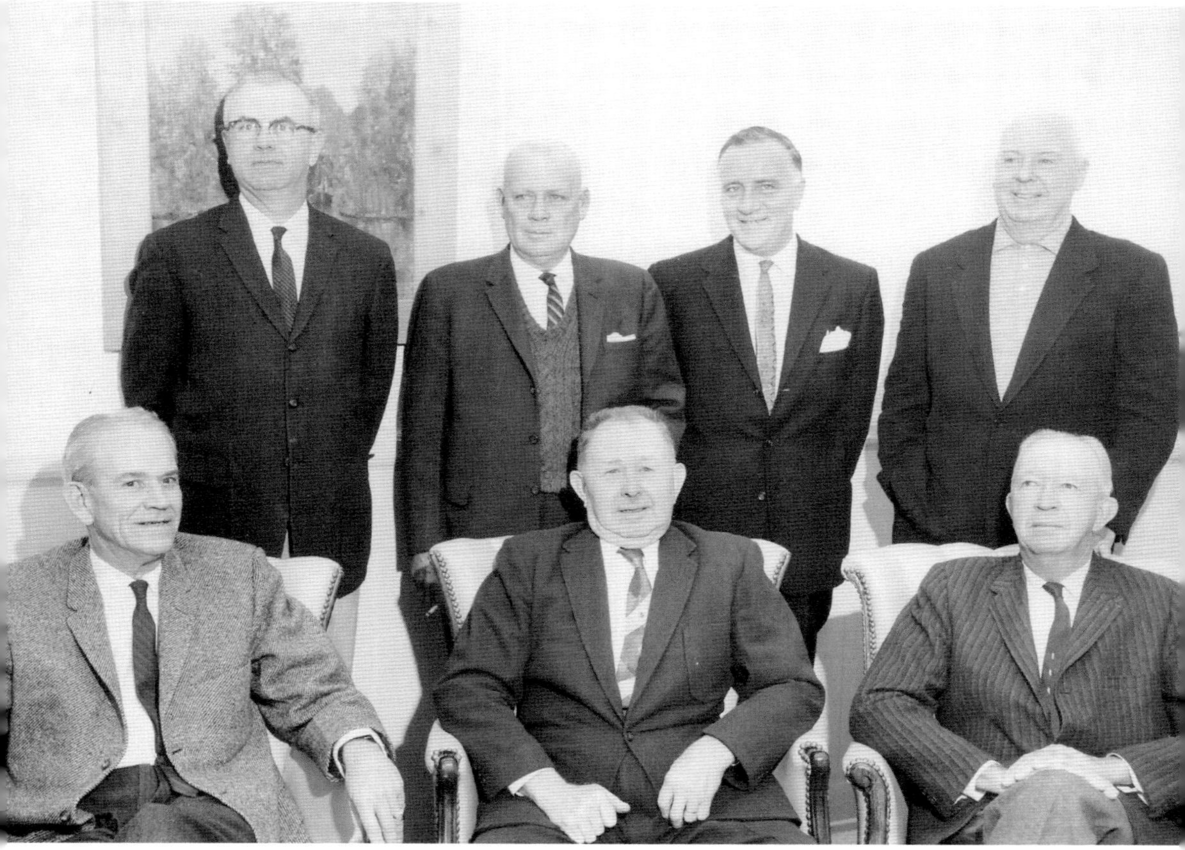

Robert Edward Lee "Bob" Brown

Born in North Carolina in 1899, Brown went to Davidson College and the University of North Carolina at Chapel Hill. He studied law and passed the bar in 1922. He married Lucille Johnston in 1931 and they had two children, Ceclia and Joy. They moved to Myrtle Beach in 1937, when he opened a retail liquor store. Shortly thereafter, he went into the real estate business with John A. McLeod. "Mr. Bob," as he was known, was a charter member of Coastal Federal Savings and Loan Association, on the board of directors, and served as its first president from 1954 until his death. Brown was a charter member of the Dunes Club, a member of the Myrtle Beach Civitan Club, the American Legion, and the Presbyterian Church, and was on the Myrtle Beach City Council in the early 1940s when they built the municipal airport and worked on getting the government to open a military base here. By 1980 he was officially retired, but he still served as bank president, and in his off time he loved to fish and travel. The original board of directors is pictured here at a meeting on June 30, 1954. They are, from left to right, (first row, seated) John A. McLeod; J.N. Ramsey Jr.; and Robert E. Lee Brown Jr., president; (second row, standing) Arthur W. Holler Jr.; G.W. Bryan, vice president; Gerbrand Poster Jr., secretary and treasurer; and John Divine Jr. (Courtesy Ruthie Schiller Kearns.)

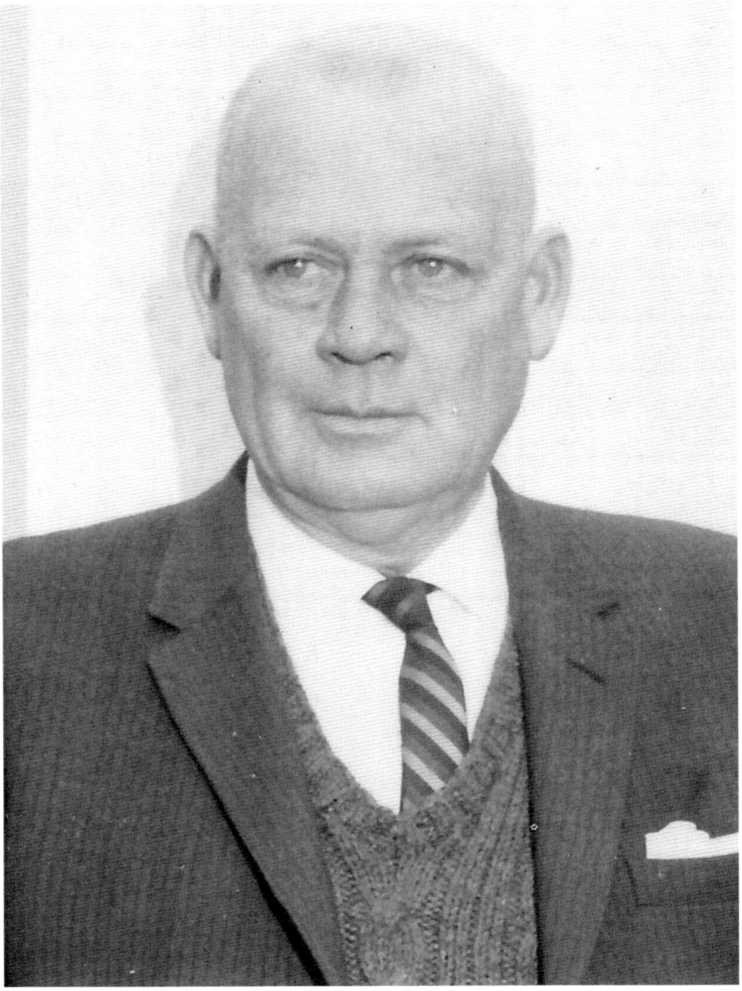

George Waller "Buster" Bryan

Son of Jim and Susie Bryan, Buster was born in 1913. He began his career as an attorney and practiced law with Claude Epps Sr. Deciding to change direction, he quit law and built the Caravelle Motel—it opened its doors on March 1, 1960, with 30 units and three floors. In 1962, the motel had the first covered pool on the Strand. The Caravelle Resort has expanded to over 500 condos on 15 floors since then. Buster was an owner of Pine Lakes in the 1940s, a founder of the Dunes Golf and Beach Club, and the golf package creator in 1962. He also built Robbers Roost Golf Club and Possum Trot Golf Club and created Golf-O-Tels, the first golf promotion group. As Cecil Brandon said, "He really was the foundation of all the things we did, the starter of the golf business in Myrtle Beach."

He was a member of the historic meeting that created the Coastal Education Foundation Inc., which eventually became USC–Coastal Carolina College and today is known as Coastal Carolina University. Buster was also part of the group that purchased and developed what was then called Floral Beach in 1952. His wife, Marge, came up with the name Surfside, and "Beach" was added so that it is now known as Surfside Beach.

Buster and Margaret "Marge" Cline had two children, Bo and Suzanna. He lived a full life, leaving his mark early in Myrtle Beach history. He died unexpectedly of pneumonia in 1969 at the age of 55. (Courtesy Ruthie Schiller Kearns.)

J. Marcus Smith Sr.
Born in Florence in 1925, Smith's family moved to Conway, where he graduated from high school. After receiving his degree in optometry in 1946, he moved to Myrtle Beach and opened his optometry practice here in 1947. He was the first eye doctor in Myrtle Beach. Smith established himself and married his childhood sweetheart and love of his life, Frances "Frankie" Marian Johnson, in 1950. Very active in the community, he joined the Jaycees and in 1957 was named Jaycees Young Man of the Year. He was involved in the youth program at the First United Methodist Church for many years. Smith researched and collected area history and wrote a local history column in *The Sun News*. He and Frankie had three sons: Marc, Frank, and David. Always wanting to put his writings in a book, but not having the time, he asked his son to realize his dream for him. Marc made that dream a reality in 2013 when he published his father's writings in the book *I Remember Myrtle Beach When . . .: A Collection of Local History, Personal Stories, Photographs and a Brief Biography of Dr. J. Marcus Smith.* (Courtesy J. Marcus Smith Jr.)

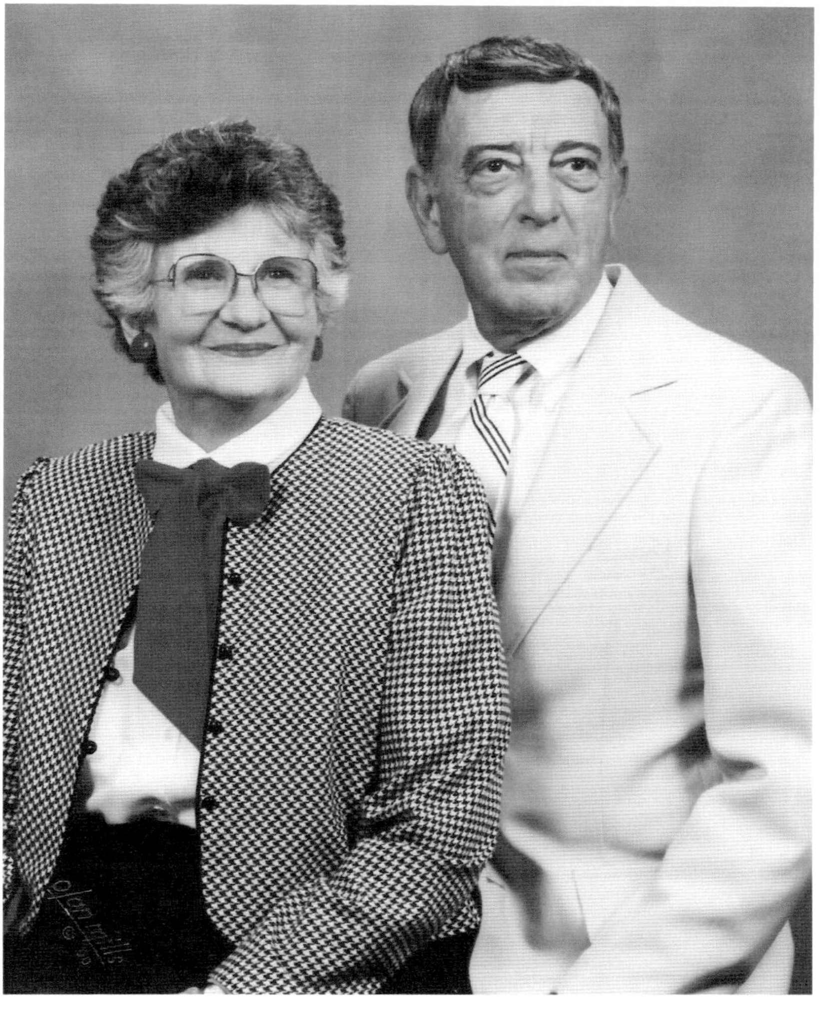

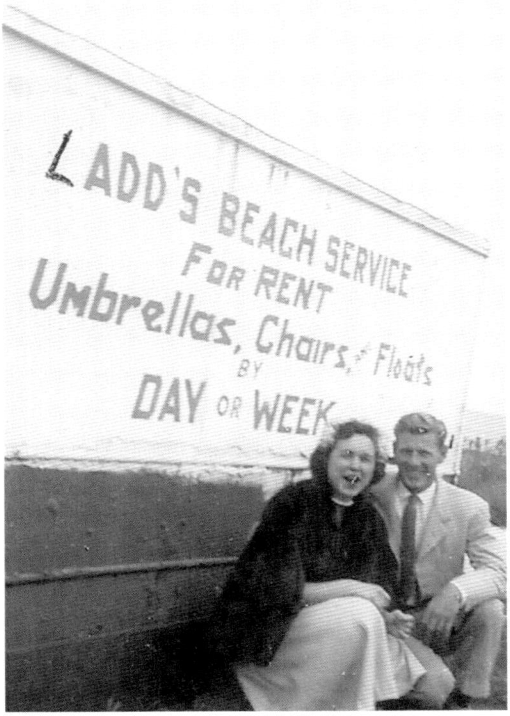

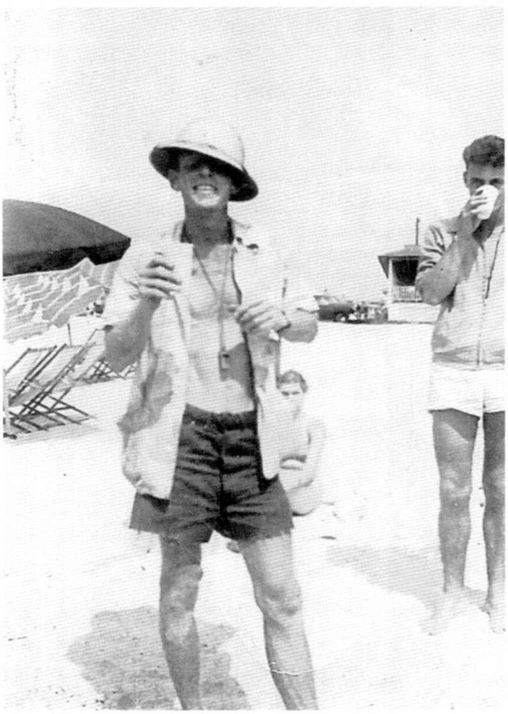

Thomas Moultrie III and Elizabeth Anne Ladd

Ladd's Beach Service was one of the first beach concessions in Myrtle Beach; it began in 1946 after he served in World War II. A family business, it was run by Moultrie and Elizabeth for 30 years. Their daughters Susan and Luanne grew up in the business and on the beach. Every summer they would set up their chairs and beach umbrellas, renting them to the sun worshipers who had discovered the white sandy beaches and family atmosphere. Their trained lifeguards would watch the waters and the bathers for potential dangers—always keeping water safety a high priority. Lifeguard positions have always been considered a prestigious summer job by locals and visitors wanting to spend their days at the beach and get paid for it. (Courtesy LuAnne Ladd Schmidt.)

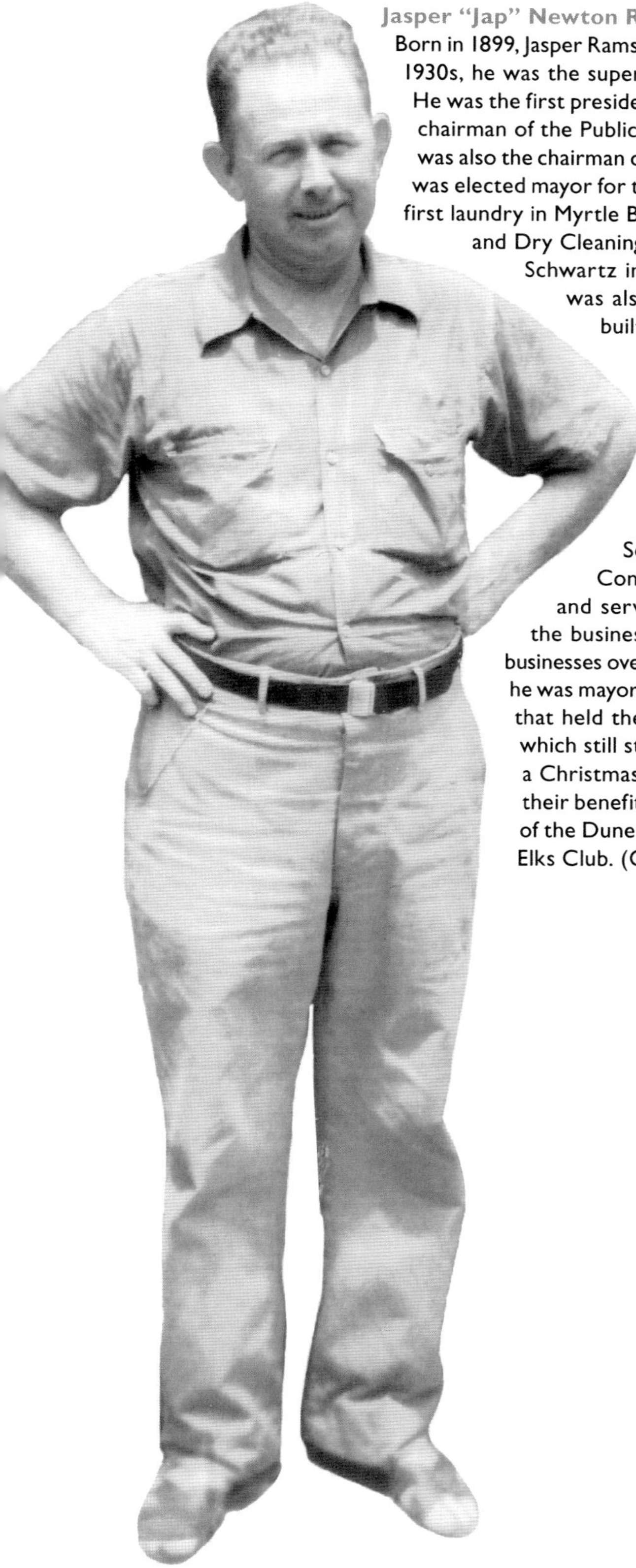

Jasper "Jap" Newton Ramsey Sr.
Born in 1899, Jasper Ramsey came to Myrtle Beach in 1928. In the early 1930s, he was the superintendent of relief work in Horry County. He was the first president of the chamber of commerce in 1938 and chairman of the Public Works Commission for six years. Ramsey was also the chairman of the Myrtle Beach Airport Commission. Jap was elected mayor for two terms: 1949 to 1954. He established the first laundry in Myrtle Beach in 1930, and owned Nu-Way Laundry and Dry Cleaning for many years before selling it to Lambo Schwartz in the 1960s when Lambo moved here. He was also head of Federated Construction, which built the first sewage disposal plant, and was the head of Ramsey Construction Co., which graded Kings Highway for the Woodside brothers and Myrtle Beach Estates. While the Ocean Forest was being built, he would haul their construction products—brick, steel, and cement—from the railroad to the hotel. Along with G.P. Seagle, he organized Myrtle Beach Lumber Company in 1947. In 1949, he bought out Seagle and served as president until 1953, when he sold the business. Jap Ramsey was involved in many more businesses over the years, too numerous to mention. While he was mayor, the city hall was built along with the building that held the first fire and police department, both of which still stand today. During his tenure, he instituted a Christmas bonus for the city employees, still part of their benefit package today. Jap was a founding member of the Dunes Golf and Beach Club and a member of the Elks Club. (Courtesy J.N. Newton Jr.)

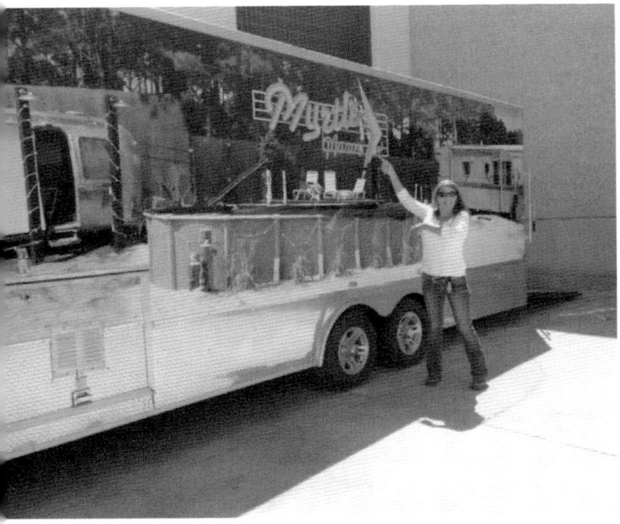

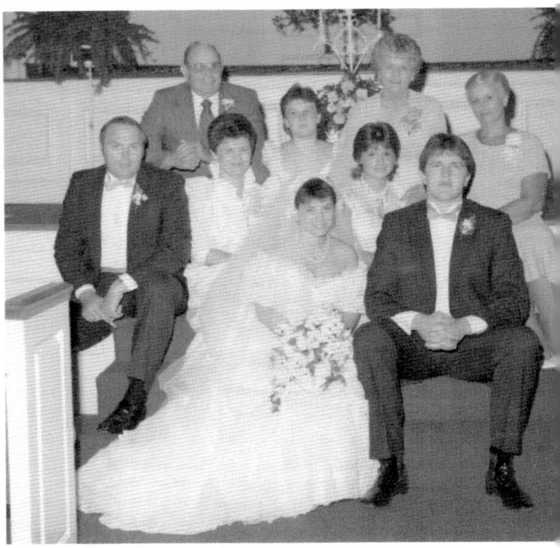

Cecil Patrick Family

Cecil Patrick Sr. was the original owner and operator of Patrick Mobile Home Park. It was a quiet little mobile home park nestled in the tall pines along Highway 15 just off Harrelson's Boulevard and the entrance to the airport. It was quiet until they started filming a reality show in 2012. Now everyone from beauty contestants to other reality show stars (including Swamp People and Honey Boo Boo) as well as regular tourists stop by to get their "Keep Calm and Trailer On" T-shirts to commemorate their visit to the "Myrtle Manor" Trailer Park. Cecil's grandfather Joseph moved to Myrtle Beach in the early 1920s, living with his family in a house on Alder Street and owning several acres up to Highway 501. He may have been a brick mason by trade, but "once a farmer always a farmer," so he swapped the land for some land out in the country (present day Highway 15, where the park is now) so he could plant a garden. He would drive his freshly picked produce into town with a mule and wagon, selling to the day-trippers and the locals. Joe eventually bought more property with Cecil Sr. and Jr., slowly adding to the family holdings over time. Cecil Sr. opened the mobile home park in 1968 with only nine spaces, enlarging it to what it is today. Cecil Jr. and his wife Barbara currently run it. The photograph above right was taken at the wedding of their daughter Dana and her new husband Dennis Painter. With Cecil Jr. in the second row are Barbara and Sherry Causey (a niece). In the third row are Cecil Sr., Becky (daughter), Helen (mother), and Ann Patrick Causey (sister). Jeana Futrell is pictured on the left with the new Myrtle Manor merchandise trailer. (Courtesy Patrick Family.)

CHAPTER FOUR

Myrtle Beach Air Force Base

When the Army Air Corps first came to this area and built the base, they were embraced by the local community as their own. After World War II the base was decommissioned, but the local community worked together to get it reopened. Through hard work and perseverance, the base reopened as the Myrtle Beach Air Force Base in 1956. Residents shared the budding city with them and they lived amongst the other citizens, sent their children to the same schools, shopped at the same stores, and worshipped in the same churches. They became as much a part of the community as the community became a part of them. When the Sun Fun Festival began they were included, opening the parade with the color guard. The base would open up to visitors for tours and demonstrations, people would be allowed to sit in the planes for pictures, and the Air Force Band would play. The jets would fly overhead and the brass would all come out in their dress uniforms.

There were many changes on the base over the years, and many wars fought. Thousands of men and women were stationed here, and they trained here and went to war. They fought in Europe during World War II, went to Vietnam and Korea in the 1960s and 1970s, and traveled to the Middle East in the 1980s. Most of them returned home, but some did not.

The Myrtle Beach Air Force Base closed in 1993, much to the disappointment of the City of Myrtle Beach. Eventually, the Redevelopment Authority was formed and a plan was put together. Under the lead of Buddy Styers, the chairman of the Myrtle Beach Air Force Base Redevelopment Authority, the land was disposed of and the new Market Common was established. The historic Myrtle Beach Air Force Base Museum Project was enacted and several museums were completed in existing buildings on the old base property, including the Crabtree Gymnasium and the Whispering Pines Golf Course. In memory of the base and the people stationed here, there are plaques on historical sites commemorating events and persons. Most of the streets have been named for people in honor of their service. The memorial Wall of Service is located near the front entrance, with names of people who worked on the base—military personnel as well as civilian. There is also a MIA/POW Freedom Tree and plaque that was put in place in 1973 after Colonel Shine went missing in 1972, in honor of all the MIA/POW soldiers, past and present.

While the base has been closed for over 20 years, it is forever in local hearts because of the role it played in the history of the area.

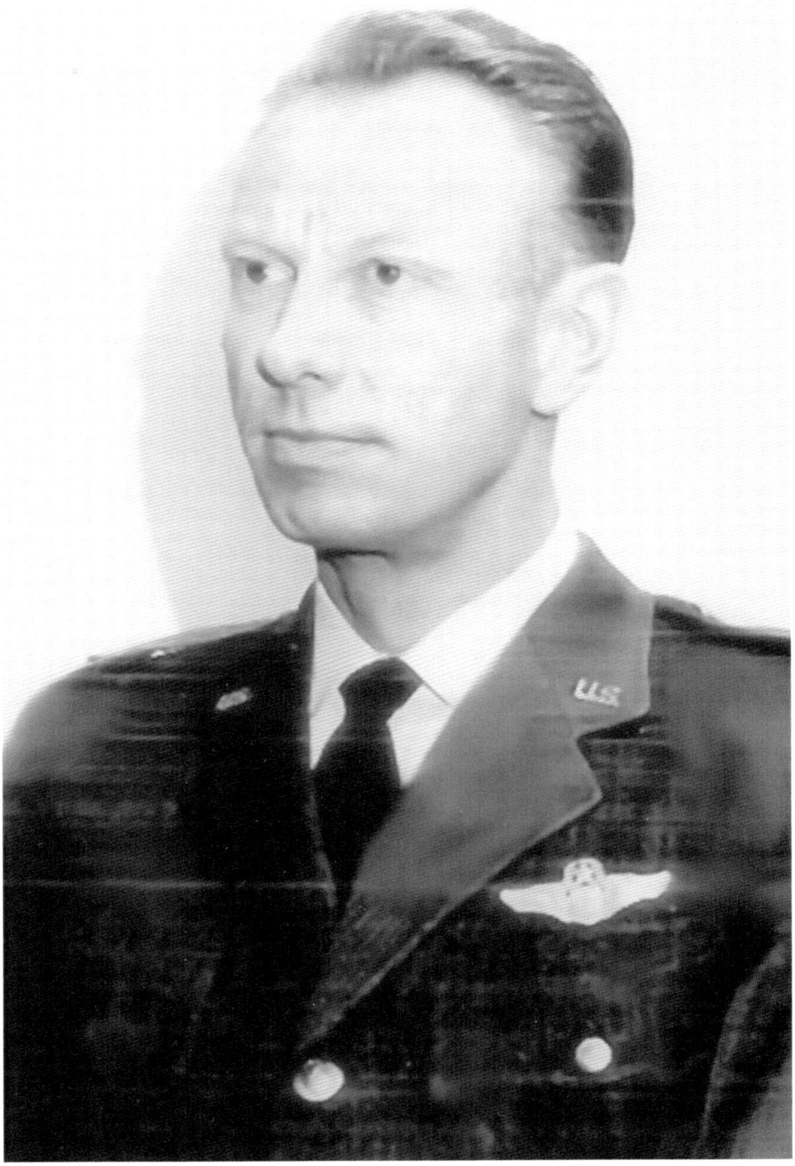

Col. Robert G. Emmens

Arriving in Myrtle Beach in 1955, Colonel Emmens was here to command the newly activated 4434th Air Base Squadron and to supervise rehabilitation of the base prior to opening on July 25, 1956. Once activated, Colonel Emmens was the wing commander until September, when he assumed the role of deputy base commander. Prior to his assignment here, he flew many missions including one that he later wrote a book about called *Guests of the Kremlin*. As part of Jimmy Doolittle's Tokyo Raiders, he was lieutenant and copilot in Crew No. 8 when they dropped bombs on Tokyo. Of the 16 crews, Crew No. 8 was the only crew not to crash or bail out. Low on fuel, they landed in Vladivostok, Soviet Union, where they were held as prisoners of war for 13 months before escaping to the British embassy in Iran. Then, they made their way to India and came home to the United States. At Market Common, Emmens Avenue and Emmens Preserve is named in his honor. (Courtesy Diane Moskow-McKenzie.)

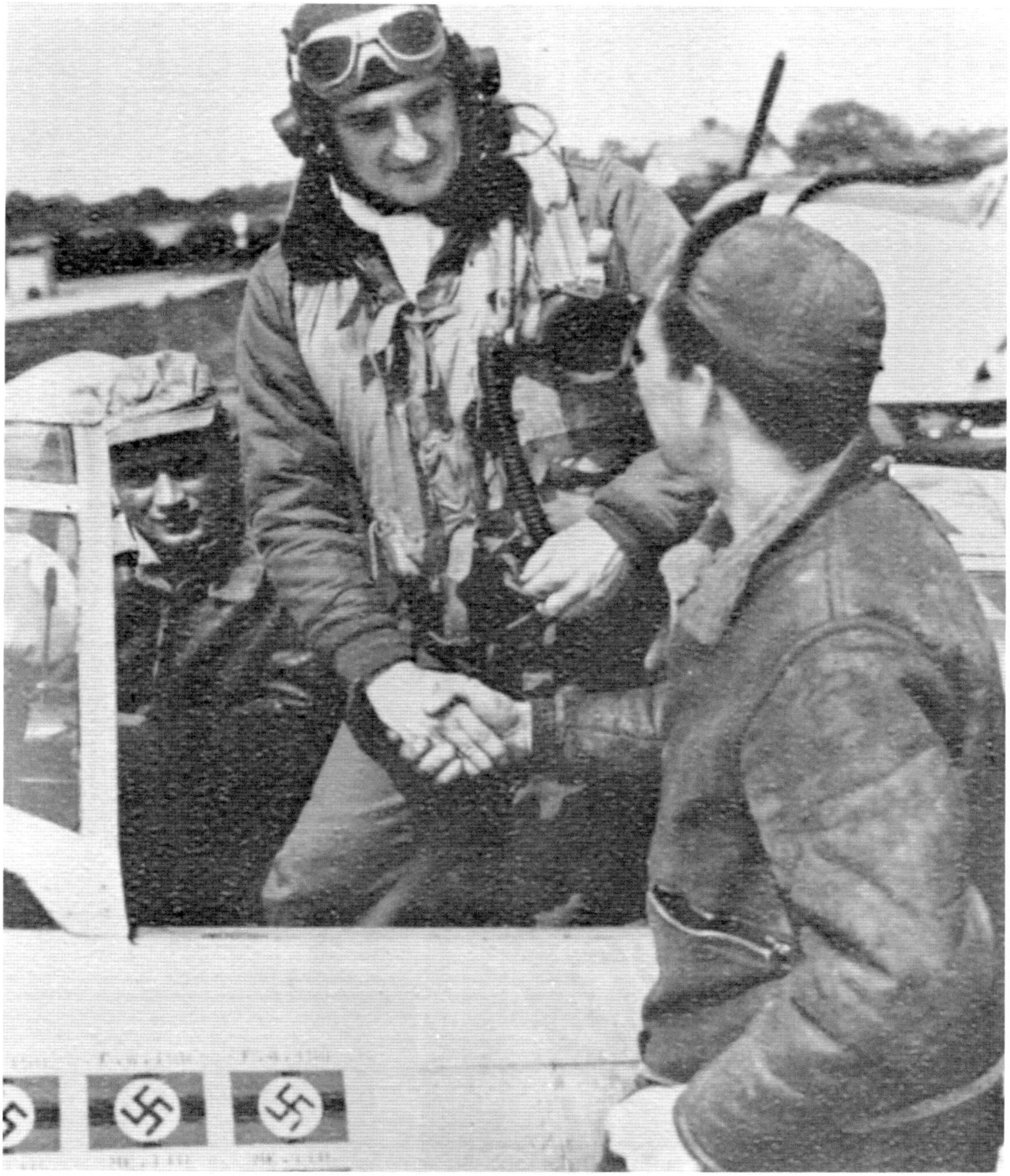

Francis S. "Gabby" Gabreski

Colonel Gabreski (center) was the commander of the 342nd Fighter-Day Wing of the Myrtle Beach Air Force Base from September 10, 1956, until November 19, 1956, (when it was inactivated and succeeded by the 354th Tactical Fighter Wing) and commander of the 354th Tactical Fighter Wing from then until July 13, 1960. Gabby Gabreski retired in 1967 with over 5,000 flying hours, and received an unprecedented 13 Distinguished Flying Crosses, the most earned by any individual. During World War II, he joined the 56th Fighter Group "Wolfpack" flying Republic P-47 Thunderbolts. During his tour, he destroyed 28 enemy aircraft in aerial combat and many others on the ground. In July 1944, he crashed in enemy territory and was a prisoner of war until the war ended. Known as "America's Greatest Living Ace" he passed away in 2002. Gabreski Lane at Market Common is named in his honor. (Courtesy CML.)

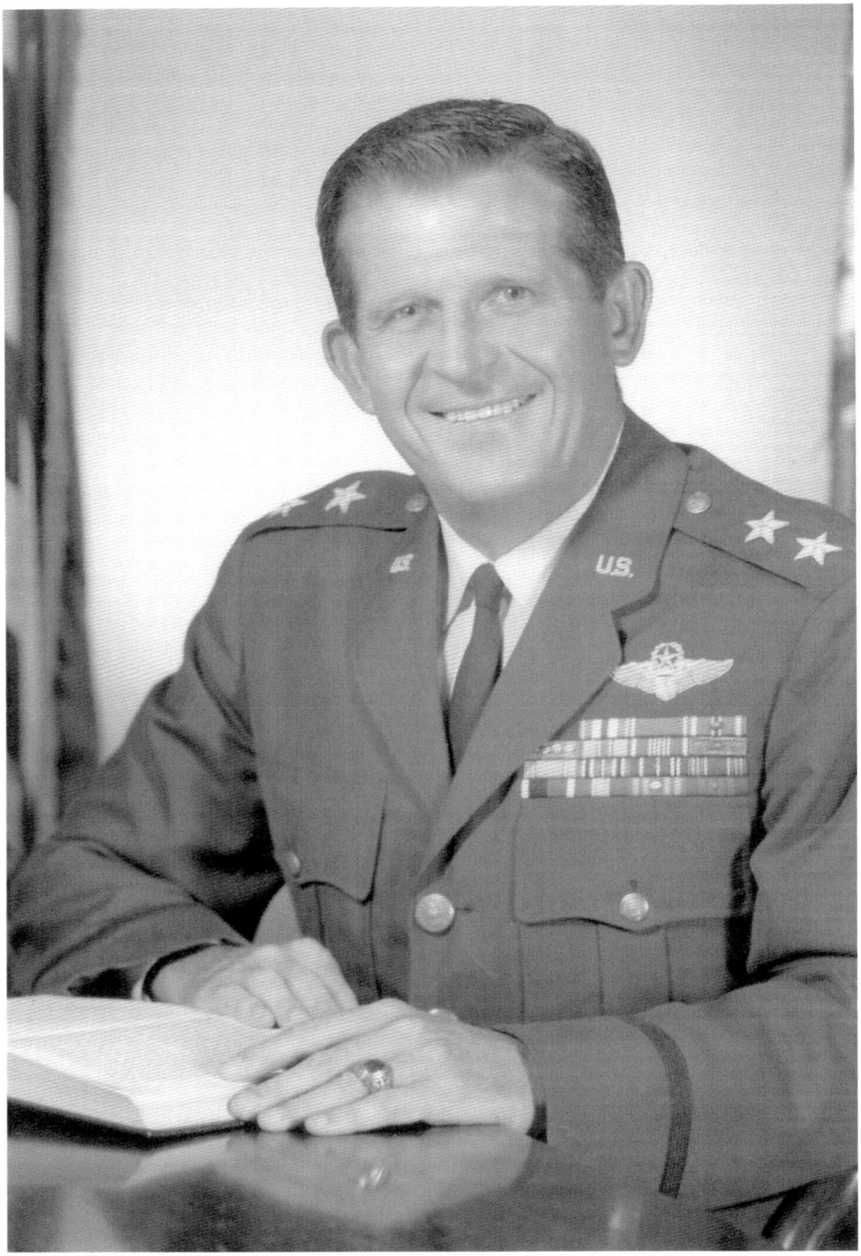

Maj. Gen. James Franklin Hackler Jr.
General Hackler first came to Myrtle Beach when he served as director of operations for the 354th Tactical Fighter Wing in 1956. While here, he met Buster Bryan and, seeing the potential of the area, he became partners with him in the Caravelle Resort. After Buster suddenly died in 1968, Jim made a decision to retire early and move here permanently to manage the hotel and some of his other investments. Hackler dissolved Golf-O-Tels and joined Golf Holiday, giving it more weight and opening it up for more expansion. He was a partner in Possum Trot, Robbers Roost, Bay Tree Golf Courses, and others. Hackler's legacy lives on through a golf scholarship at CCU and Hackler Street at Market Common. (Courtesy CML.)

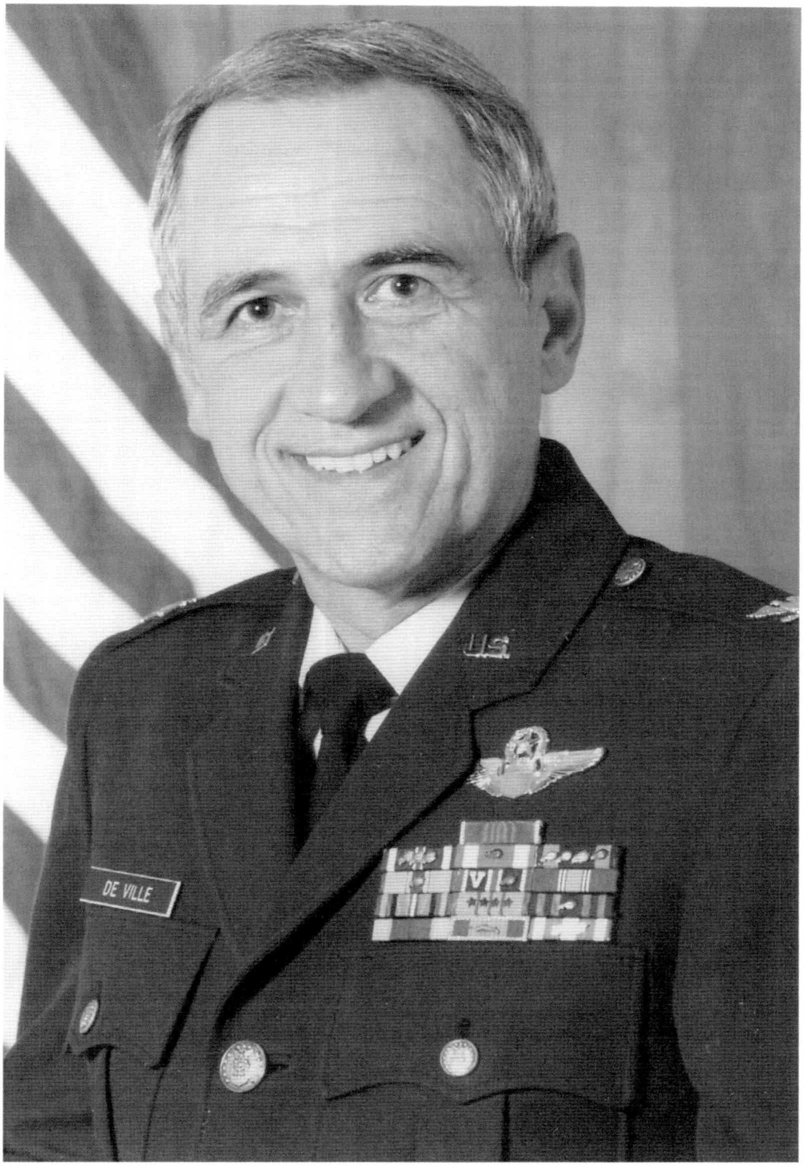

Edsel J. "Coupe" DeVille
First assigned to Myrtle Beach Air Force Base in 1978, DeVille was commander of the 355th Tactical Fighter Wing flying the A-10. He returned several years later in 1987 as base commander before he retired with the rank of general in 1989, having served 28 years. As a fighter pilot, he logged over 5,000 hours in 12 different aircraft and was awarded the Legion of Merit with two oak leaf clusters, among other numerous decorations. He was a designated Top Gun in the A-10 aircraft and volunteered for two combat tours in Vietnam. After retirement, he made Myrtle Beach his home and has been very active in the community, working with the Horry County Red Cross, the South Carolina Aeronautics Commission, the Myrtle Beach Area Chamber of Commerce, and the Palmetto Pride board of directors. He worked tirelessly on the Myrtle Beach Air Force Base Redevelopment Task Force. Among the streets in Market Common, there is a DeVille Street in honor of General DeVille's many years of service. (Courtesy Diane Moskow McKenzie.)

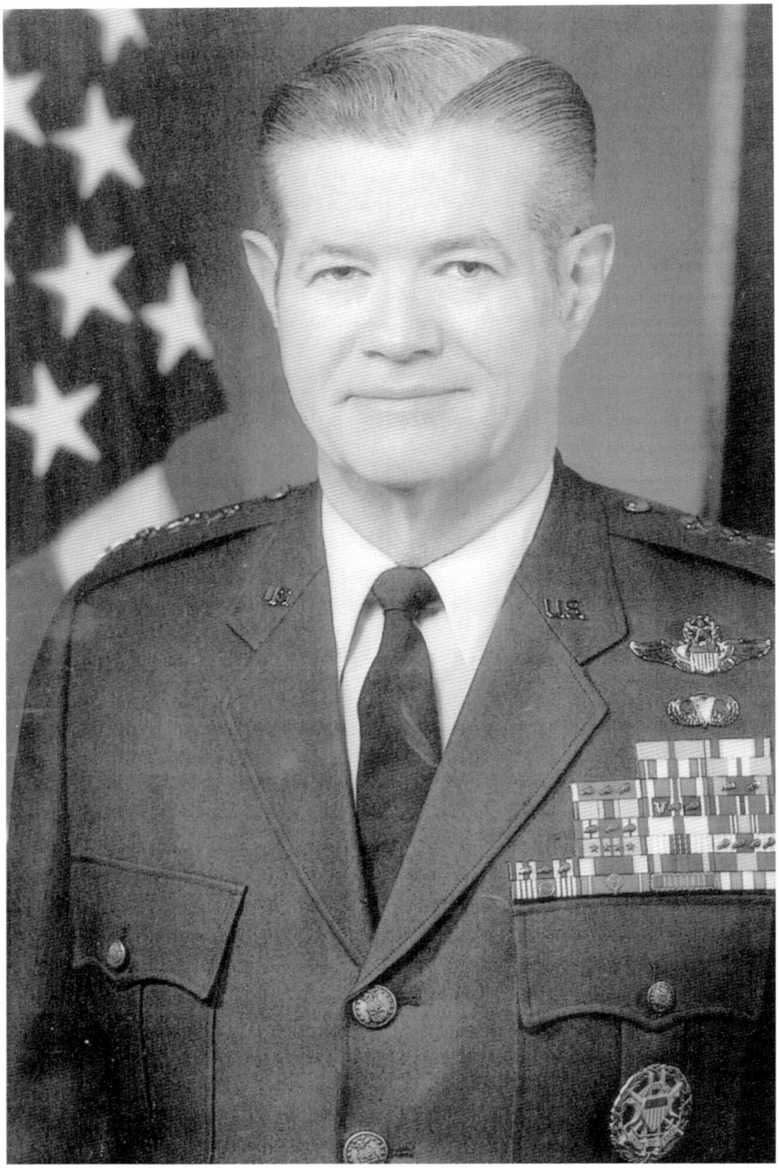

Gen. Michael Patrick Chamberlain Carns
Born in Kansas, General Carns is a graduate of the United States Air Force Academy and Harvard University. He served in the military from 1961 to 1994 and was base commander of the Myrtle Beach Air Force Base from 1979 to 1980. During his time here, he created a "unique combat readiness training program centered on deploying and operating aircraft from an austere forward operating location under simulated combat conditions," according to an anonymous biographical sketch. The area on base where this training was held was called FOLTA, or Forward Operating Location Training Area. This program was used by other bases to update and train their flying units. During his career, Carns has logged more than 6,400 flying hours and received numerous awards and medals, including the Defense Distinguished Service Medal with oak leaf cluster. Prior to retirement in 1994, General Carns was the vice chief of staff of the United States Air Force. He is currently vice chairman of PrivaSource Inc. (Courtesy CML.)

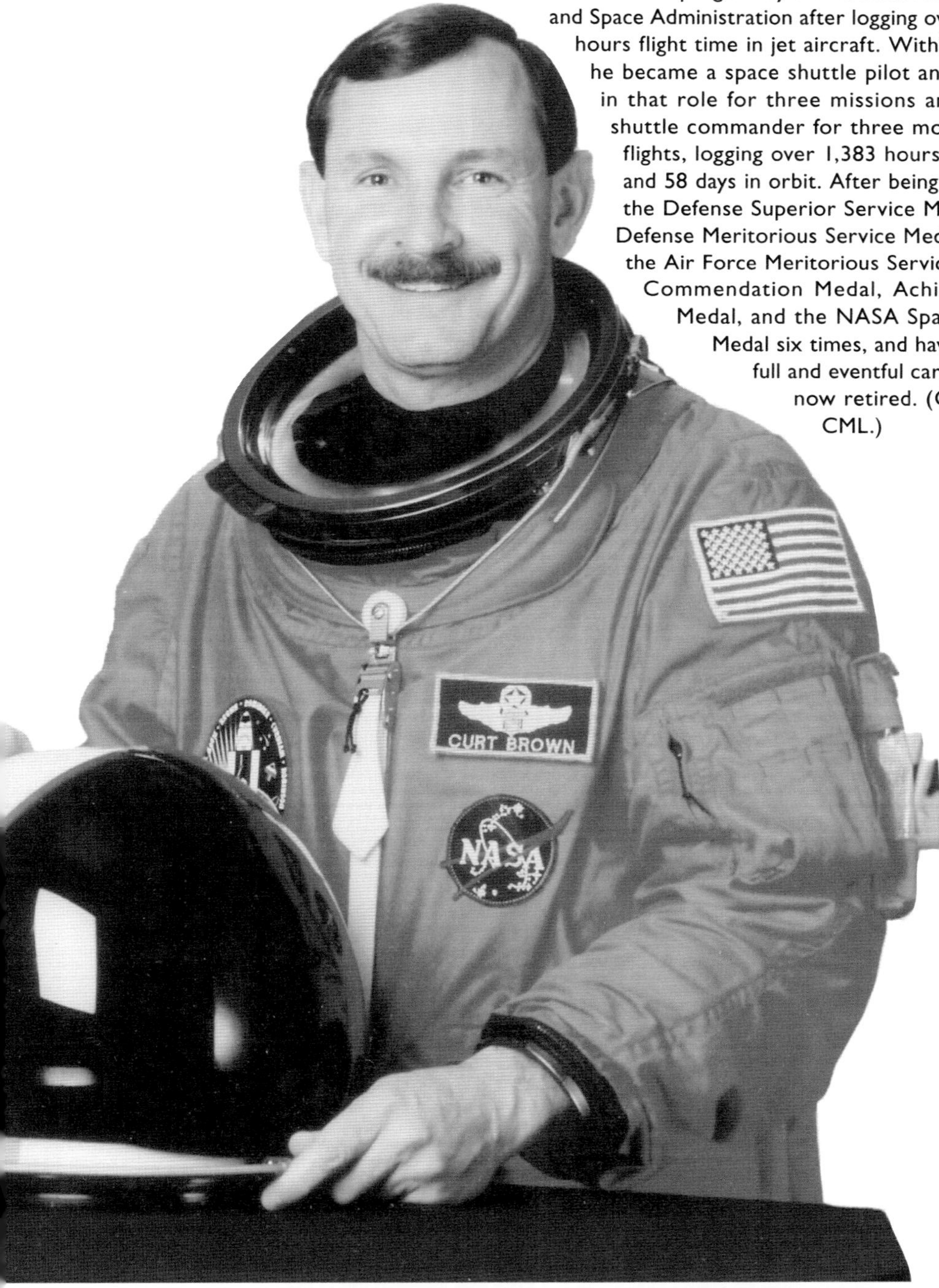

Col. Curtis L. Brown

From North Carolina, Colonel Brown was stationed at Myrtle Beach Air Force Base from January 1980 to March 1982. He graduated from the United States Air Force Academy and completed his pilot training at Laughlin Air Force Base in Texas. He was assigned here as an A-10 pilot. After he left, he went on to more training and became an instructor pilot for the A-10. Several years later, in August 1987, he was selected for the astronaut program by the National Aeronautics and Space Administration after logging over 6,000 hours flight time in jet aircraft. Within a year, he became a space shuttle pilot and served in that role for three missions and was a shuttle commander for three more space flights, logging over 1,383 hours in space and 58 days in orbit. After being awarded the Defense Superior Service Medal, the Defense Meritorious Service Medal twice, the Air Force Meritorious Service Medal, Commendation Medal, Achievement Medal, and the NASA Space Flight Medal six times, and having led a full and eventful career, he is now retired. (Courtesy CML.)

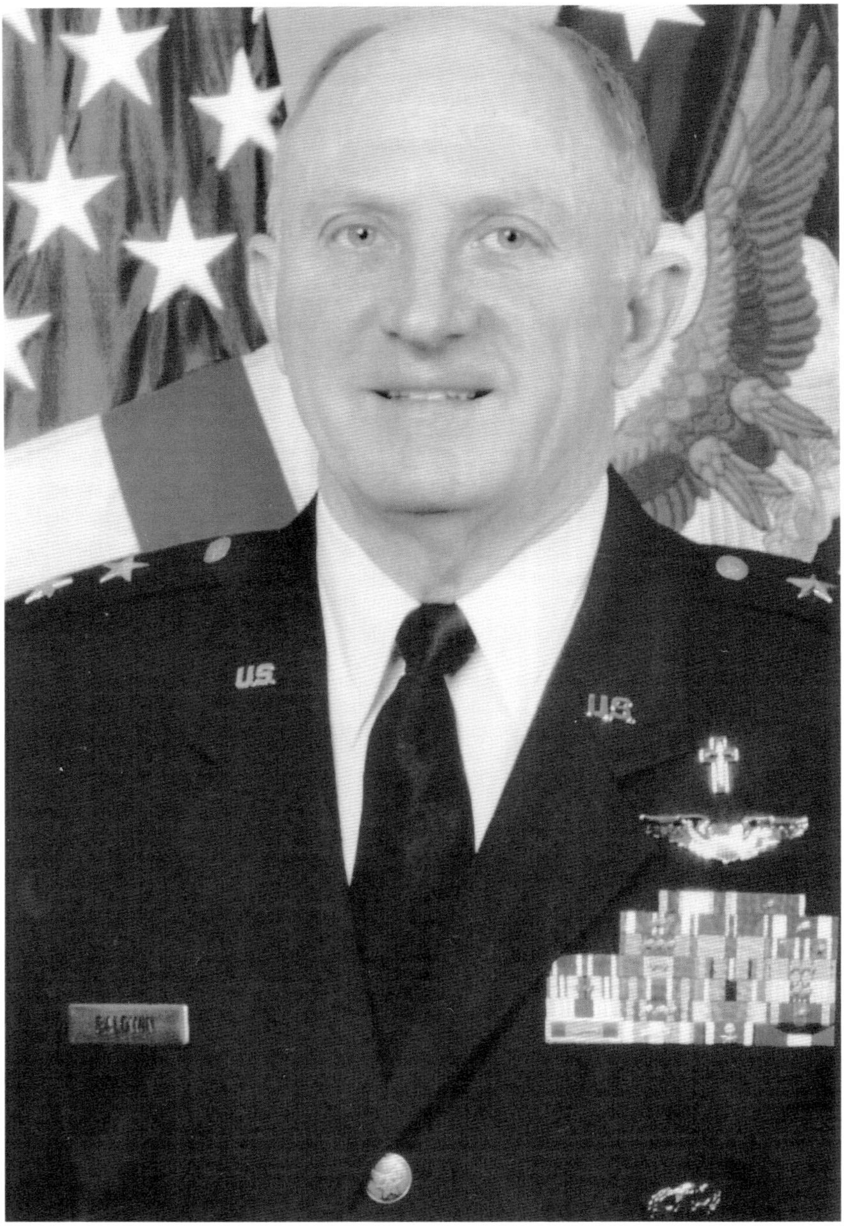

Maj. Gen. Charles C. Baldwin

Chaplain Baldwin was stationed at Myrtle Beach Air Force Base from June 1989 to June 1992, where he served as the senior installation chaplain. During Desert Storm and Desert Shield, he accompanied the 354th Tactical Fighter Wing to Saudi Arabia when they were deployed. Prior to coming here, Baldwin served in South Vietnam as an HH-54 rescue helicopter pilot. He left the service to earn his master of divinity degree and returned to the Air Force as a Protestant chaplain. Baldwin has received many awards over the years, including the Distinguished Service Medal with oak leaf cluster, and is currently in Washington, DC, serving as the Air Force chief of chaplains, which includes advising the secretary of defense and the Joint Chiefs of Staff on religious, ethical, and quality of life concerns. (Courtesy CML.)

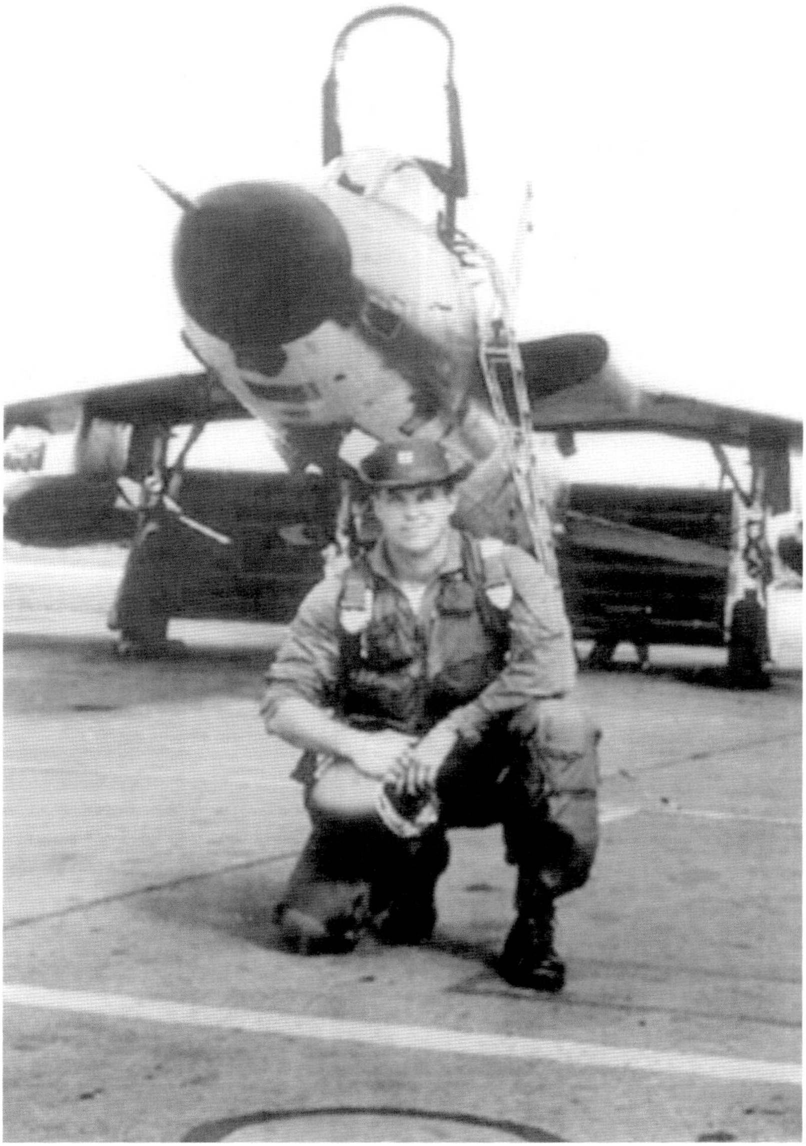

Maj. Anthony "Tony" Cameron Shine
Major Shine was deployed with the 354th Tactical Fighter Wing to Thailand in October 1972. While piloting his A-7D aircraft on December 2, descending below cloud cover to get a better look on a reconnaissance mission, he disappeared. An extensive search by a rescue team was unable to find him or his aircraft. He became missing in action December 10. It took almost 24 years, but Major Shine's remains were located and finally brought to rest on American soil in Arlington National Cemetery after they were identified on August 2, 1996. Along with the Joint Task Force Full Accounting Group that never forgot, his daughter Colleen Shine kept looking for him. She traveled to Vietnam and, after extensive searching, found evidence of his plane. She was the reason his remains were brought home. In remembrance of Major Shine, and in honor of his service, Shine Avenue in Market Common is named after him. For his sacrifice, he was awarded the Purple Heart. (Courtesy Diane Moskow McKenzie.)

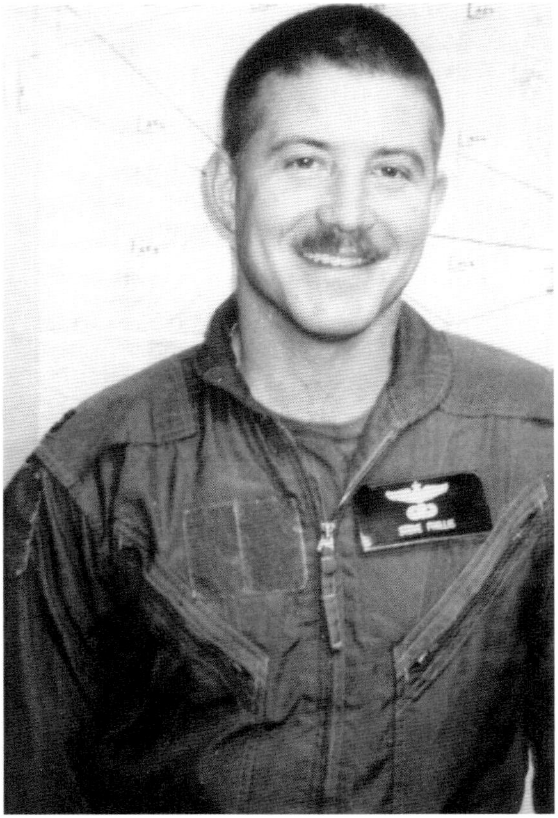

Capt. Stephen Richard Phillis

Captain Phillis was an A-10 pilot and deployed from Myrtle Beach Air Force Base when his unit was ordered to Saudi Arabia in 1990 during Operation Desert Storm. During a combat mission, his wingman was shot down by enemy fire. He immediately organized a search and rescue mission for him and was hit by enemy fire and killed when his A-10 crashed. His wingman, Lt. Bob Sweet, was captured by the Iraqis and repatriated after the war. To preserve Captain Phillis's memory in a small way, Phillis Boulevard on Market Common is named in his honor. (Courtesy CML.)

Brig. Gen. James Howell Howard

In 1943, when he was promoted to major, he was given command of the 356th Fighter Squadron, part of the 354th Fighter Group at Myrtle Beach Air Force Base (then the Myrtle Beach Army Air Field). In the European and Pacific theaters, he was the first fighter ace and the only fighter pilot awarded the Medal of Honor for his heroics in Europe during World War II. Howard Avenue in Market Common is named in his honor. (Courtesy CML.)

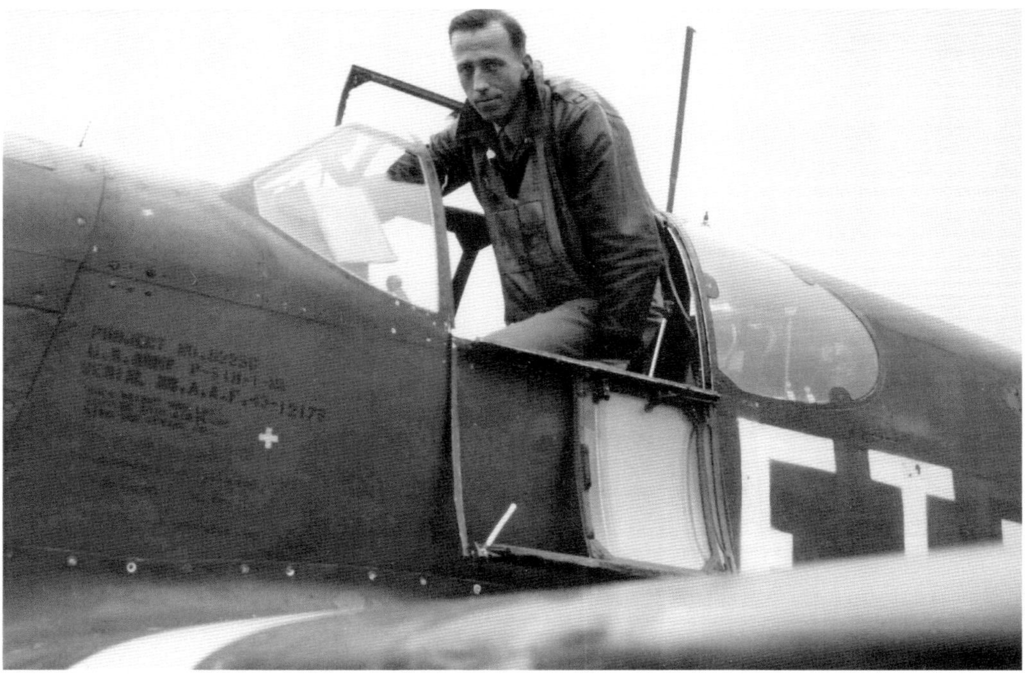

CHAPTER FIVE

Locals with Character

Since the city was incorporated in 1938, quite a few people have passed through; some stayed, some did not. Locals are thankful for those who invested so much of themselves into the community. The larger a place becomes, the more services are needed for all walks of life. Kids need help, so someone cared enough to open up Myrtle Beach Haven. There was no newspaper, so someone decided to publish one. The kids on the block needed some fun, so someone's dad built a little roller coaster. Students needed to learn science, so there was a teacher who puts chameleons on her ears. These are but a sampling of our community leaders and educators—people who make our world a better place to live.

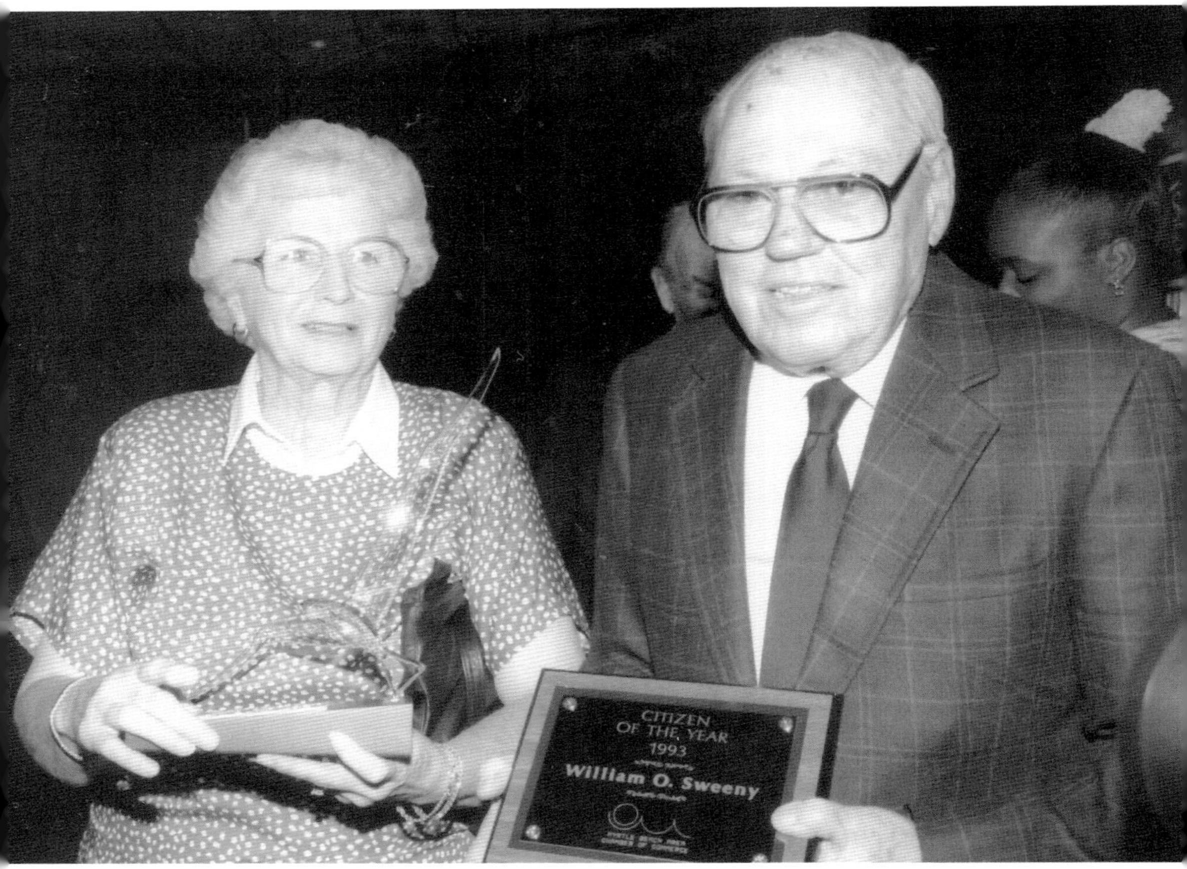

William Oglesby Sweeney

Originally from Lexington, Kentucky, Sweeney and his wife, Odette, moved to Myrtle Beach after he retired in 1974. Using his time wisely, he became very active in community and civic work. He was best known for his deeds at the shelter home, Myrtle Beach Haven, of which he was one of the founders. He was also on the board of directors for United Way, Helping Hands, and the Franklin G. Burroughs–Simeon B. Chapin Art Museum. A member of the Dunes Golf and Beach Club, he was a past president and treasurer. For all of his work he received many awards, including the Service to Mankind Award from the Sertoma Club and Citizen of the Year Award in 1993 by the chamber of commerce. He died at the age of 82 in 1998. (Courtesy MBCC.)

Henry Trezevant "Trez" Willcox

Originally from Marion, Trez came to Myrtle Beach in 1926, working with Myrtle Beach Investment Company for several years. After the town incorporated in 1938, it appointed Trez town secretary and recorder. An avid writer, he began writing and editing the first news bulletin for the area, *Myrtle Beach News of Charming Myrtle Beach*, which he distributed to locals and visitors. He also wrote news articles, sending them to the Associated Press, which would sometimes pick them up and publish them throughout the Carolinas. He loved Myrtle Beach and wanted others to know about it. Trez was most proud of the news release with the headline "Myrtle Beach on map First Time in History" with a Washington dateline published in 1928. He retired from the city in 1967 after giving 28 years of service as the publicity director, recorder, and secretary. Always involved in the community, he was a member of the Civitans Club, named Civitan of the Year 1958, and in 1957 he was elected a lifetime honorary member of the club. For his continued work in promoting tourism, the chamber conferred upon him an honorary life membership. He was a member of the board of directors of Associated Charities, a member of Toastmasters of Myrtle Beach, and a member of the Outboard Boating Club of America. Trez was also a member of the Huguenot Society of South Carolina, the Elks, the Moose, and the Mason Lodges. (Courtesy CML.)

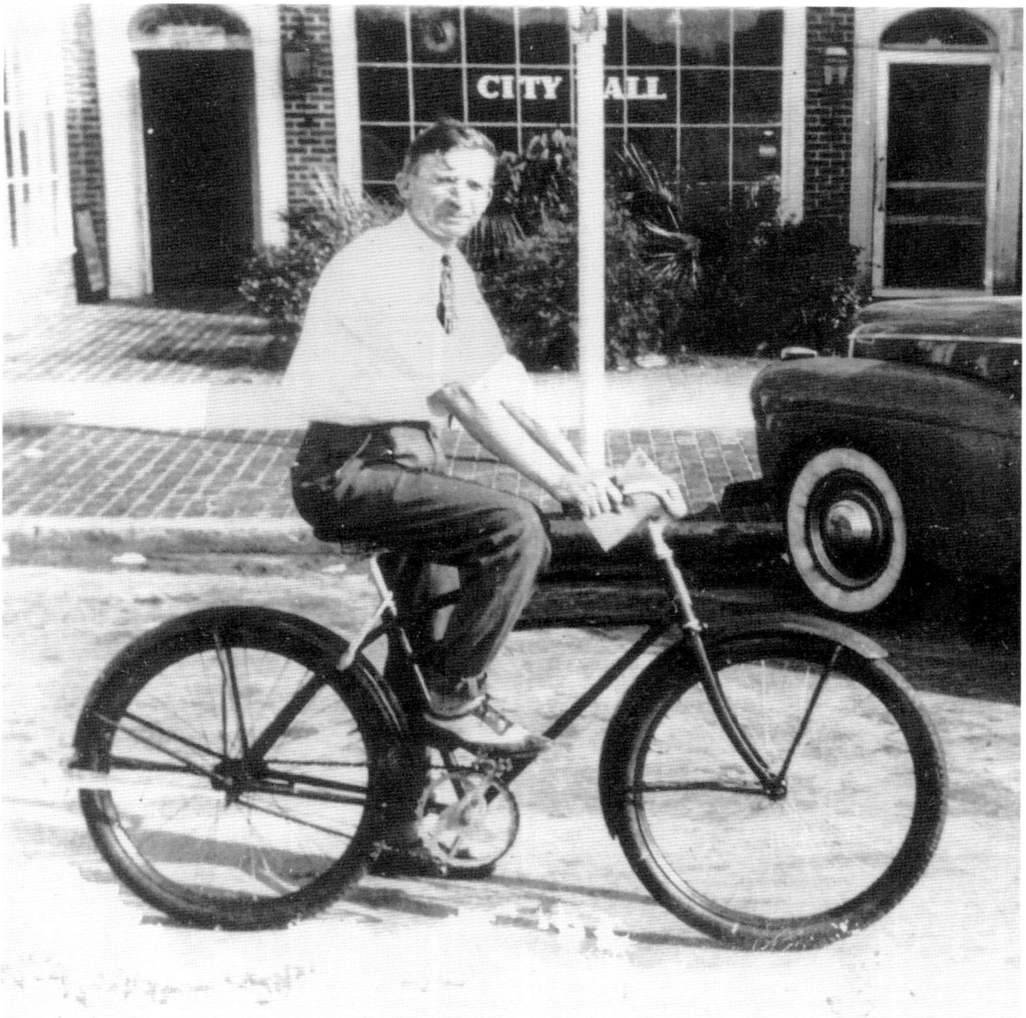

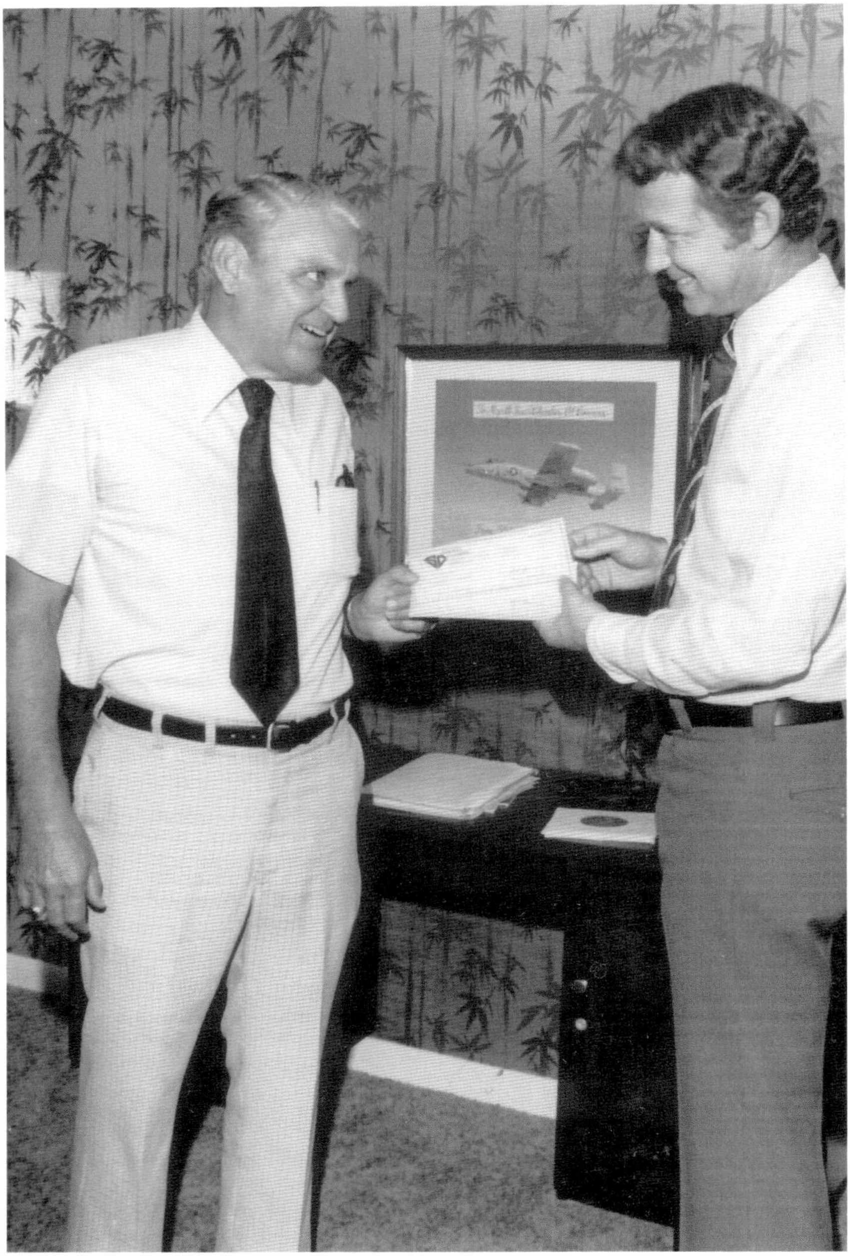

Curtis Williams

Williams was a fighter pilot in the Korean War and later in the South Carolina Air National Guard, retiring as a major. He went on to receive his bachelor's degree in electrical engineering from the University of South Carolina in 1960. He worked with Santee Cooper and retired after 28 years as vice president of the Horry Georgetown Division. Very service oriented, Curtis was a member of the Rotary and served as president. He was the first president of the Myrtle Beach Better Business Bureau and a member of the Elliott Springs Flight Order of the Daedaleans. He had worked with Associated Charities of Myrtle Beach since 1993, and was president when he passed away in 2012. (Courtesy MBCC.)

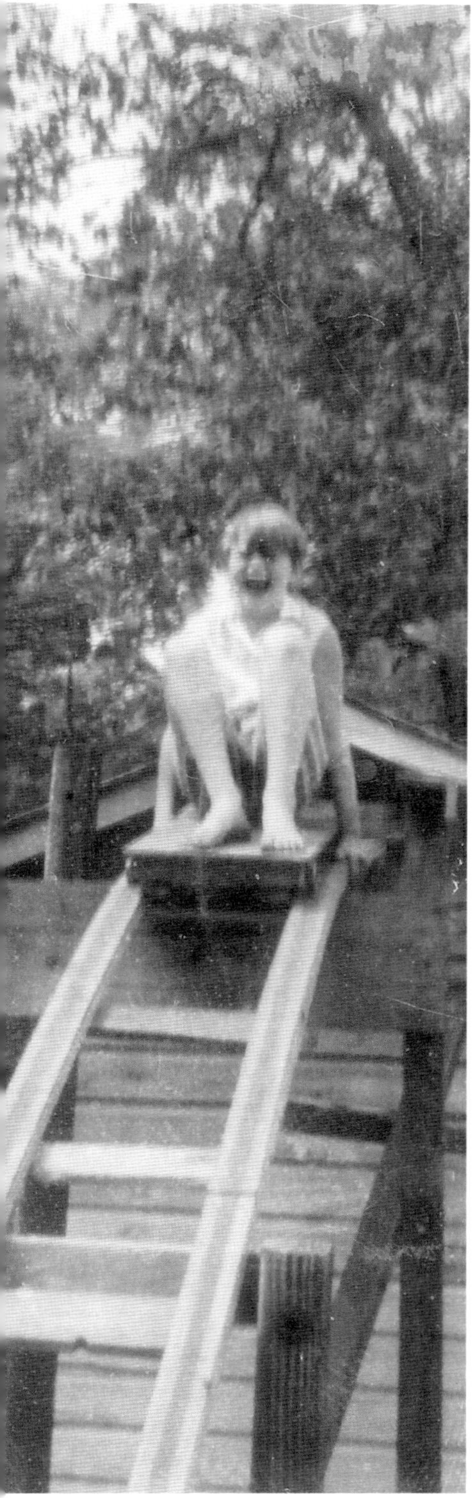

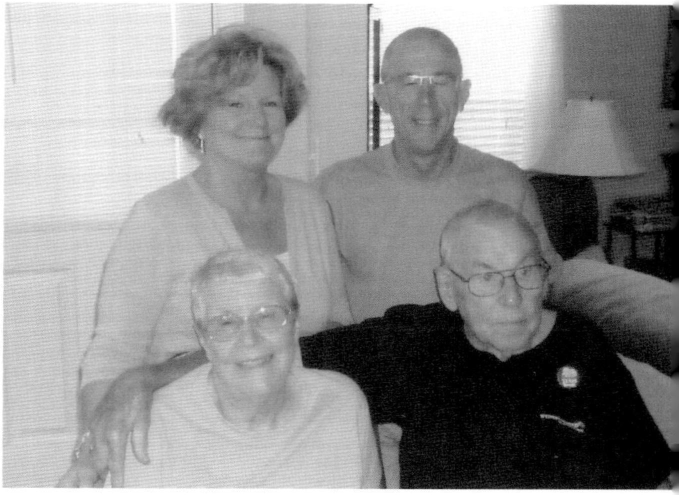

Jack Nixon

Known for his sense of humor, Jack Nixon was elected into the lifetime position as humorist for the Myrtle Beach Lions Club by unanimous decision. Full of pranks that he pulls out of a hat and off the top of his head, it only takes a few moments to be sitting with him before spontaneous laughter erupts. He and his wife, Irma, raised their family (Jo and Byron) in the Knox Acres Section of Myrtle Beach between Twenty-ninth and Thirty-eighth Avenues North. She worked for the county school system as a mathematics teacher and he worked at Santee Cooper. He was always fascinated with electricity and was an inventor. He created and built a roller coaster for his children and the neighborhood kids. His daughter Jo is pictured at left getting ready for the ride of her life starting on top of their tree house, another design of Jack's. He is best remembered for the Halloween Carnivals. It started out small, just dressing up while giving out candy to trick-or-treaters. Then he mentioned it to his friends and coworkers and several people got in on the act. They ended up taking it on the road to various church groups in the area. There was a casket with a skeleton that sat up when the lid was opened, and a Frankenstein's monster that sat on a slab with electricity zapping between two metal bars, while they (dressed in lab coats) would yell, "more power, more power," while turning a huge wheel and laughing like maniacs. Life has never been dull in the Nixon household. (Courtesy Jo Nixon Lacey.)

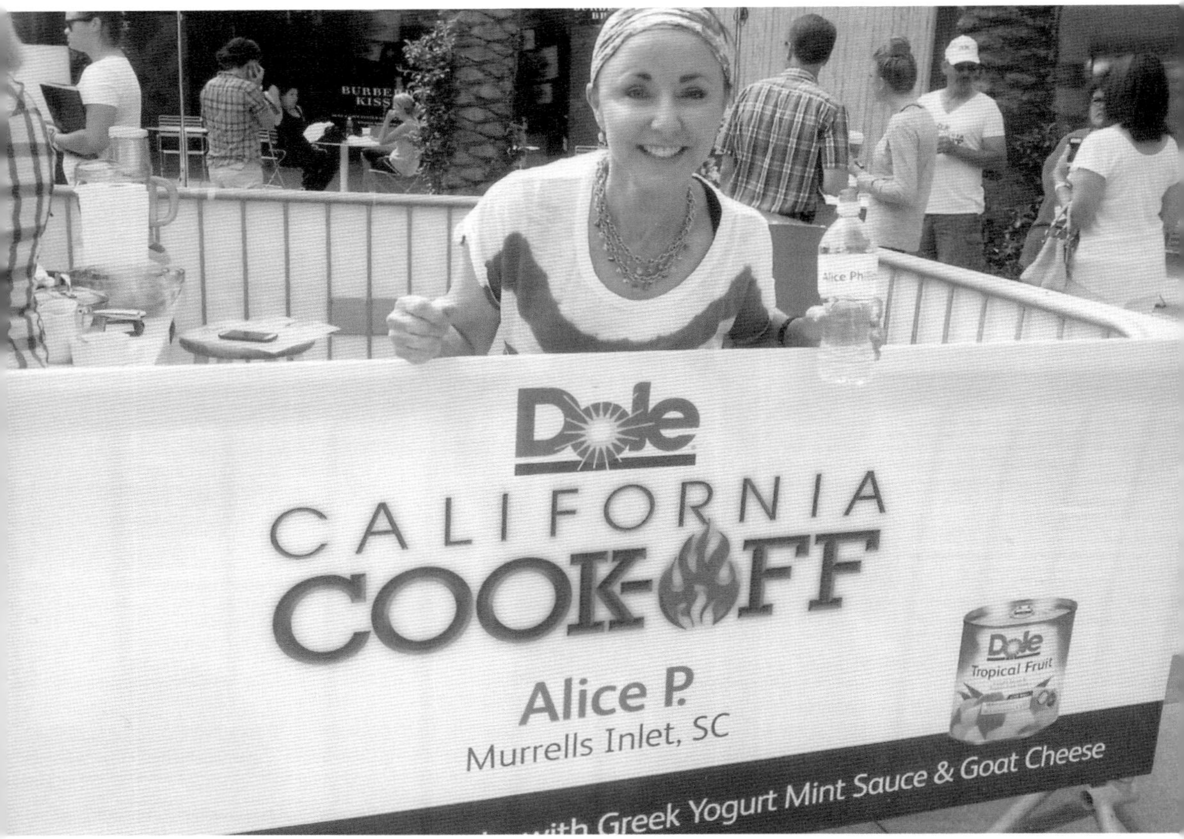

Alice "Allie" D'Antoni Phillips

Allie received her undergraduate and master's degree in special education and orthopedic conditions from Marshall University, where she met and married Dan D'Antoni. They moved to Myrtle Beach where he worked at Socastee High School as a coach and started the popular Beach Ball Classic, while Allie became the guidance counselor at Myrtle Beach Junior High School. After receiving her doctorate in psychology from USC, she went into private practice. She raised her three boys and ran a successful business for 30 years. Over those years, life changed. She had remarried, and her new husband needed to move to another city. She decided to close up shop and move with him and, once again, her life changed. She started cooking more, and ended up entering cooking contests and winning them. Recently, she entered the Dole California Cook-Off and was the grand-prize winner. She was the National Cooking Champion in 2013. Those who like diverse, healthy recipes with a flair for good taste should visit her food blog at allyskitchen.com and find out "What's for Dinner?" (Courtesy Janice McDonald.)

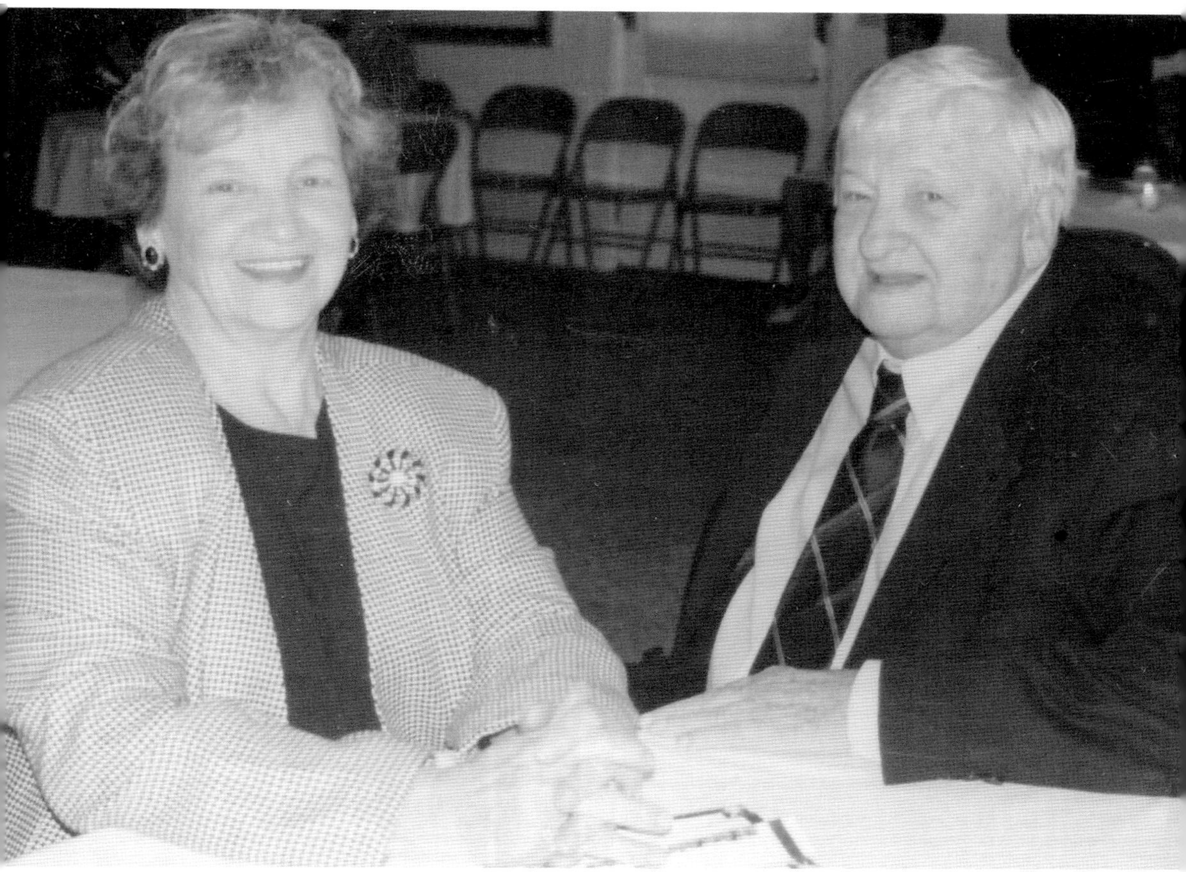

Henry Thomas Newton Sr.
Tommy Newton was filled with a lust for life. To see if he liked something, he tried it. He rode and broke wild horses. He was an auctioneer, and opened a radio station in Clio. He worked for AT&T and owned and operated several communication companies including T&C Communications. He operated the Rambi Raceway and was a stock car driver and go-cart racer. He was a coach for the Myrtle Beach Recreation Department for over 20 years and ran the Pickin' Parlor. This is just a partial list. He married the love of his life, and he and Gresta raised four children: Tommy, Scott, Lisa, and Kaye. He was a devoted Gamecock fan and loved traveling to the games with his family. He was a president of the MLC Shrine Club and a member of the Beachcombers, Horry Shrine, and the Masons. Tom loved his family and doted on his grandchildren. He passed away at the age of 79 in 2011. (Courtesy Gresta Newton.)

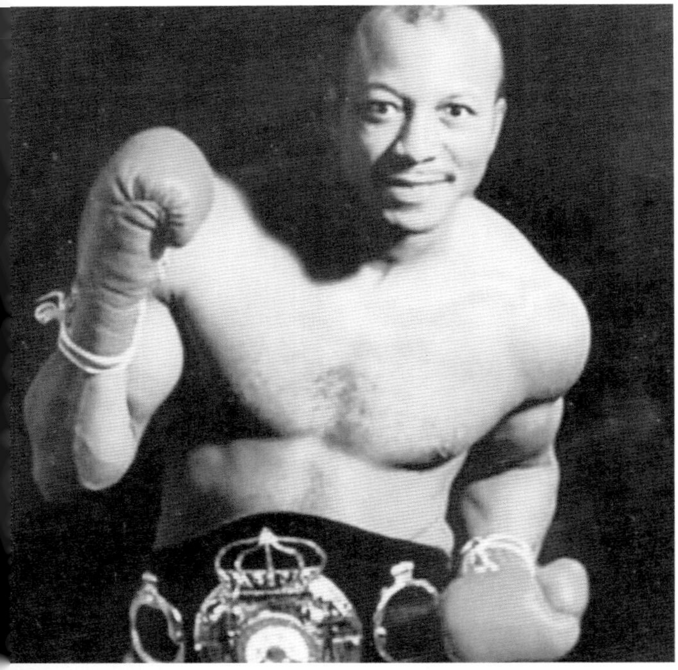

James "Bonecrusher" Smith
Smith was the first heavyweight champion to have a college degree when he defeated Tim Witherspoon in Madison Square Garden on December 12, 1986, to win the World Boxing Association title. He has written a book to motivate readers to set a goal and work to obtain that goal, entitled *M.A.D.: Make a Decision*. He tours, lecturing young children on daily decisions and consequences and how to live with them, to gain confidence in their life, to stay in school, and to work toward goals. Proceeds from the book sales benefit his youth-oriented mentorship, Champion for Kids Inc. Born into a large family in North Carolina, he recently moved to Myrtle Beach where he runs a summer boxing camp and is looking to open a boxing museum. (Courtesy James Smith.)

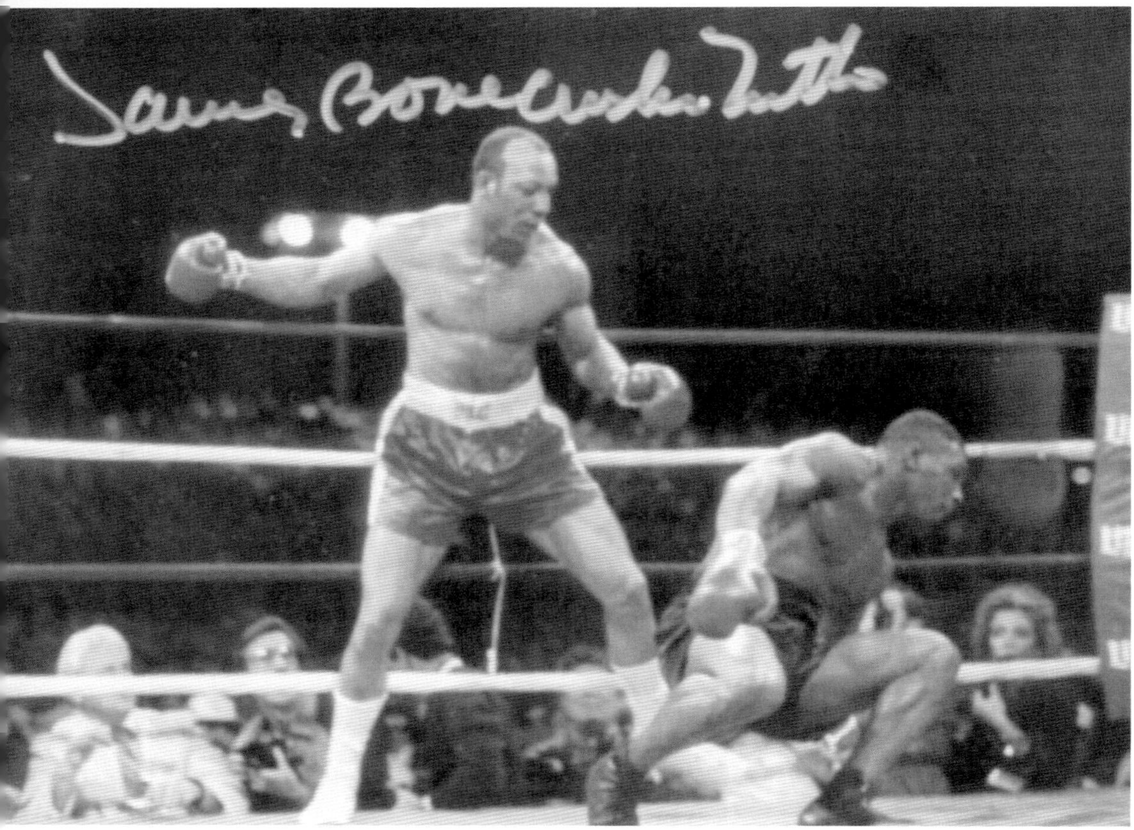

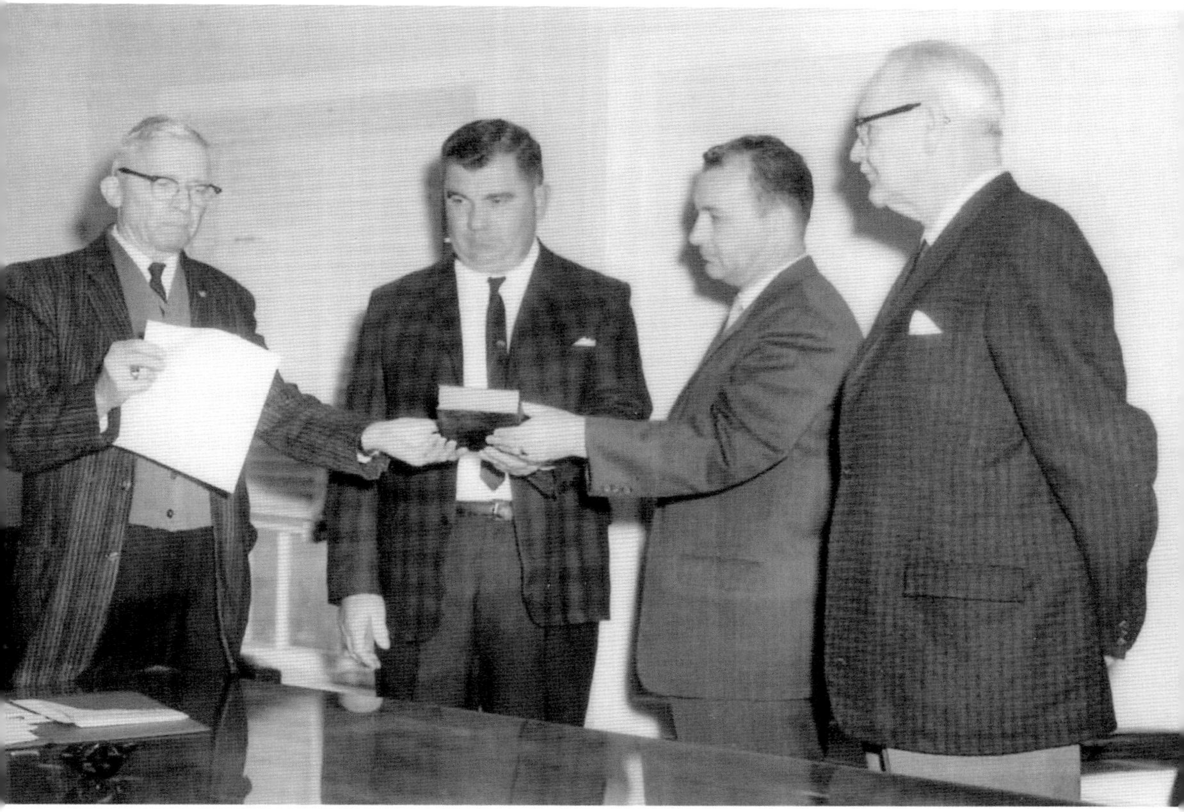

Robert "Bob" Grissom

Bob served Myrtle Beach for many years, first on the city council from 1960 through 1973 and later as mayor from 1986 to 1998. He was "Mr. Myrtle Beach," working to promote tourism here and along the Grand Strand for most of his life. A consummate politician, he always had time to listen to issues, and if it was for the good of the city, he worked on making changes. During his tenure, the Convention Center doubled its size, a minor league baseball team was established here, public housing was built, and the obscenity laws were updated. Mayor Grissom worked very hard for this city and the surrounding communities. He was a true ambassador, always wanting what was best for Myrtle Beach and striving to accomplish it. (Courtesy MBCC.)

Ray Clardy

Ray Clardy was a loyal and dedicated volunteer at Myrtle Beach Parks and Recreation for many years before he became an employee for the city. He had a sweet and generous nature that showed in his actions. He was Santa for the children in the After School Program for many years. Each week he would bring the ladies who worked in the After School Program Tootsie Roll Pops and Bazooka gum because he thought they needed a little pick-me-up to handle the children. He was also firm in his beliefs. When he was a volunteer scorekeeper for the adult softball leagues, he would not allow the men to argue, curse, or misbehave. He would give them one warning and if they acted up after that, Ray would quietly leave the press box, turn off all the ball field lights, hop in his golf cart, and leave. The men would be left standing in the dark on the field.

His dependability and devotion to the "Wreck" Center was always evident and never questioned; however, his reasoning sometimes was. Thus began the phrase "Rayisms, verbal misfires." Many are guilty of Rayisms in one form or another, but Ray was the first one to be caught. Thus began the book *The World According to Ray* and its nine editions since 1994. The first book was mainly filled with his Rayisms, but as time went by, employees in different departments would write them down when they heard someone say something and send them in for the next edition. It was an honor to be included in the next book. It allowed people the opportunity to laugh at themselves and to see language in an entirely different light. These books are archived in the Shirley W. Boone South Carolina Reference Room at the Chapin Memorial Library. Ray died at the age of 45 after a long, hard, four-year battle with male breast cancer. He is pictured here with a car of his favorite driver, Dale Earnhart. (Courtesy Pam Stone.)

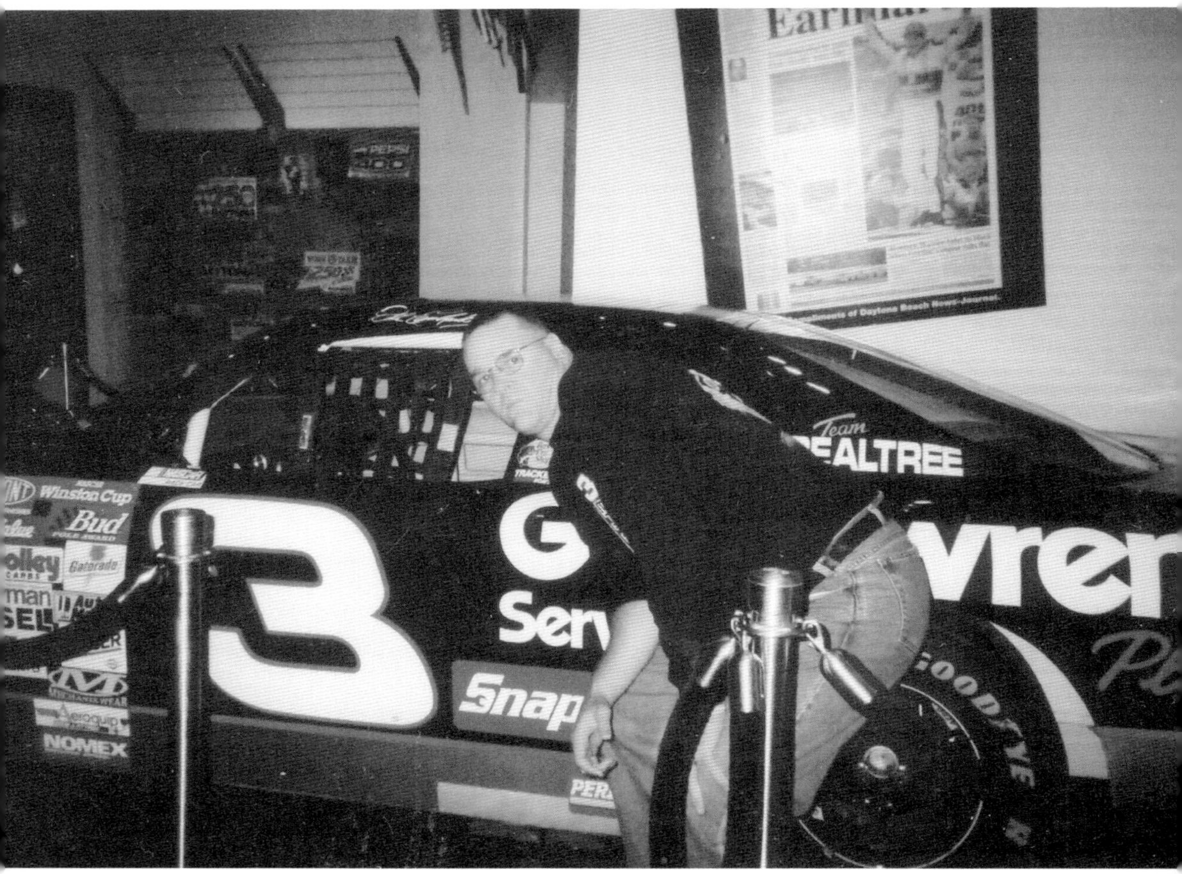

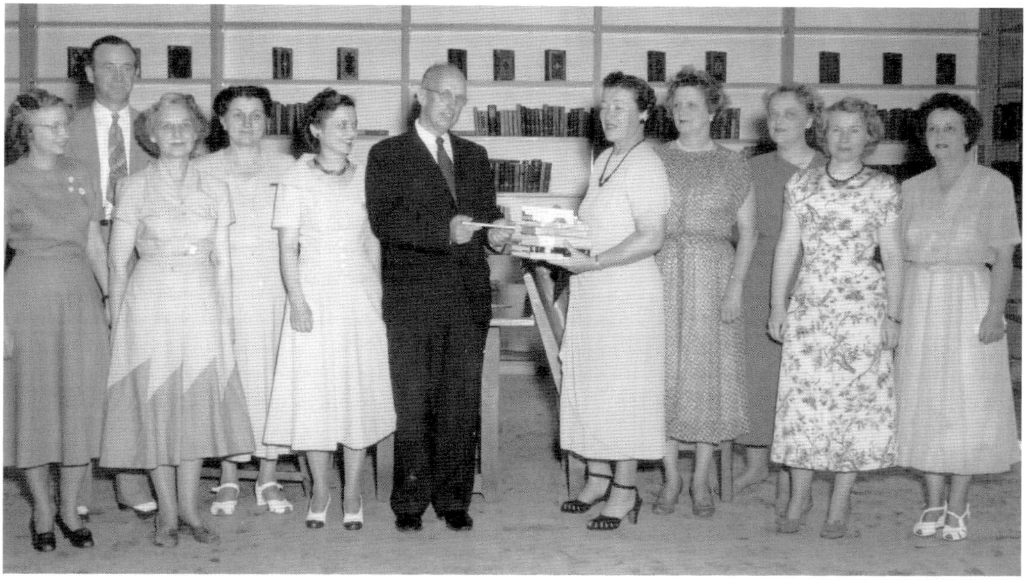

Norment, Martha

Martha was the first director of the Chapin Memorial Library when it opened June 1, 1949, as the first library built in Horry County. Prior to that time, public libraries around the county could be found in public buildings, local businesses, or in people's homes. The original Myrtle Beach Library had been housed in many locations, including the Chapin Company at one time. Pictured here from left to right are Mary Parham, Claude Epps, Mrs. Frank (Martha) Norment, Mrs. Holmes B. (Sarah) Springs Sr., Mrs. James E. (Sarah) Bryan Jr., the Rev. Cecil Brearley (chairman of the library board), Mrs. Sherwood Forest, Mrs. Ed Lawton, Mrs. Bill James, Mrs. Bill Hart, and Mrs. E. Redfern. (Courtesy CML.)

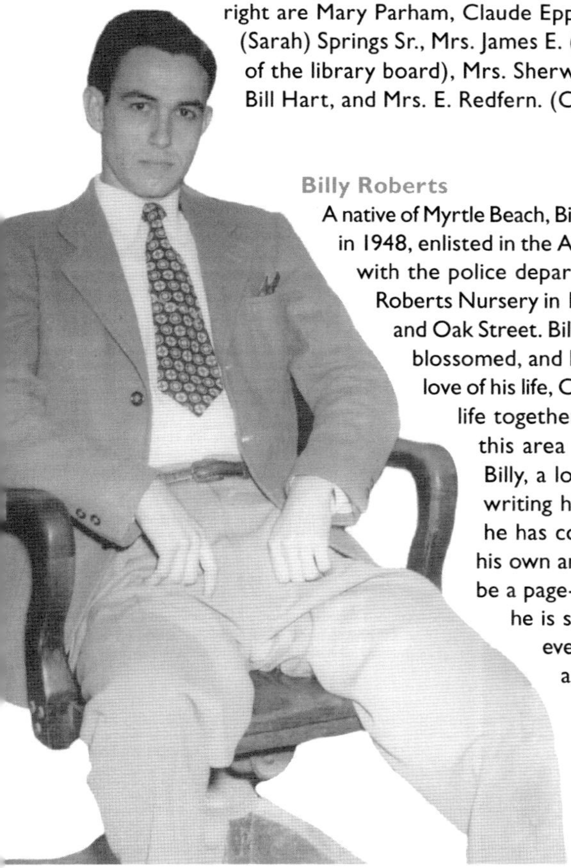

Billy Roberts

A native of Myrtle Beach, Billy Roberts joined the Myrtle Beach Police Department in 1948, enlisted in the Air Force for a while, and then came back and worked with the police department again for several years. His parents opened Roberts Nursery in 1964 on the corner of Twenty-seventh Avenue North and Oak Street. Billy went into business with them in 1966. The business blossomed, and he continued there until his retirement. He met the love of his life, Carolyn, and married her in 1960. They built a beautiful life together across the street from the nursery. With ties to this area dating back long before incorporation as a town, Billy, a local historian and photographer in his own right, is writing his own history of Myrtle Beach. Filled with stories he has collected from family members and recollections of his own and of people he has met over the years, it is sure to be a page-turner when it is complete. When people see him, he is sure to have his camera with him, taking pictures of everyone he comes across and surprising them later with a photograph. Considered a true southern gentleman with a sentimental, warm heart, Billy is one of the local treasures. (Courtesy Billy Roberts.)

Frank Beckham

Frank Beckham is better known as the first recreation director, for whom the current and newly remodeled recreation building on Oak Street is named after. Beckham began his career on the first floor (called the basement) of the Chapin Memorial Library over on Fourteenth Avenue North. He later moved his operation to a new building on Oak Street, allowing the library to spread out to both floors. Beckham brought sports to the youth of Myrtle Beach. He would be proud to see his vision of multiple recreation buildings spread throughout the city, fully staffed with up-to-date equipment. His vision was filled with baseball fields, soccer fields, basketball courts, tennis courts, and the teams to fill them. Those visions have become a reality today. (Courtesy Anna Beth Doig.)

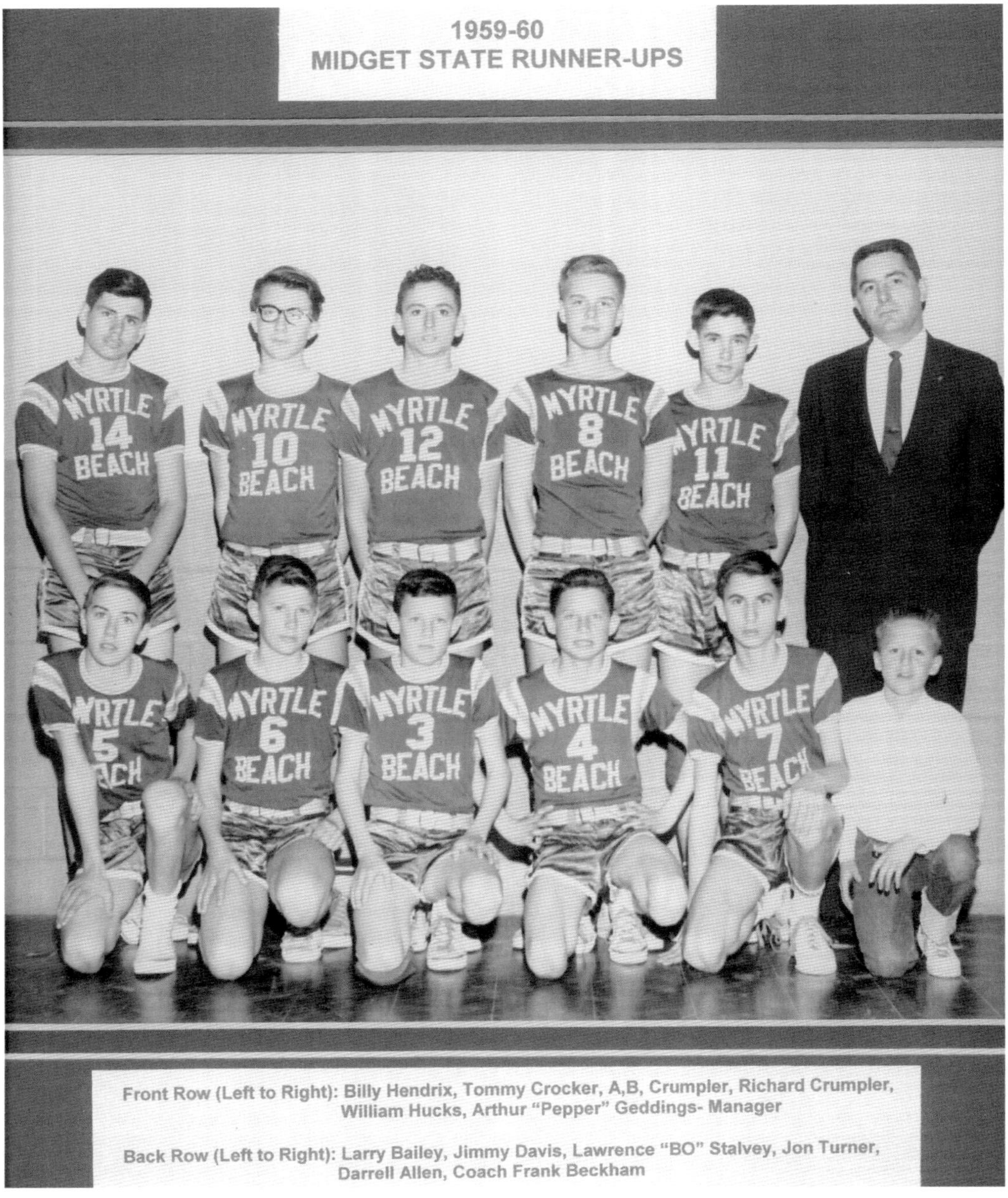

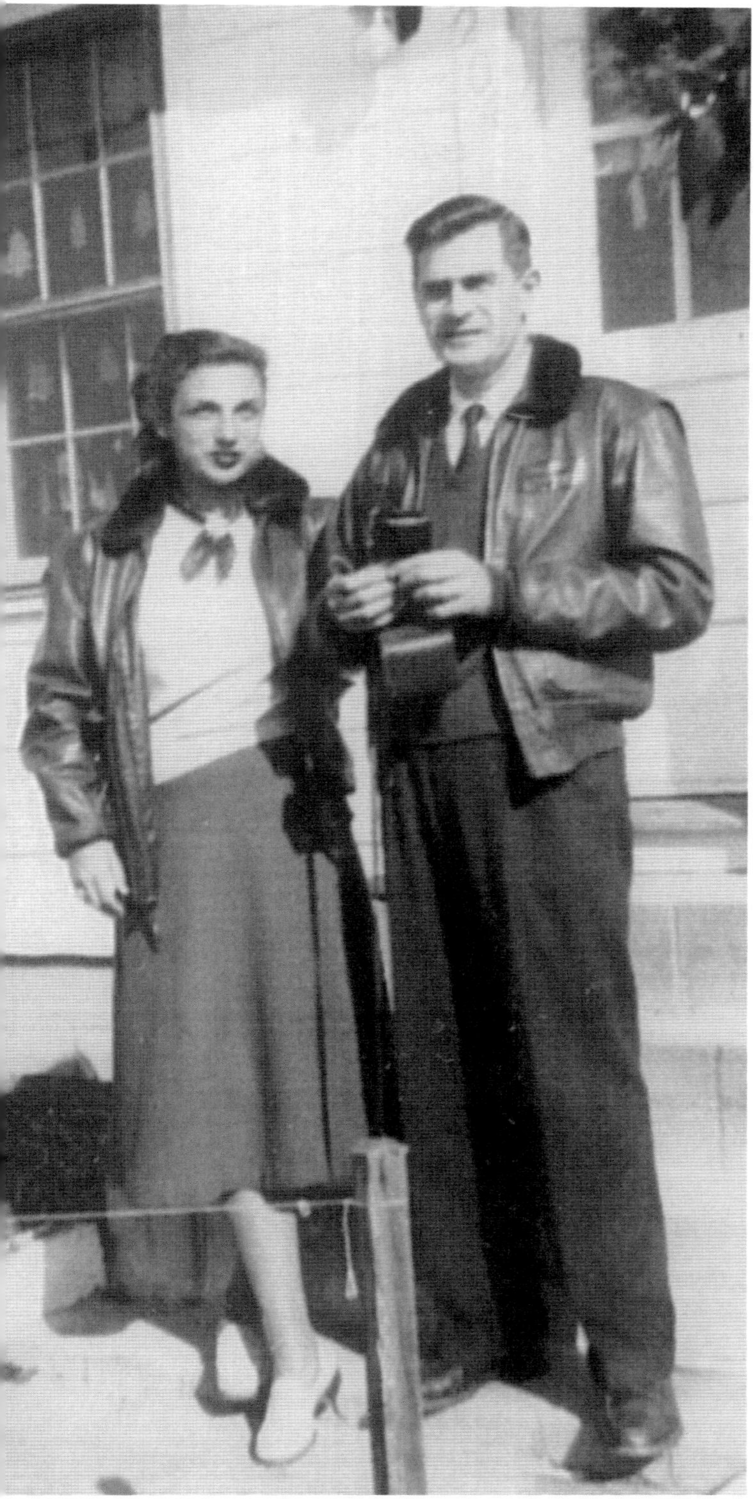

Judith "Judy" and Richard "Brad" Bradford
Judy and Brad met in Florida after they had both joined the Navy—she as an airplane mechanic and he as a pilot. It was a great love. They married, and after having their first child, Rock, they moved to Myrtle Beach in May 1950. From Florence, Brad first came to Myrtle Beach in 1937 and wanted to make this area their home. He set up his dental lab and she went looking for a kindergarten for her son. She found it in the basement of the Chapin Memorial Library, run by Lucille Jordan. She and her husband ended up buying the kindergarten and moving it to their home on Thirty-second Avenue, where they ran the school for 14 years. They added to their family when their son Jim came along shortly thereafter. They helped start the Presbyterian church kindergarten and the Lutheran church added its monkey bars to their playground. During the war, Brad sold his dental lab to his partner and went back into the Navy. When he came back home, he worked for the United States Postal Service and managed the South Wind Hotel for many years. In 1973, he opened the Bradford Frame Shop, and in 1989, moved it and the family south to Murrells Inlet. (Courtesy Dr. James Bradford.)

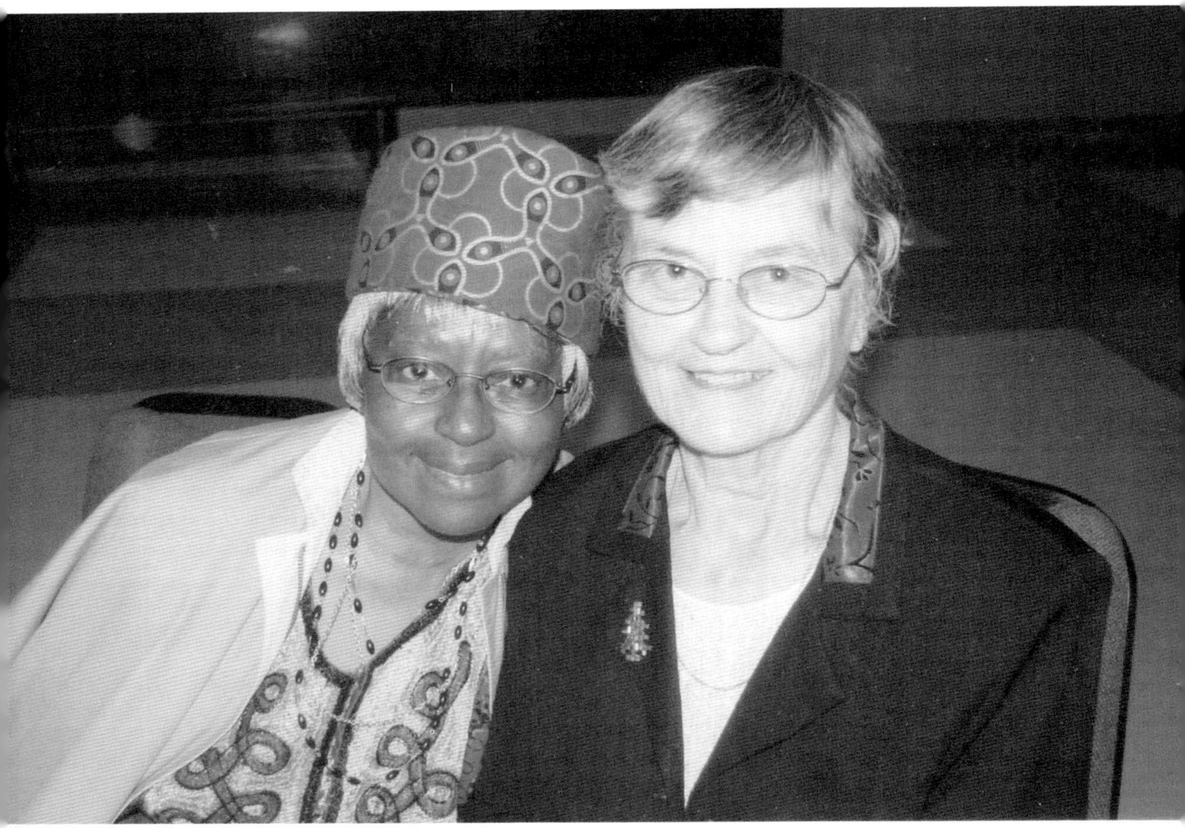

Mary Catherine Brantley Canty
Mary (left) was born here in Myrtle Beach in 1933. She is daughter of Arthur Brantley and Martha Dennison. Her grandparents Moses and Ellen (Scrap) helped raise her—he was a trumpet player and worked at the Ocean Forest as a chef until he retired. She and her husband, Isaac Canty Jr., had six children, Martha, Cookie, Cynthia, Cassandra, Millicent, and James (Beaver). Dennison Street is named after her grandfather Moses. She was on the board to restore the Myrtle Beach Historic Colored School and contributed to the cookbook they produced to raise funds for ongoing upkeep of the building and community projects. She volunteers there weekly. On February 22, 2013, Mayor Rhodes declared Mary Canty Day in honor of her passion and community work over the years. Mary is pictured here with Mary Catherine Hardee at the book launch for Barbara Stokes's *Myrtle Beach: 1900–1980*. (Author's collection.)

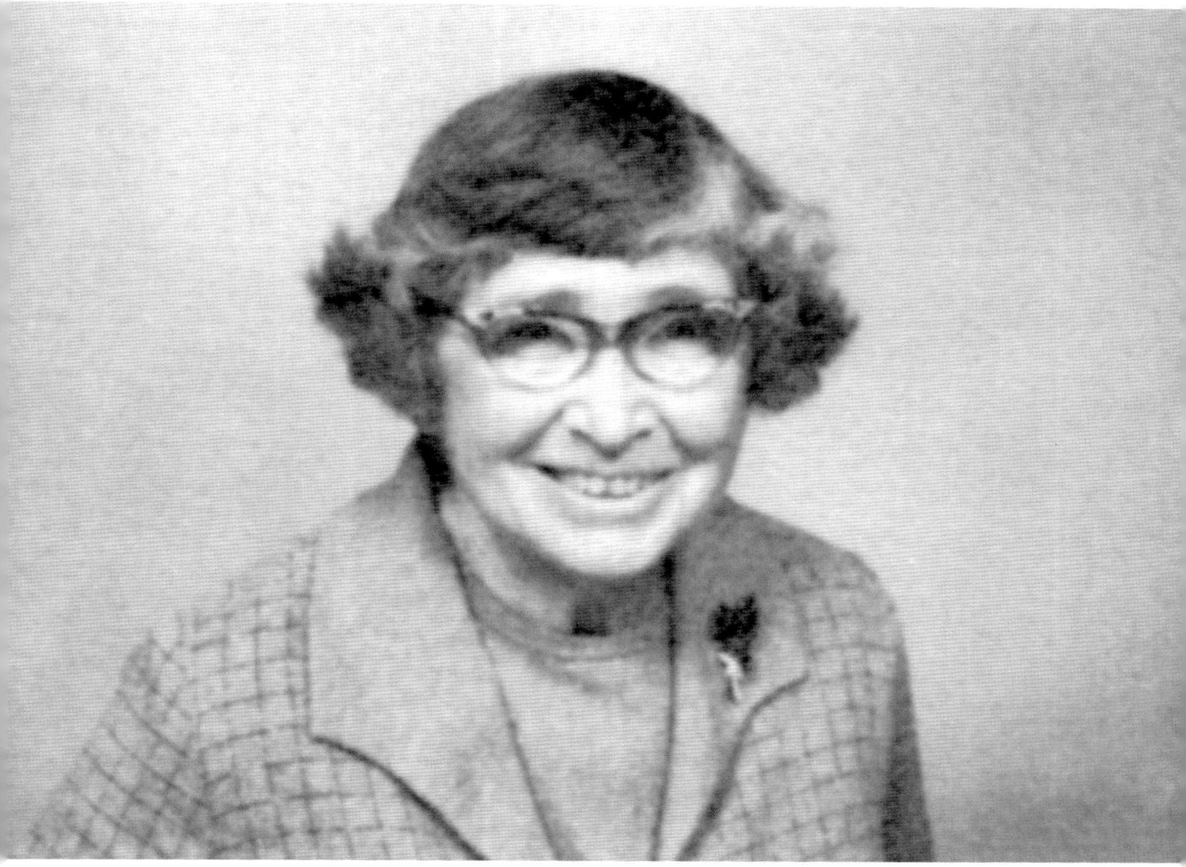

Marion Byrd
Byrd was one of the early teachers at Myrtle Beach High School, when they still called themselves the "White Caps." She was voted Teacher of the Year by her students several times. She taught science and was considered one of the "cool" teachers. As one student put it, "She'd hunch over and then stand up and she would have two chameleons biting on her ears, like earrings. She'd say, 'I don't know what I'd do without chameleons.' And then she would put on a shawl, a scarf, or something that was green or brown and they would change." (Courtesy MBCC.)

Shirley Walker Boone

Shirley moved to Myrtle Beach two weeks after Hurricane Hazel. She always said from the reports she had heard that she was not sure that she had anything to come to. She came anyway as the director of Chapin Memorial Library, a position she held for 36 years until her retirement. A great storyteller, she would mesmerize people with tales about those she had met during her time here, always marveling at the changes she had seen. She would begin with, "Let me tell you about . . ." Everyone remembers her with a smile. She helped many children write their papers, and some say they might not have graduated if it was not for her. Shirley had a zest for learning and her enthusiasm for sharing what she knew with everyone that she came in contact with endeared her to all. Knowing that she had to give up her keys to the library when she retired, she returned home to her native Laurens and passed away in 2007 at the age of 80. After her retirement, the South Carolina Genealogy Reference Room was named in her honor. The Friends of the Chapin Memorial Library established a yearly Shirley W. Boone scholarship fund for area high school students. (Courtesy CML.)

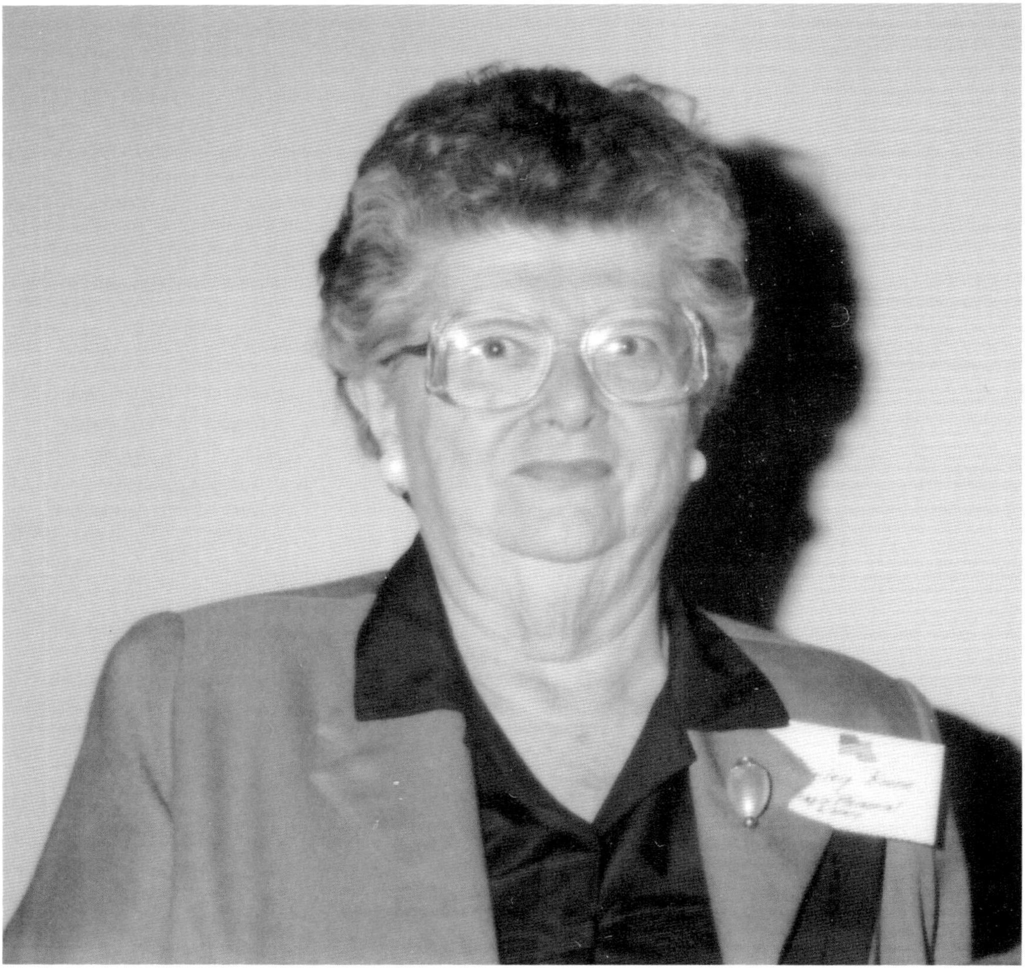

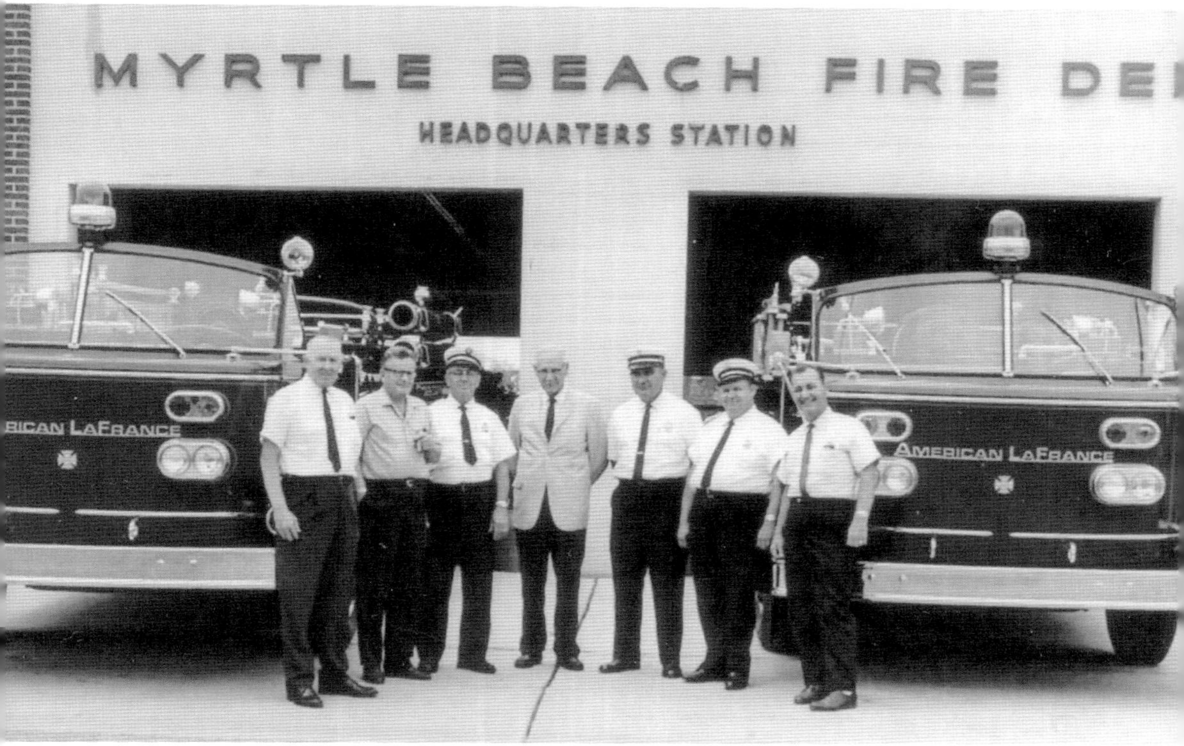

Fernie E. Faulk

Fernie joined the city fire department in 1954, rising up through the ranks to chief before he retired in 1986. He is remembered as a mentor to his fellow workers and employees, fair with a positive attitude, a smile on his face, and his signature cigar. An Army veteran of World War II, he was awarded the Bronze Star, the Purple Heart, the Combat Infantry Badge, and five Campaign Stars for his service. A member of numerous state fire associations, he was also inducted into the South Carolina Firefighter Hall of Fame. Fernie passed away in May 2000 at the age of 75. (Courtesy CML.)

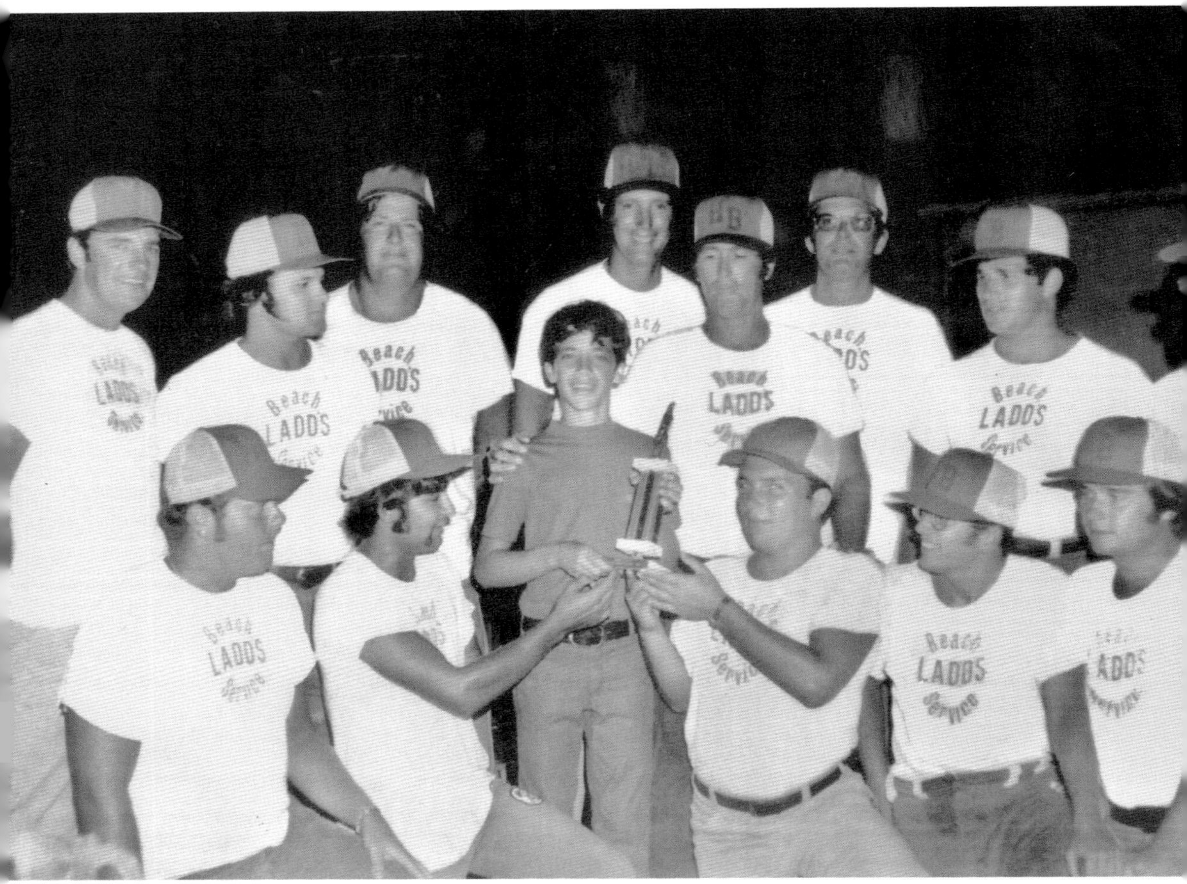

Doug Shaw

Coach Shaw was the Myrtle Beach High School head football coach for 25 years. During his tenure, his teams won four state championships and sixteen conference titles, and competed in playoffs 23 of his 25 years. He passed away suddenly at the age of 52 in 1994. The football stadium that he played in for those 25 years was named Memorial Stadium, and in 1995, the city council passed a resolution to rename the facility for him. His wife, Cecelia, accepted the resolution during a ceremony on September 12, 1995. Renovated in 2008, it is a state-of-the-art facility and the largest in the city. (Courtesy Anna Beth Doig.)

Dr. Carl Compton

Dr. Compton served as the First Baptist Church of Myrtle Beach pastor from June 1949 until he retired in 1987. During his tenure, he helped create four other churches, the First Baptist Church of Surfside, the Ocean View Baptist Church, Socastee Baptist Church, and the Forestbrook Baptist Church. In 2007, the church dedicated its Family Life Center to Dr. Compton and his wife, Martha, and renamed it the Compton Center in their honor. After retirement, Dr. C, as he was lovingly called, continued his work in the community when an anonymous donor wanted to fund an oral history project. This became known as the Hearing Horry History series, with over 50 interviews in the set. It is now housed in the archives of the Chapin Memorial Library. (Courtesy Mary Catherine Hardee.)

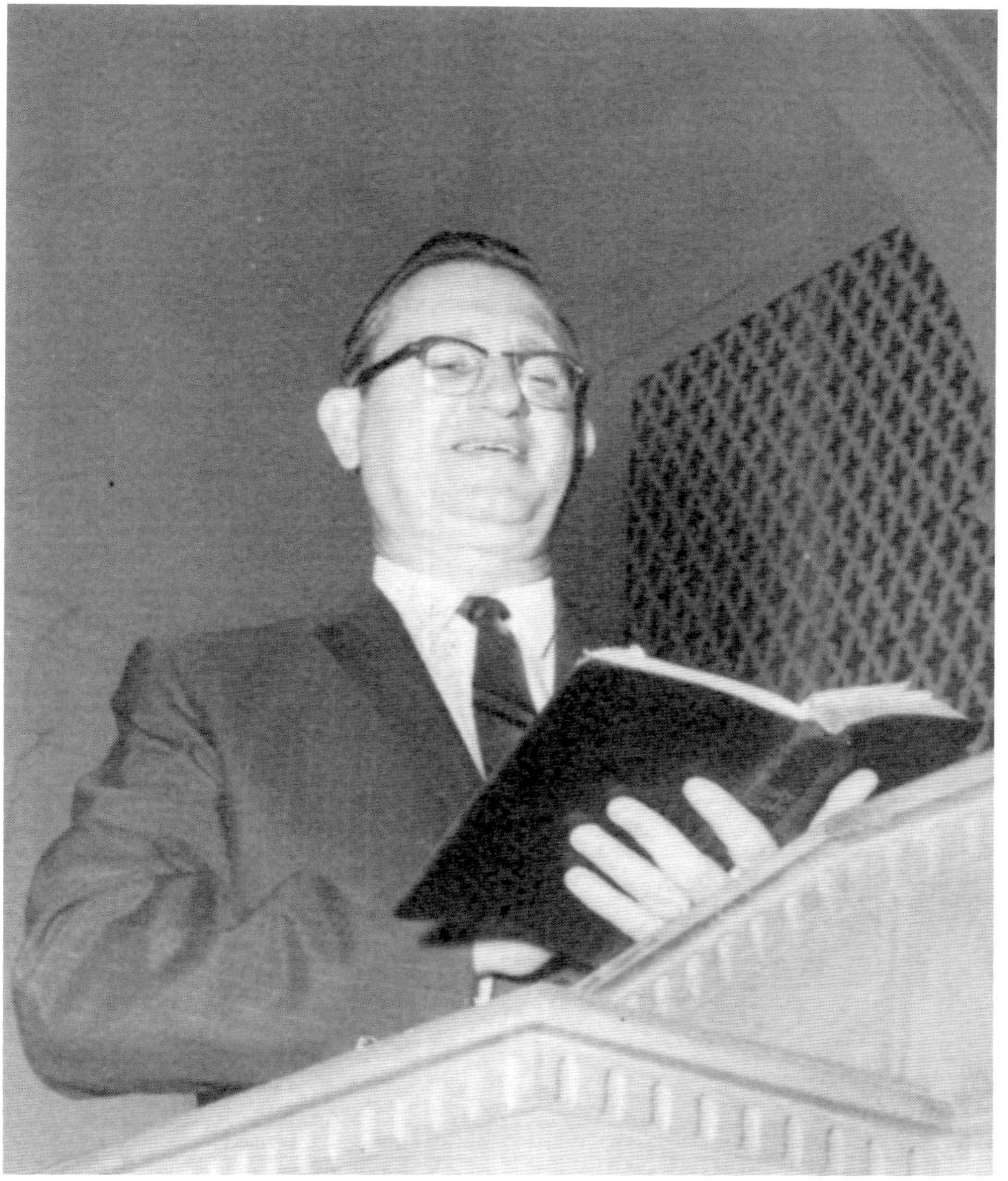

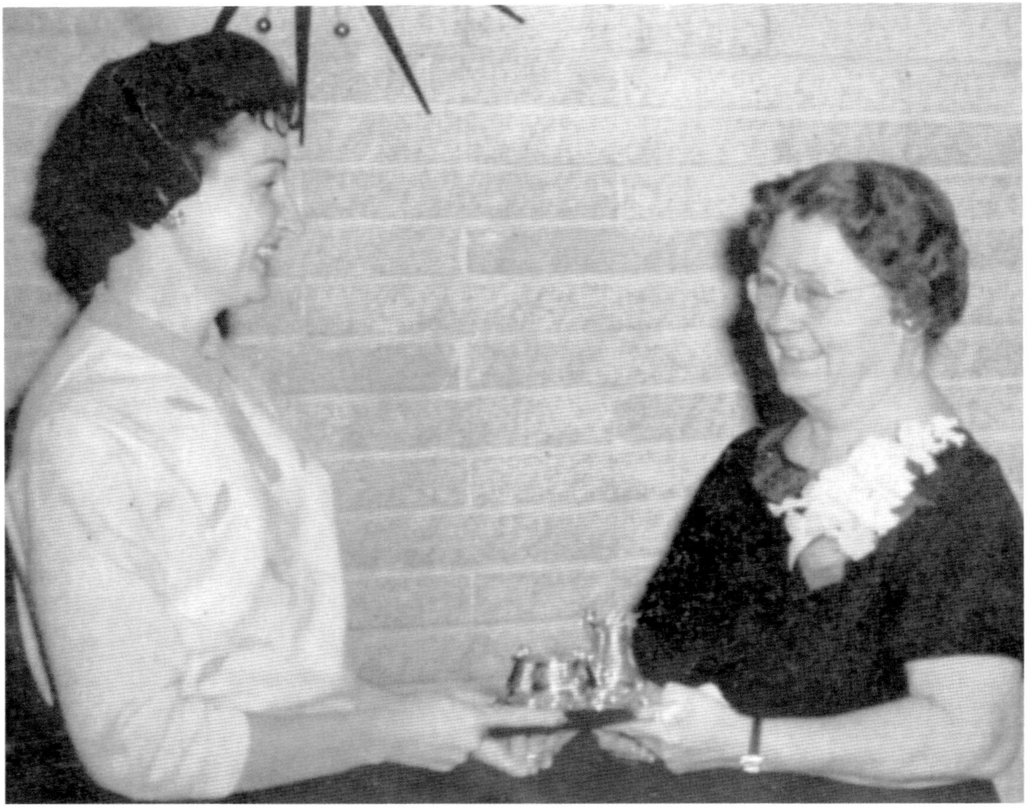

Mable Fleming

Mable, her husband, Alex, and their children moved to Myrtle Beach in 1941 when she accepted the job as the only telephone operator in town. The office was in the front room of their home. They offered payphone service, collected bills, and were the chief source of information in town. A 24-hour job, her daughters, Evon and Marian, would help by taking shifts during the night to answer the phone system whenever it would ring. Since there were very few phones in the city, they would sometimes take messages. Evon and Marian would ride their bikes to deliver them. Evon said that on some trips, her little dog would run along by her side, and when he would get tired—especially on the trips from the house on Chester Street all the way to the Ocean Forest Hotel—she would put him in the basket for the trip back. Mable continued to work with General Telephone until she retired in 1963. (Courtesy Eddie and Sabrina Benton.)

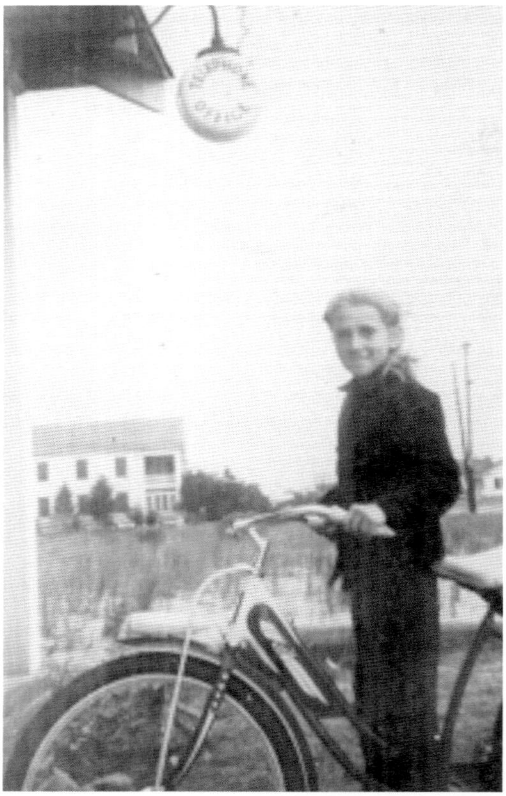

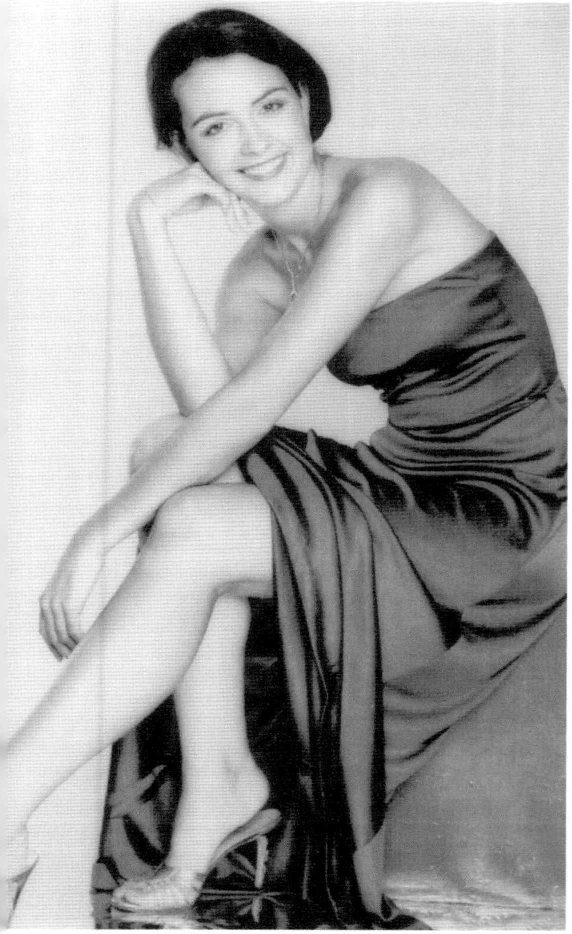

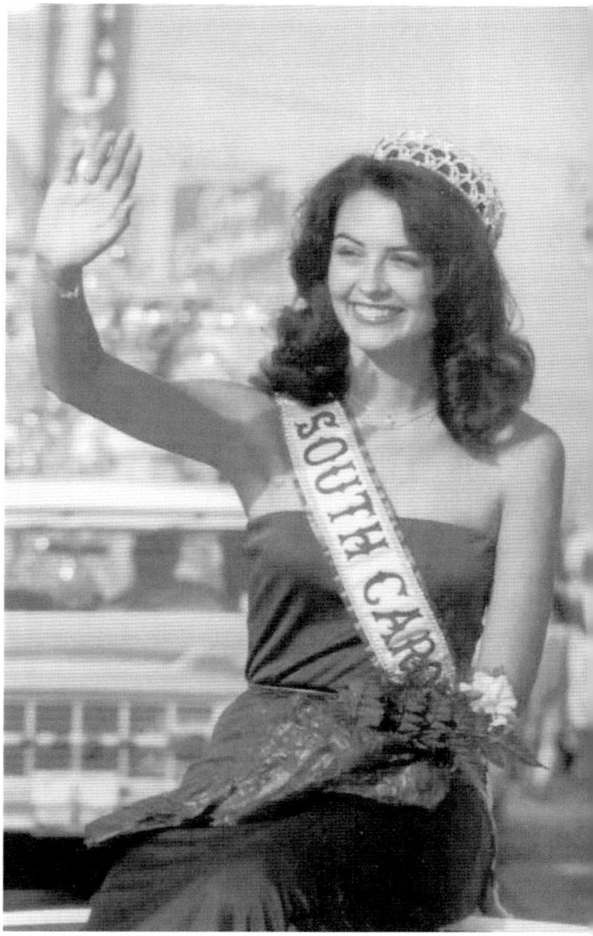

Janice McDonald

A native of Myrtle Beach, Janice McDonald is the second child of Weyman Texas McDonald and Dorothy Briles McDonald. She, along with her siblings (Paula and Anna), grew up swimming in the Atlantic Ocean and riding rides at the Myrtle Beach Pavilion. During the late 1970s, Janice won many pageants including Miss Myrtle Beach and Miss South Carolina USA in 1979. After graduating from the University of South Carolina with a major in broadcast journalism, she began her career in Charleston and Savannah before landing a job at WTBS in Atlanta. Janice helped launch CNN2 (now CNN Headline News) and traveled the world with CNN as a producer, writer, reporter, and anchor. Nominated for eight Emmys, she left CNN in 2001 to start the Atlanta based J-Mac Productions. Janice has visited all seven continents, and among all of those memories some of her highlights are visiting Antarctica with the late Jacques Cousteau in 1990 and again in 2009 with Prince Albert II of Monaco, planting trees in Ethiopia, building houses in Mongolia for Habitat for Humanity, and sailing on a Viking ship in Iceland with a descendant of Leif Ericson. Janice has authored several pictorial books including Images of America: *The Varsity*, and coauthored *The Myrtle Beach Pavilion* and *Aiken*. With her love of travel, she has also written several travel books including *An Historic Walking Guide: Bruges*, *Day Trips From Atlanta*, and *The Insider's Guide to Myrtle Beach and the Grand Strand* to name a few. Still traveling, producing, and writing, Janice always seems to have her passport up to date, her phone and camera charged, and her bags packed, ready for the next adventure. (Courtesy Janice McDonald)

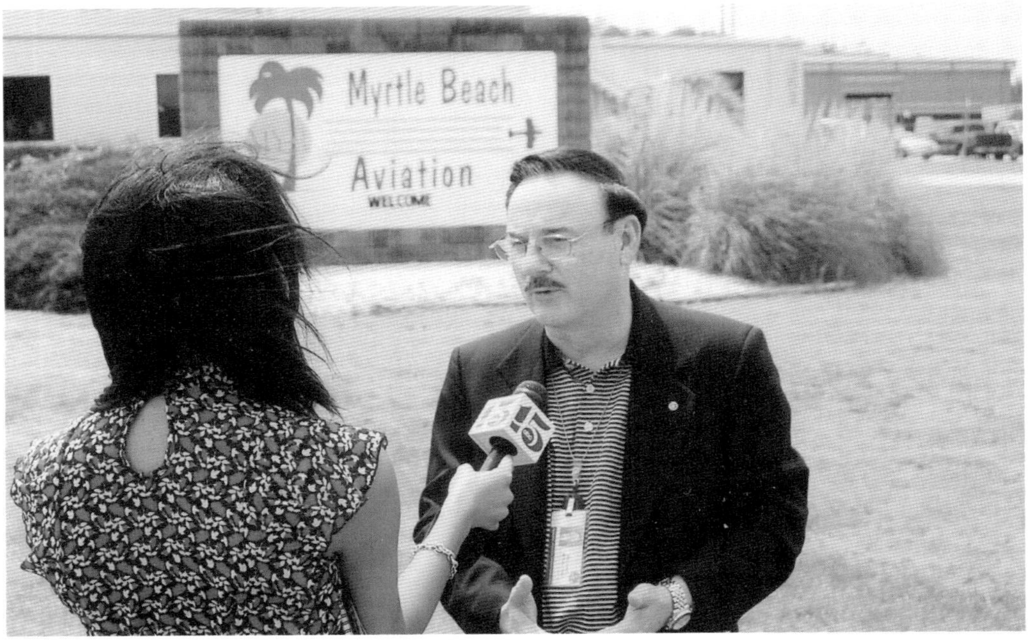

Mike Marlowe

Mike began his aviation career in 1970 as an Air Force pilot. After flying combat in Vietnam, he was stationed back home to Myrtle Beach Air Force Base in 1977. When the base closed in 1993, he and his wife, Diane, created the Myrtle Beach Flying Club with one plane and 20 members. It has grown to four aircraft and over 100 members today. In 1995, Mike was hired as general aviation manager for Horry County Department of Airports. In 2005, the South Carolina state legislature appointed Mike to the new South Carolina Aeronautics Commission as the district one commissioner, which includes Horry and Georgetown Counties. The commission created a plan to modernize the public airport facilities across the state. Commissioner Marlowe raised $4 million through grants. Construction was completed for the award-winning General Aviation Terminal in October 2009.

Mike was the first general aviation pilot to fly into the then Myrtle Beach Jetport after the base closed in 1993. He was honored in 2003 as the General Aviation Airport Manager of the Year. Mike retired from the Horry County Department of Airports in 2012. He and Diane are very active in their flying club and find it hard to keep their feet on the ground. (Courtesy Mike and Diane Marlowe.)

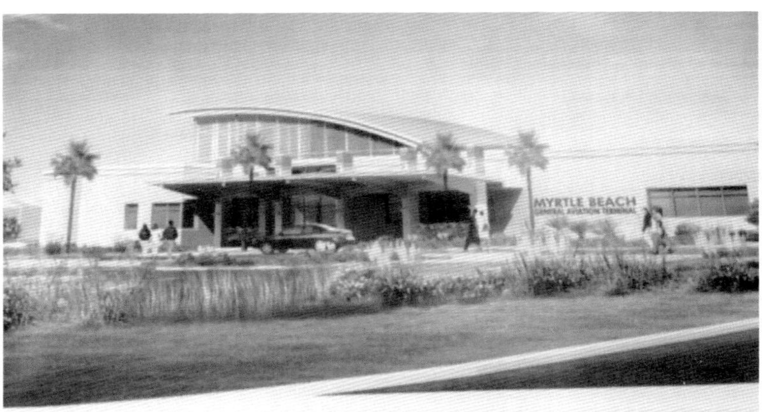

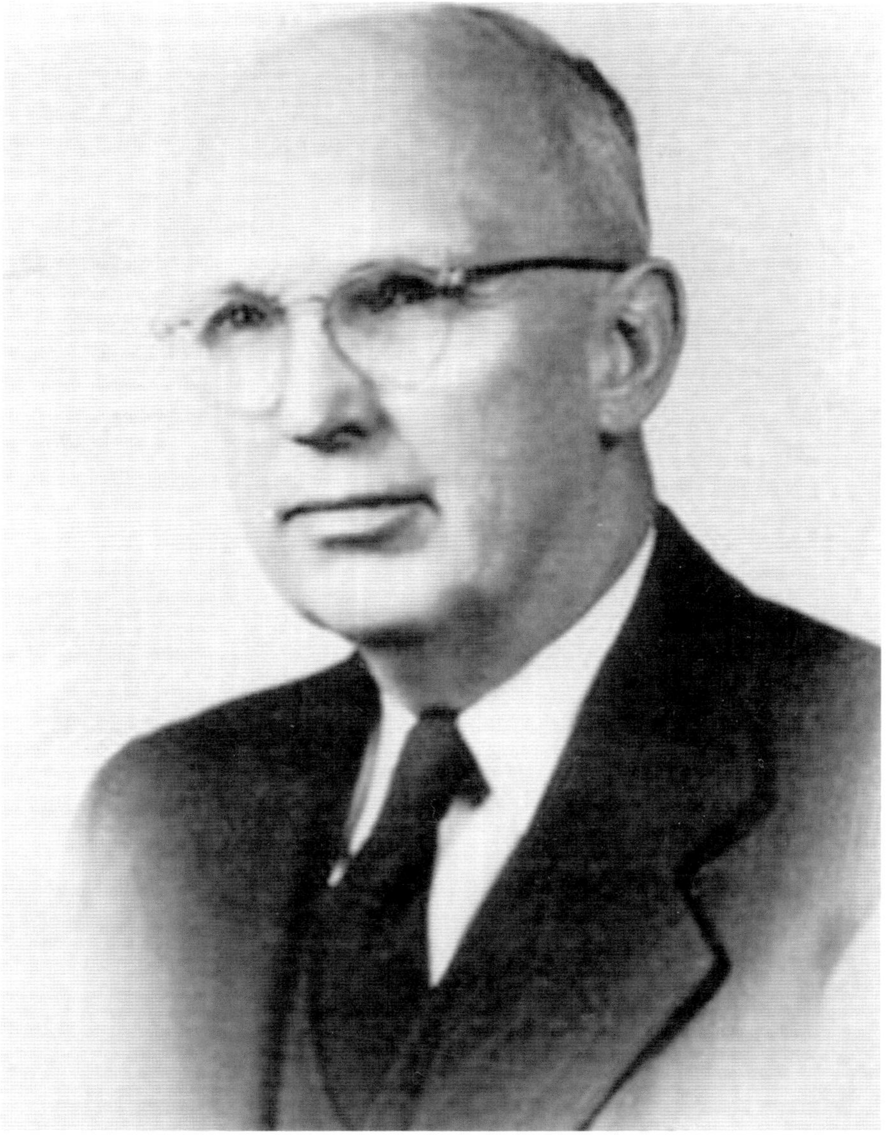

Cecil DuBose Brearley

Brearley moved here February 1, 1928, and on the 18th held the first Presbyterian service at the First Methodist Church of Myrtle Beach. By the end of the year, the congregation had built its first church at Tenth Avenue and Kings Highway (now Mr. Joe White Avenue), where Mammy's Kitchen now sits. As the minister of the Kingston Presbyterian Church in Conway, he would visit on the first and third Sunday evenings of the month until they were able to hire a full time preacher. In 1945, Reverend Brearley became the full-time pastor until he retired in 1961. In 1948, a new sanctuary was built between Thirteenth and Fourteenth Avenues North, and the first church was moved and attached. It was later named Brearley Hall in his honor. He was called Dr. or Reverend Brearley by some, Bishop of Horry by others, but preferred to just be called preacher. Very active, he also started the Presbyterian church in Pawley's Island in 1946, was on the first Chapin Memorial Library Commission board, and was a member of the Myrtle Beach Rotary Club. (Courtesy CML.)

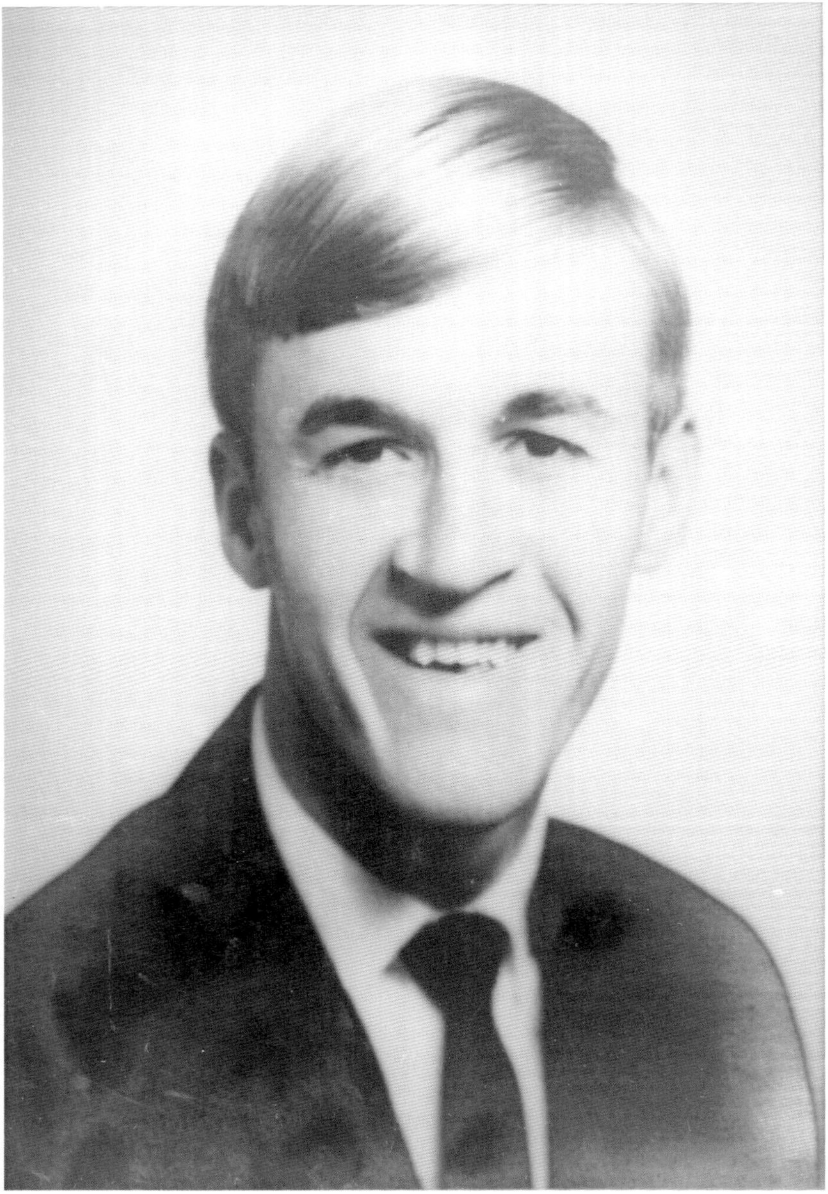

Arthur Joseph "Pepper" Geddings Jr.
Nicknamed "Pepper" for his lively personality and competitive spirit, Geddings took part in the city recreation programs for years and was well known and loved by all. Small in stature, his infectious smile would attract people to him, especially children. He made a profound impression in the short time he was here on earth. He graduated from MBHS and went off to college, graduating from Wingate Junior College in 1967. Pepper continued school at Appalachian State University, but during a baseball game he was accidently struck in the head by a pitch and died of the injury when he was 20. The recreation center was in the process of being built at that time, and in 1968, they named the new facility in his honor. Pepper Geddings Recreation Center is located at 3205 North Oak Street in the Frank Beckham Complex. (Courtesy Anna Beth Doig.)

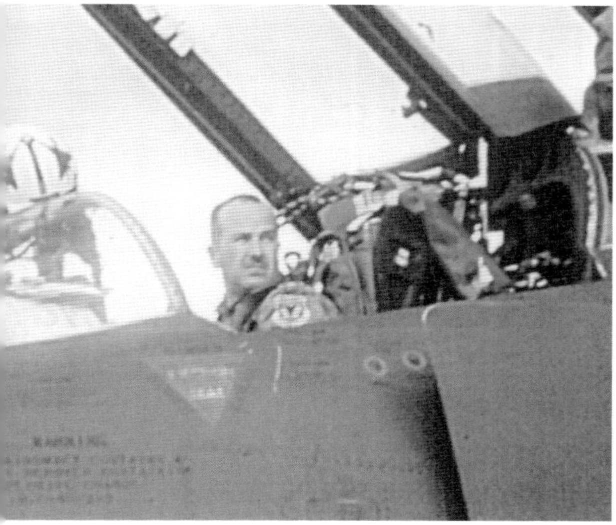

Col. Robert P. "Pancho" Pasqualicchio
Colonel Pasqualicchio was a combat fighter pilot with three combat tours and over 350 combat missions during the war. He came to the base in 1956 as part of the first team that opened it and was the first commander of the newly formed 356th Fighter Squadron of the 354th Fighter Group. After the war in Korea in 1951, he was invited to the White House to be personally commended by President Truman for his role in rescuing five American airmen who had been shot down behind enemy lines. He was a Top Gun member of the United States Air Force Fighter Group gunnery competition in 1956 and the recipient of many decorations and awards for his service. (Courtesy CML.)

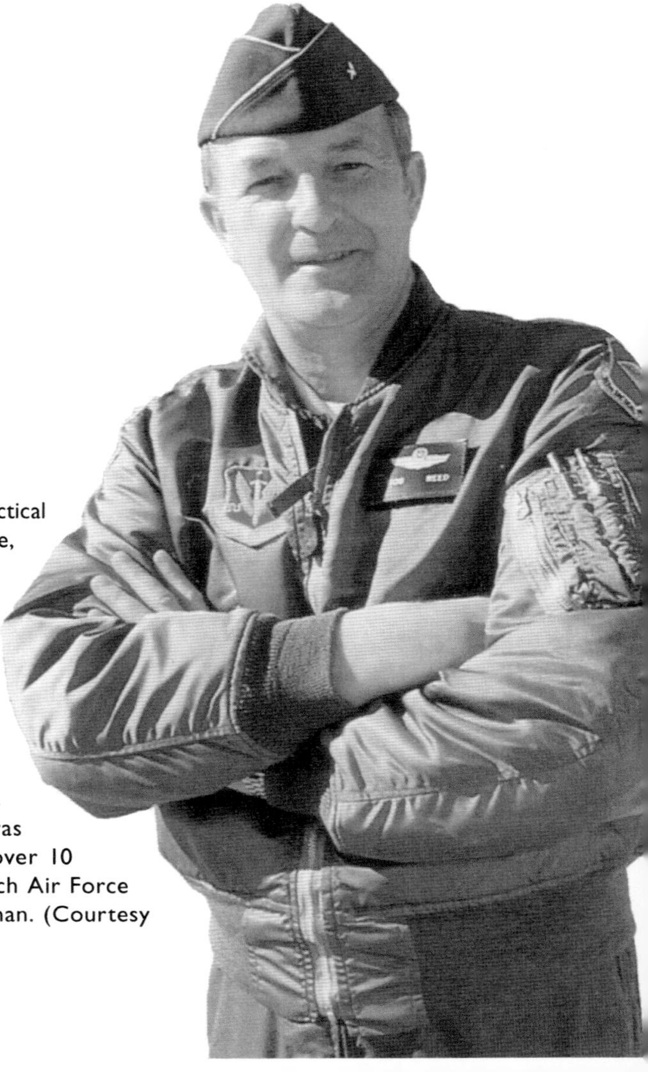

Gen. Robert H. Reed
General Reed was the commander of the 354th Tactical Fighter Wind from 1976 to 1979. While he was here, the 354th became the United States Air Force's first combat operationally ready wing of the A-10 aircraft and set many firsts in the field. A command pilot with over 6,000 flying hours, he was a highly decorated officer including the awarding of the Distinguished Service Medal and the Distinguished Flying Cross.

Pasqualicchio and Reed loved Myrtle Beach and both decided to retire here with their families and become part of the community. Pancho was director of airports for Horry County for over 10 years until 1986. Reed joined the Myrtle Beach Air Force Base Redevelopment Authority as vice chairman. (Courtesy Diane Moskow McKenzie.)

Blanche Floyd

Floyd moved to Myrtle Beach in 1950 with her husband, James K. "J.K." Floyd Jr. She worked as a schoolteacher for 30 years in the Myrtle Beach Schools. After retirement, she spent more time writing and published several books on local history including *Tales Along the Grand Strand of South Carolina* and articles for local newspapers and regional magazines. She was very active in her church, First United Methodist, and spent much of her time as the church historian. Blanche was also president of the South Carolina Conference Historical Society (Methodist Conference) and served on the Commission on Archives and History. She lived a long and full life, and her writings and contributions to local history will live forever. (Courtesy Beth Floyd Szostak.)

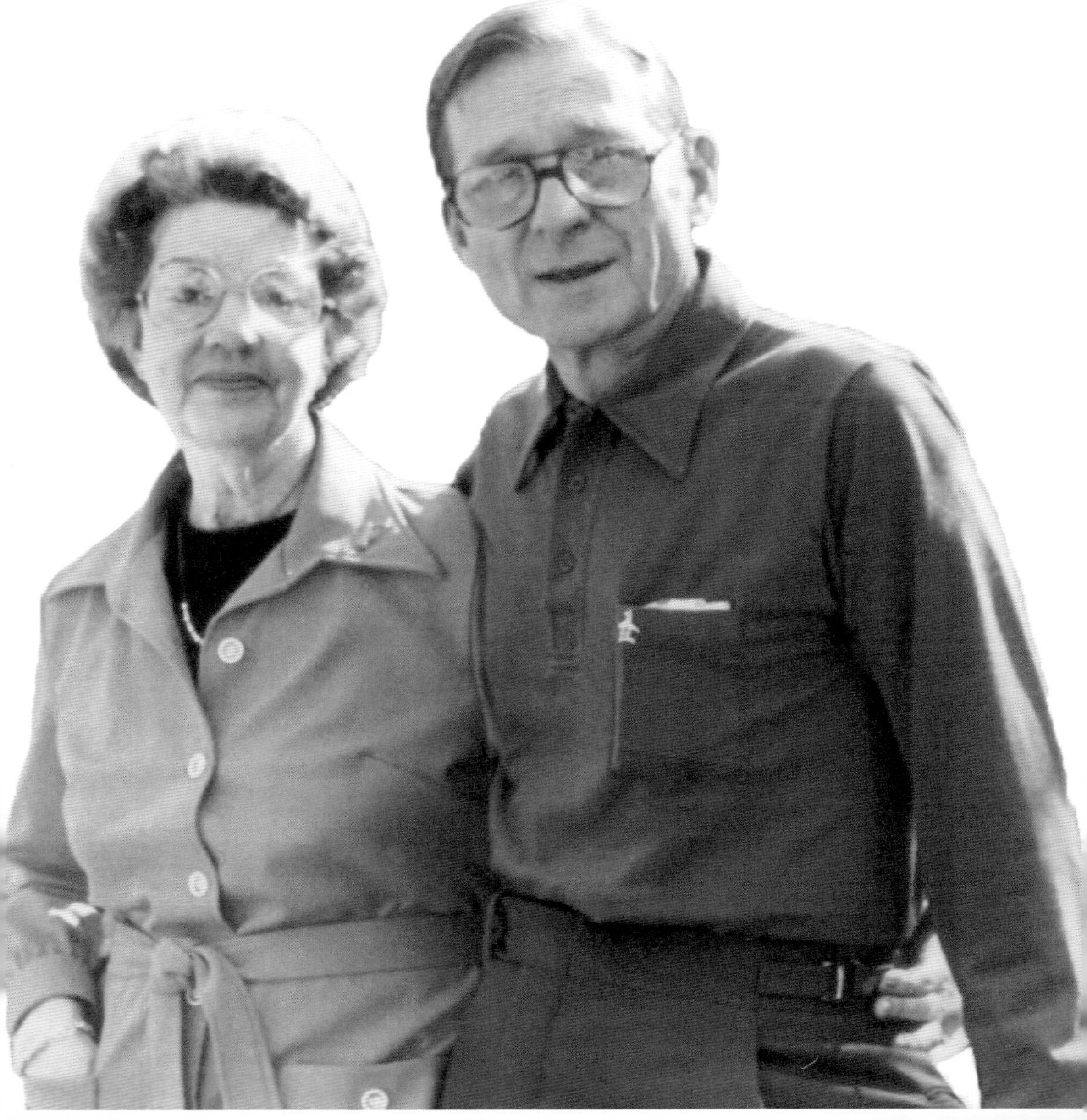

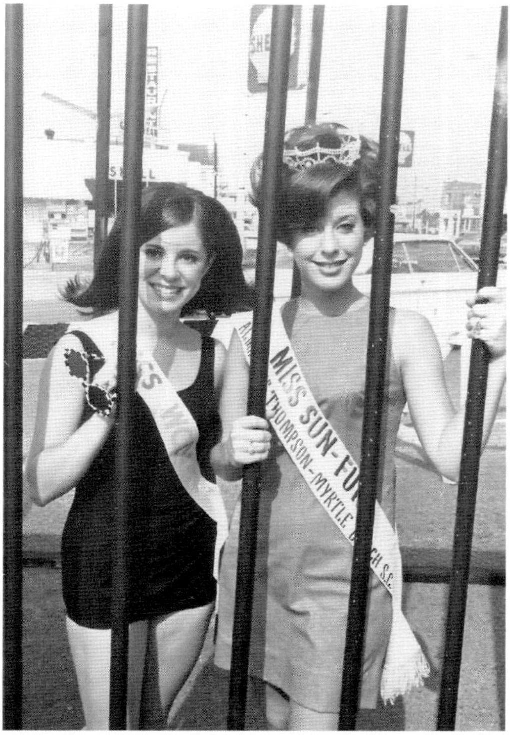

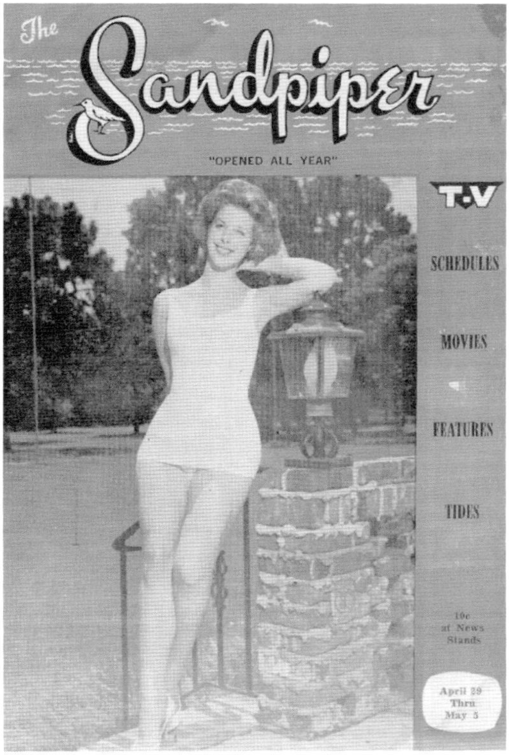

Alma Lynne Thompson Hayden

Alma Lynne still looks like she did when she won her beauty pageant titles of Miss Sun Fun, Miss Rambi Raceway, Miss Myrtle Beach High School, Miss Myrtle Beach, and even Miss Bemco Mattress. Always beautiful inside and out, her broad smile brightens her path everywhere she goes. While in high school, she drew and painted the Myrtle Beach Seahawk on the east wall of the gymnasium. The pirate lived there until the Myrtle Beach High School was torn down. She received her art degree at Columbia College and then came home to teach art at the high school and raise her family. Ever the artist, Alma Lynne went on to design needlework and needlecrafts that can be found all over the world in her books from Alma Lynne Designs and Alma Lynn Originals. She loves to decorate, and her home is a reflection of her creative spirit. When she is not spending time with her family, she also illustrates greeting cards for women. (Top, courtesy MBCC; bottom, CML.)

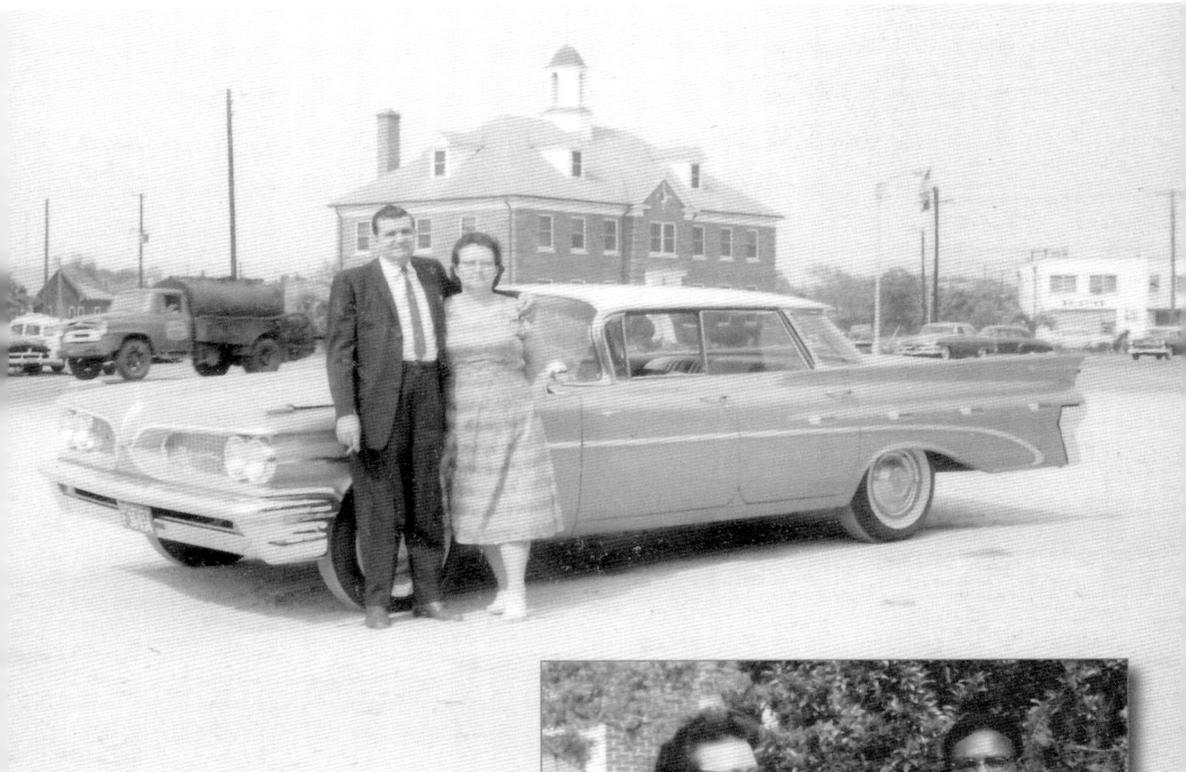

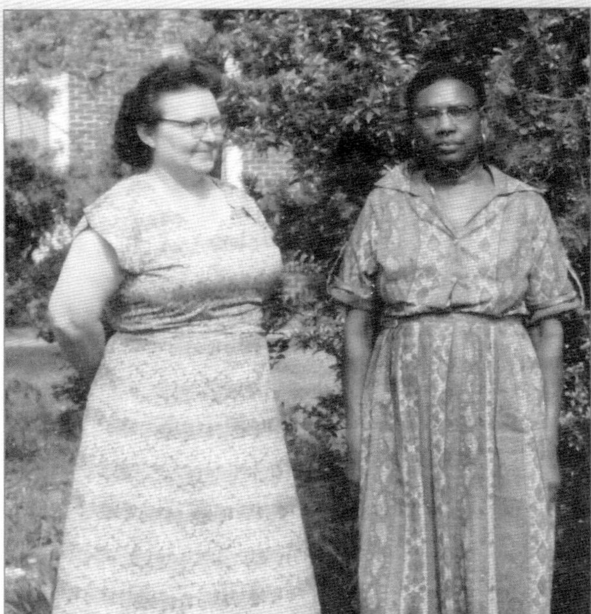

Ida DeLeslin "Lessie" Elvis Hardee and Archie Wade Hardee
Both Horry County natives, their move to Myrtle Beach in 1954 was precipitated by the offer of owning the Queen City Trailways franchise at the Union Bus Terminal off of Broadway in downtown Myrtle Beach. Archie and Lessie operated the bus station together for 10 years before they retired. Known for its great restaurant featuring home-cooked southern meals, families would stop by for Sunday dinners after church. Hester's famous fried chicken is still remembered by many. After retirement, they managed Hardee Apartments on Third Avenue South until their deaths—Archie in 1967 and Lessie in 1985. Lessie is pictured at right with Hester. (Courtesy Mary Catherine Hardee.)

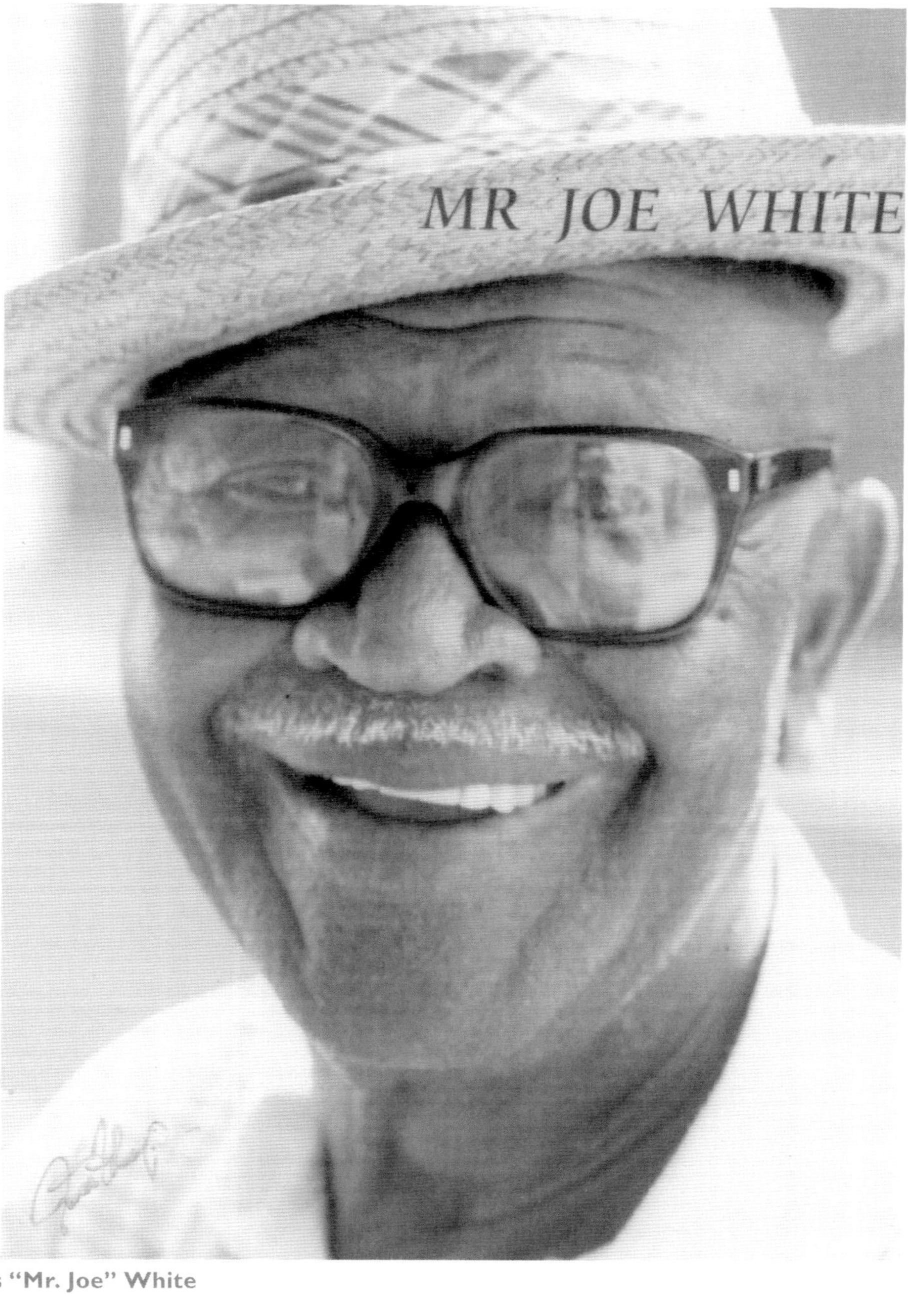

Julius "Mr. Joe" White

Mr. Joe was a shoe stylist by trade, known by all for his smile, wave, and the jingle of his horn as he passed on his bicycle on his way to and from work. Mr. Joe was born in Georgetown in 1910 and moved to Myrtle Beach in 1930. He began shining shoes for a nickel in sixth grade. He worked for many years at the Ocean Forest Hotel, then at various barbershops, and finally settled at Woody's Barbershop in the Arcade Building later in life. After Mr. Joe passed away in 1997, the city changed Tenth Avenue North (the street he traveled to and from work every day) to Mr. Joe White Avenue in honor of him and his legacy. (Courtesy Jack Thompson.)

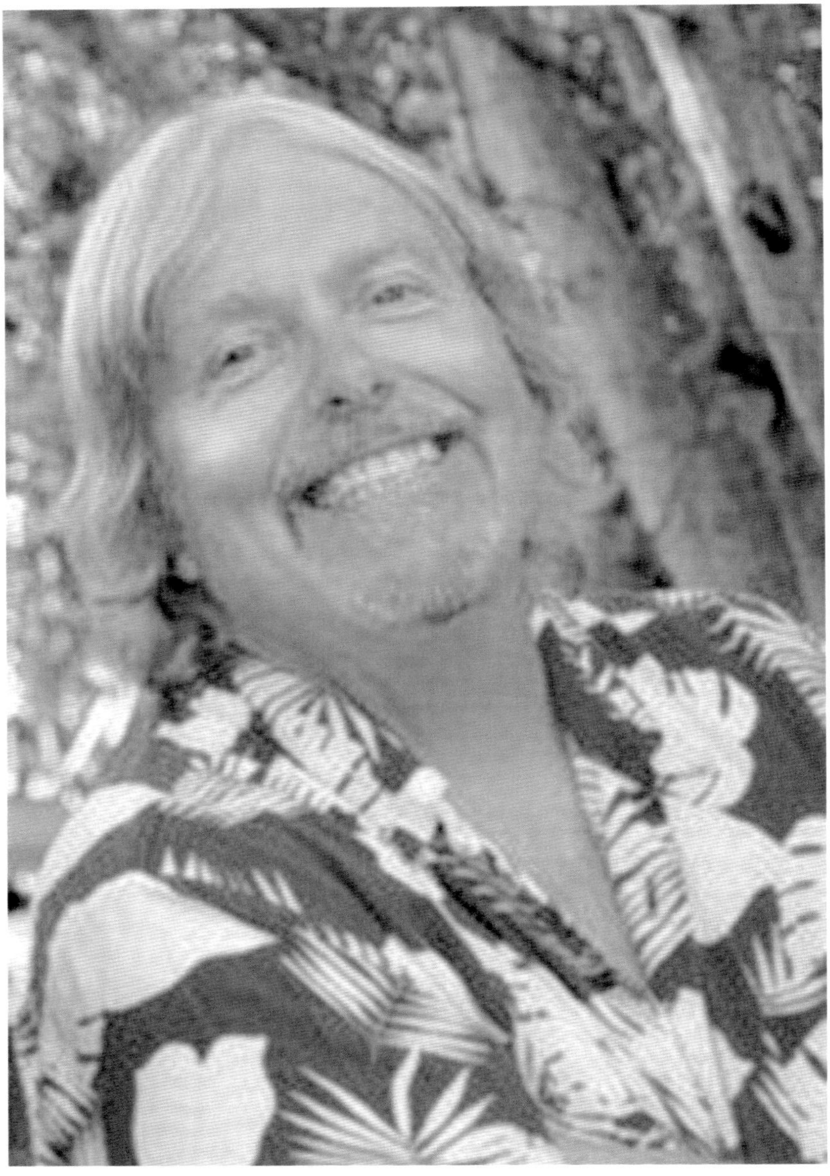

Jimmy Lathan
Jimmy's smile would light up the room and lighten one's load. He worked all over the beach, but the Myrtle Beach Pavilion and Sea Cruz were probably the two places most people knew him from. He was a fixture at the pavilion from an early age and worked there until they closed in 2006. He knew every nook and cranny in the pavilion and was often heard saying "no job too big, no job too small, General Services has it all." He managed the Magic Attic for over 30 years, bringing in acts big and small. He even had the Rolling Stones come in for one number when they were passing through in the mid-1970s. He could name every act that had come through those halls, their likes, their dislikes, and details about their act, mesmerizing people with the tales. After the pavilion closed, he later went to work with Sea Cruz and was planning to write a book with his good friend Deacon Dawson about the area music scene. Sadly, Jimmy died unexpectedly in 2011 at the age of 59. (Courtesy Deacon Dawson.)

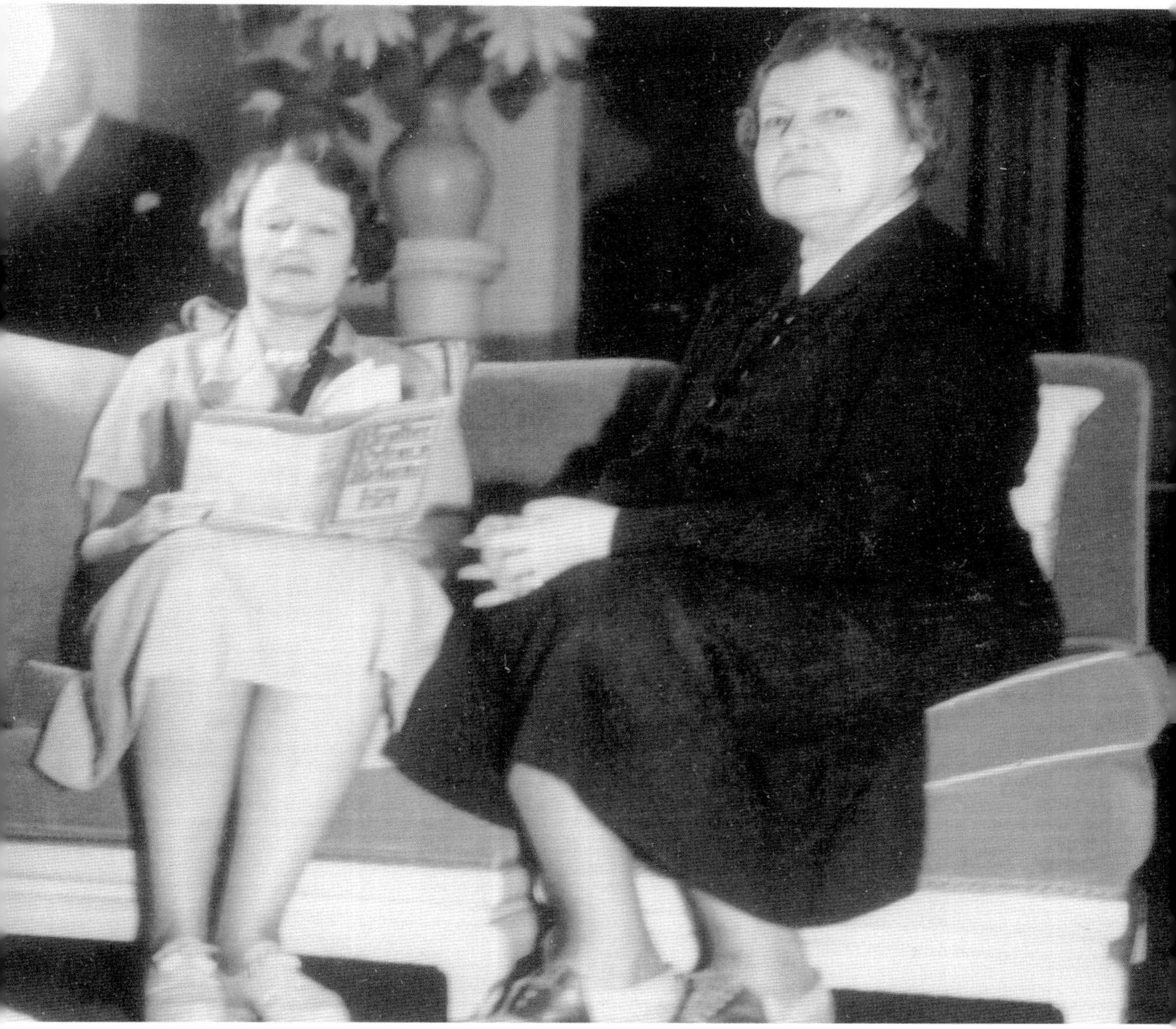

Elizabeth Chapin Patterson

Elizabeth Chapin Patterson (pictured on the right with her mother, Elizabeth Mattocks Chapin), daughter of Simeon B. Chapin (back left), filled her life with charity and good works. She started the Happy Club in 1965, and in 1967, she started CVS—the Community Volunteer Services, a local free clinic in the African American community. In 1980, a building was established at the corner of Tenth Avenue North (now Mr. Joe White Avenue) and Nance Street. During the 1970s and early 1980s, the community would come together and have a huge yard sale to raise funds for this project. The yard sale would fill the (then) small convention center, and people would line up two and three deep to get into the sale, which would last for two days and raise thousands of dollars. Some might also remember some of Patterson's other projects—Rainbows End and Friendship House. She was the powerhouse behind the building of the first hospital, Ocean View Memorial Hospital. At her request, her father donated hundreds of acres of land for the establishment of the Meher Baba Spiritual Retreat on the north end of Myrtle Beach. (Courtesy Chapin Foundation.)

INDEX

BIBLIOGRAPHY

Bedford, A. Goff. *The Independent Republic: A Survey of Horry County, South Carolina*. Second edition. Conway, SC: Horry County Historical Society, 1989.

Chapin Memorial Library archives. Myrtle Beach Air Force Base Collection, Stokes Research Collection, Oral History Collection, Trez Wilcox Collection.

Hall, John R. *Woodside history—John T. Woodside*. Greenville, SC: John R. Hall, 2009.

Lewis, Catherine H. *Horry County, South Carolina: 1700–1993*. Columbia, SC: University of South Carolina Press, 1998.

Stokes, Barbara F. *Myrtle Beach: A History, 1900–1980*. Columbia, SC: University of South Carolina Press, 2007.

Sun News newspaper, Myrtle Beach, SC: The Sun News, 1952–2013.

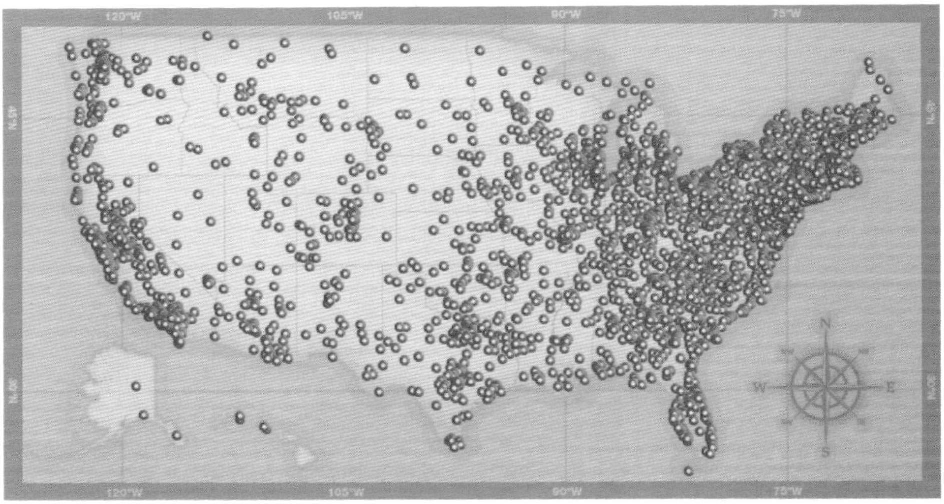

Consistent with our mission to preserve history on a local level, this book was printed in South Carolina on American-made paper and manufactured entirely in the United States. Products carrying the accredited Forest Stewardship Council (FSC) label are printed on 100 percent FSC-certified paper.